Table of Contents

T0013073

♦ Hall of Fame Player

>>>>>>>>>>>>>>> Introduction

Growing up in the Boston area, I was inundated with Red Sox propaganda and swiftly brainwashed into becoming a fan of the team. I was so young that I was not even aware of what a pennant race was, which was a good thing because in the late 1950s and early 1960s, the Red Sox were never in one.

The voice of Curt Gowdy, later much more famous for his other sportscasting, was the sound track of my youth on summer nights. I fell asleep to Gowdy's calls on the radio, even as I graduated into playing baseball as a Little Leaguer.

In 1960, when I was nine years old, my father, Joseph, and my grandfather, Jacob Kristal, led me to my first Red Sox game live at Fenway Park. It really was memorable to see the spacious green of the field stretched out when we climbed to our seats.

Over time I learned more and more about the nuances of the sport, appreciating the hows and whys of the game, and the inner thoughts of those who excelled on the field. Come October, I can watch playoff baseball day after day, week after week as the suspense builds towards the World Series without tiring of the complex game. It has always been a special aspect of baseball that you can attend a contest and see something you had never seen before.

Eventually, I became a journalist, most of the time a sportswriter, and made a career out of writing for newspapers. Over the decades, I gained access to Major League ballparks all around the country to cover games and write feature stories and columns.

Although some of the Hall of Famers, star players, and just interesting guys with stories to tell, were interviewed via telephone or in some other public settings, most of them were interviewed in their teams' clubhouses. As the years passed, I realized I had been fortunate to enjoy lengthy conversations with many of the greats of the game.

In selecting the players from the list of players I heard special stories from, when possible, I tried to emphasize different moments of their careers other than always the best-known ones. I chose these tales from the dugout because they essentially veered into the unusual, not always recounting a play that won a specific game.

Often enough, the players themselves found it refreshing to talk about an aspect of the sport dear to them that the daily beat writers on deadline hustling to get that game's result into the paper didn't have time to dwell on. When as an Anchorage Daily news sports writer, I approached Minnesota Twins relief pitcher Eddie Guardado to chat about his time spent in summer ball with the Anchorage Glacier Pilots, he memorably said, "I always have time for someone from Alaska." In a way that single sentence was a mouthful, an entire story encapsulated.

Eddie was one of the many players I spoke with over the years who didn't make the cut of 56 players included in this collection. Some 34 of them are in the Baseball Hall of Fame, plus eventual, inevitable Hall of Famers Albert Pujols, Dusty Baker, and Pete Rose (someday).

Lew Freedman

September, 2023

HANK AARON

Photo courtesy of BASEBALL HALL OF FAME

⟫⟫⟫⟫⟫⟫⟫⟫⟫⟫⟫⟫ *THE SETTING*

In July of 2012, Henry Aaron, who got his start in professional baseball with the Indianapolis Clowns of the Negro American League in 1952 for $200 a month, appeared as part of a panel discussion at the Negro Leagues Baseball Museum in Kansas City.

The discussion moderator was Dave Winfield, like Aaron a member of the National Baseball Hall of Fame in Cooperstown, New York, and the other speaker was Frank Robinson, another power hitter honored by election to the Hall in upstate New York.

The Major League All-Star game was scheduled to be played down the road in another section of Kansas City two days later. But no one carried a more experienced and impactful voice for the 200 baseball fans gathered in the room than Aaron. He was an inspiration to the crowd as one of the greatest ballplayers of all time and a man whose career carried him from poverty-like beginnings in Mobile, Alabama to being a highly respected elder statesman of the game. Aaron achieved clout by clouting home runs at an unprecedented rate for the Milwaukee and Atlanta Braves and at the end of his big-league days for the Milwaukee Brewers in 1976.

During Aaron's 23-season Major League career the signature stretch in the public eye commenced with him chasing and surpassing Babe Ruth as the sport's all-time home-run king. Rather than the pursuit be splashed with joy, Aaron's inexorable climb towards Ruth's previously unassailable mark of 714 home runs became an ordeal.

Plagued by death threats, inflammatory letters, and racial epithets, Aaron needed police protection as he sought to break a sports record, all because he was a Black man trying to exceed a famous mark recorded by a one-time phenomenon of the game whose memory was especially esteemed.

While the story Aaron told was widely known, few present had heard it from his own lips in such dramatic fashion as an African-American son of the South poured forth emotion to a rapt crowd sitting in hushed silence as if listening to the forceful words of a preacher.

⫸⫸⫸⫸⫸⫸⫸⫸⫸⫸⫸⫸ THE STORY

At no time did Hank Aaron yell. At no time did the man known for his soft-spoken nature speak venomously. There was still a scar on Aaron's heart so many years after the events before, during and after his home run chase highlighting the poison of racism still dwelling in the minds of many Americans.

"Hammerin' Hank" completed his 1974 season with 713 home runs, one shy of the former New York Yankee great's lifetime total. He simply ran out of games that year. So, the issue hung over Aaron's head all winter, allowing the attention and pressure to build and giving bigots time to mail him terrifying letters.

It was obvious when the season began in early April of 1975 that as soon as Aaron came to the plate, he would quickly blast the home runs needed to pass Babe Ruth. However, the negative backlash Aaron suffered as he worked his way to the grand moment that remains embedded in many baseball fans' heads, sadly at times superseded the ballpark doings.

At the time, Aaron had a daughter attending Fisk University in Nashville, Tennessee and she needed protection to go about her daily life. His two younger sons, still in public school, had police escorts to travel from home to the classroom and back. FBI agents read Aaron's mail, digesting with disgust much of the content. He told them not to bother, but the investigators insisted. While 99 percent of such letters may not carry true threat, the investigators had to scan them for the one percent that might be dangerous.

"The last two years of my career were probably the toughest of my 23 years," Aaron said in Kansas City. "It was kind of sad for me and it should have been joyful for me. I was merely playing baseball. I don't know where I got the strength."

The passions Aaron inflamed by excelling at his sport in the same manner as he always had, left him baffled about the world around him, one so bound up in expressing hate. Of course, a Black man growing up in the 1930s and 1940s in Alabama had not been shielded from such racist thought as a youth. And in his early days as a member of the Braves organization he was assigned to Jacksonville in the South Atlantic League, aka the Sally League, which was a Deep South-situated minor league not known for its enlightenment.

Frank Robinson, also listening in on the stage in Kansas City, also played in the Sally League years after Aaron did, only with Columbia, South Carolina. Race issues aside, Aaron left a mark as a hitter, Robinson said, with fans commenting that "Henry hit one over here." The same statements followed him around the league, said Robinson, who didn't even know who Aaron was at the time. After making such a circuit, however, and hearing about Aaron's long-ball accomplishments, Robinson said, "He inspired me."

Aaron inspired many – on and off the field. He hit that majestic, meaningful home run to move past Ruth on the all-time career list on April 8, 1974. He was able to concentrate to do his job when he stepped into the batter's box while those in Atlanta Fulton-County Stadium roared at the mention of his name.

"God had wrapped me in his hand and I was very safe when I got to the ballpark," Aaron reminisced.

To perhaps illustrate how America has matured some, improved a bit in race relations, though no one is stating such problems have evaporated, Aaron said when he told a grandson about the racism surrounding his home-run chase, about the racist letters and threats, and the need for FBI intervention, the younger family member was incredulous. His observation? "It's only a baseball game," his grandson said.

At the time of his talk, Aaron was 78 years old, his hair was going white and he walked with a bit of stiffness in his stride. He seemed very much a man at peace with all that he had achieved.

When Henry Aaron finished his story, those in the room – Black and white – leapt to their feet and gave him a standing ovation. The affection for the man, more than the player, was palpable.

CAREER

Henry, or Hank, Aaron was a 25-time All-Star during his big-league career spanning 1952 to 1976, with a lifetime total of 755 home runs, the record of 2,297 runs batted in, and a .305 batting average. He appeared in 3,298 games, led the National League in homers four times, and played right field well enough to win three Gold Gloves. He won a Most Valuable Player award and was a member of the Braves' 1957 World Series championship team.

When Aaron retired, the 755 was the all-time-record for homers, but has since been surpassed by Barry Bonds in 2007. Aaron's final home run was caught by a Milwaukee County Stadium groundskeeper and it was later auctioned for $650,000. It was well-known, and seen on television, that when Aaron hit the shot that passed Ruth's total, the ball was caught in the Braves' bullpen by teammate relief pitcher Tom House.

House, who was in a kind of zombie frame of mind during the occasion, ran directly to home plate and gave that ball to Aaron. He called obtaining the ball the highlight of his own eight-year Major League career during which he won 29 games and saved 33.

"People tell me I made a great catch," House said years later. "If I had stood still, the ball would have hit me in the forehead."

While Aaron was affiliated with the Braves' front office for years in retirement, he became a very successful businessman. His automobile dealership earned him a spot on the cover of a magazine not connected to sports – Black Enterprise. In 2002, as more of a symbol of enduring fame, he was invited to have his face appear on a Wheaties box.

In 2007, Aaron started a charitable organization called Chasing the Dream Foundation, to guide children between the ages of nine and 12 realize their goals.

Historically Black College Grambling State University of Louisiana presented Aaron with an honorary degree in 2015 at its spring commencement.

It was only a year prior to that in an interview with USA Today, Aaron admitted he still owned the hate mail sent to him during the home run pursuit, keeping the letters in his attic. When asked why, he said, "To remind myself."

For the remainder of his days, after concluding his decade-plus stay in the Braves' front office, Aaron associated himself with good causes and only enhanced his already stellar reputation. In 2020, Atlanta Technical College renamed a building on its campus for Aaron, who had been a generous donor.

Former baseball commissioner Bud Selig, whose baseball roots stem from Milwaukee, and who knew Aaron for decades, said, "I can't think of a better human being to achieve what he did and carry himself the way he has, and, as a result, baseball is better because of him."

Henry Louis Aaron passed away at 86 in January of 2021.

GEORGE ALTMAN

THE SETTING

A genial man who had an accomplished athletic career, George Altman and I spent several days talking about his life, especially his baseball career, in O'Fallon, Missouri, long after his retirement.

We were working on a book together, in his first person, which was published in 2013. Altman attended college at Nashville's Tennessee State University, a historically black institution previously known as Tennessee A&I. The Tigers won three straight NAIA national crowns between 1957 and 1959 under the tutelage of legendary coach John McLendon. Altman played football, basketball, and baseball for the school between 1954 and 1957 and is a member of Tennessee State's athletic Hall of Fame.

That was one of the lesser-known chapters of Altman's wide-ranging sports career. He is best remembered for his nine seasons in Major League Baseball between 1959 and 1967, most notably as an out-fielder with the Chicago Cubs. Selected to appear in three All-Star games, Altman had the good fortune to not only play basketball under McLendon, but be noticed by another legend in baseball. Buck O'Neil, formerly the manager as well as a star for the Kansas City Monarchs of the Negro leagues, became the first Black big-league scout. As such, O'Neil steered such luminaries as Ernie Banks and Billy Williams to the Cubs – and Altman.

What stood out to me, almost beyond anything else that Altman and I talked about, was that he was part of the answer to a trivia question that not even most experts think to ask. Altman is one of only three men to have played professional baseball in the Negro leagues, the majors, and in Japan. The other two players who played at this level were Larry Doby, the Cleveland Indians Hall of Famer of the late 1940s and early 1950s, and pitcher Don Newcombe, winner of the first Cy Young Award for the Brooklyn Dodgers.

⟫⟫⟫⟫⟫⟫⟫⟫⟫⟫ THE STORY

Altman grew up in North Carolina, where he was an all-around high school sports star. He said he was a better basketball player than baseball player as a teenager and hoops is what got him noticed by Tennessee State.

Even though the Tigers did not have a baseball team his first two years of college, Altman excelled after that and a contact from Tennessee brought him to the attention of the Kansas City Monarchs. The Monarchs were coming to the end of their storied run while Major League Baseball was making strides with integration.

Altman's connection with the Monarchs was very brief and he was already 26 as a rookie for Chicago. Altman hit more than .300 two years in the early 1960s for the Cubs, but as he approached athletic middle age of 35, he was invited to play in Japan.

Once he accepted the role of being one of just a small number of Americans allowed on a Japanese team at one time, Altman had adjustments to make, ones he felt were worthy as he grew to love the Asian nation.

Food was one forced adaptation for an American in Tokyo in the 1960s. Altman said he had never been a fussy eater, usually devouring anything, but when in doubt generally wedded to the staple eats of hamburgers and cheeseburgers.

"I'm pretty diverse in my choices," Altman said. "I'm not difficult to please. It was fine whatever they (the team) gave us. It was not cheeseburgers. Well, it was not the all-beef cheeseburger I was used to eating. Sometimes there were hamburgers and cheeseburgers available. You could find them to eat around Tokyo, but they weren't the genuine article. They were laced with something that was a bit fishy. There was fish meal or something in the burgers."

He described the average boxed lunch for players at the ballpark as including a pickled egg, rice, tofu, and "some kind of sardine-type fish."

However, overall, playing for the Tokyo Orions, or Tokyo Lotte Orions, was a treat for Altman. He spent eight seasons playing baseball in Japan, made a lot of friends and took a Berlitz course to learn how to speak Japanese.

As a 6-foot-4 Black man, it was not easy for Altman to blend in on the streets. He was often followed and pointed at by citizens. Yet he got used to that, too, and didn't let it bug him.

Altman may have been out of the majors, but he didn't disappear. He was interviewed reasonably often by American sportswriters about his experiences and talked favorably about how it was a bonus aspect of his career, providing a nice way to stay in the game and play at a high level.

"The caliber of baseball?" Altman said. "Well, the fielding and running is big league, but the pitching and hitting is about Triple A."

Six times in eight seasons in Japan, Altman hit better than .300, including a high of .351 in 1974. He also smacked 205 home runs in Japan.

He accomplished a great deal in the lineup as he gradually got used to new customs, including taking hot baths with teammates, dealing with five-hour practice sessions, as well as those unexpected menus.

As was formerly talked about during Altman's era in Japan, there was sometimes umpire discrimination against Americans. Teams wanted the Americans to succeed and help the team, but unofficially, unstated, the administrations did not want the Americans to out-do native players by doing too well, as in winning batting titles or home-run crowns.

"They thought it was a bad reflection on their league if Americans who weren't playing in the majors anymore came over and could win hitting titles," Altman.

Over the last half-century, since Altman first traveled to Japan, many homegrown Japanese players have made the grade in the majors, especially highlighted by Ichiro Suzuki, who set his own records in the United States and is bound for the Hall of Fame.

When Altman batted around .330 his first season in Japan, he was very pleased. It proved what he believed – that he could still play.

"That was very satisfying to be able to show that to people who felt I was washed up and should retire," Altman said.

⟩⟩⟩⟩⟩⟩⟩⟩⟩⟩⟩⟩⟩⟩ CAREER

George Altman, born in March of 1933, turned 90 in early 2023 and he was no longer playing in any baseball league. However, for many years into retirement Altman was a successful competitive horseshoe player.

He and Etta raised three children and during his stay in the majors, Altman played not only for the Cubs, but also the St. Louis Cardinals, with a single season as a member of the New York Mets.

In all, Altman batted .269 lifetime in the majors, in just shy of 1,000 games, clubbed 101 homers and had a high of 96 runs batted in during the 1961 season.

In one big-league game Altman hit two home runs off Dodgers great Sandy Koufax. He briefly overlapped on the Monarchs on one of Satchel Paige's sojourns with the team, an experience he felt was almost otherworldly given Paige's mythic stature.

Expressing gratefulness to his short time connected to the Negro Leagues, Altman admires the efforts made to perpetuate the history contained in the Negro Leagues Baseball Museum in Kansas City as one by one the last survivors of a bygone era pass away.

LUIS APARICIO

THE SETTING

One of the greatest shortstops of all-time, Luis Aparicio was born in and came from Venezuela. Although he played well for some other teams over his 18-year Major-League, Hall-of-Fame career, he made his biggest mark with the Chicago White Sox.

Unlike many other ballplayers of prominence, Aparicio, now well into his eighties, has been somewhat reclusive during his retirement, maintaining his home in the country of his roots, and only periodically making appearances for fans in Chicagoland. At times he even turned down interviews through his agent.

This followed a period, though, when he had regularly showed up at baseball-related events in Cooperstown, New York, at the hall, and elsewhere.

One notable exception for Aparicio making himself visible a bit later in life, was in 2006 when the White Sox unveiled a dual statue of Aparicio and his old second-base partner Nellie Fox performing a double play. Aparicio's strong allegiance to Fox and their infield combination identification came through.

The bond between Aparicio and Fox, who died young from cancer at 47, was tight. Fox had already passed away and could not be present for the ceremony in the outfield at what was then called U.S. Cellular Field and is now Guaranteed Rate Field. Fox had yet to be selected for the Hall of Fame, though he was subsequently chosen.

The statue is actually two-in-one, cementing the connection between the men. The Fox figure is depicted after having fielded a ground ball and flipping the baseball to Aparicio. The Aparicio figure is shown holding up his glove in anticipation of receiving the toss from Fox.

While it is ironic that Luis' nickname was "Little Louie," Aparicio and Fox's human dimensions were similar, Aparicio being listed as 5-foot-9 and 160 pounds and Fox as 5-10, 160. Both men were slightly built, as was routine for middle infielders of the 1950s and 1960s.

They were more esteemed for their fielding prowess than their hitting, but they were also offensive sparks in their own ways.

»»»»»»»»»»»»»» *THE STORY*

The ballpark Luis Aparicio and Nellie Fox called their home field for much of their careers was actually the original Comiskey Park. It opened in 1910 and was replaced by a new Comiskey Park adjacent to the old one in 1991. The old home plate was maintained in a parking lot nearby when the original Comiskey was torn down. After that the new stadium changed names through sponsorship naming rights payments.

Compared to most other teams, the White Sox have been more active in preserving their club history with life-like bronze statues. Alongside the artistic sculpture of Aparicio and Fox, several others decorate fan-convenient places within the park. Fans can revisit baseball greats such as Minnie Minoso, Carlton Fisk, Billy Pierce,

Harold Baines, Frank Thomas, Paul Konerko and Jim Thome. Plus, Charles Comiskey, the namesake of the original park himself, who is in the Hall of Fame.

The unveiling of each statue has been a special occasion and that was true on the Aparicio-Fox day. A small crowd assembled during the day-time event and one fan shouted, "Way to go, Luis!" from among the group of onlookers. Clearly pleased by the anonymous supporter, Aparicio raised a fist in the air.

Aparicio was in his seventies at the time, dressed immaculately in a suit, and wore glasses, an accessory not needed when he was playing in the big leagues between 1956 and 1973.

"It's a great honor for me to be here today," Aparicio said in his official remarks. "I would not rather be anywhere else today. Baseball is the best game. Thank you, God, for giving me the ability to play this game."

When Aparicio broke in with the White Sox in the mid-1950s, Fox was already inhabiting the neighborhood at second base. Fox was older, playing his first Major League games in the late 1940s with the old Philadelphia Athletics and joining the White Sox in 1950.

Fox was a veteran presence and he offered heady advice to the younger rookie as the duo became regulars together in the American League All-Star game lineup. Fox was also Aparicio's biggest verbal supporter, to sportswriters and other baseball people, saying his partner was such a slick fielder he was even claiming ground balls on the second-base side of the bag. And nobody was talking about that as the consequence of a shift.

"I learned a lot from him," Aparicio said on the emotional day of the statue's unveiling, when he was thinking of his long-time teammate, "about how to play this game, about how important this game is for us."

In 1959, Aparicio was the shortstop, and Fox the second baseman, when the White Sox broke a team curse. It was 40 years since the team disparagingly was labeled "The Black Sox" for fixing the outcome of the World Series of 1919 versus the Cincinnati Reds.

Although the Sox did not win the World Series in '59, they did win the American League pennant.

Statue day, however, was more about the two men who occupied the middle of the infield together, sharing special moments and now frozen in time together in bronze. Only one of the two was present to savor the honor and Aparicio was feeling the loss of his old ally keenly.

"Nellie would have been happy today," Aparicio said. "We all miss him."

CAREER

Aparicio was good right away. At 22 years old, he won the American League rookie-of-the-year award in 1956. A 13-time All-Star who won nine Gold Gloves for his fielding prowess, Aparicio gained considerable renown in other baseball cities for his skill on the basepaths. Nine times Aparicio led the AL in stolen bases – the first nine seasons of his career in a row. Aparicio was a main reason why the White Sox were called the "Go-Go White Sox" during that era.

Overall, Aparicio stole 506 bases with a high of 57 in one season. He batted .262 in 2,599 games. Besides his 10 seasons with the White Sox, Aparicio spent five years with the Baltimore Orioles and three with the Boston Red Sox. He was 39 when he retired.

By comparison, his pal Fox played 19 years in the majors, 14 of them with the White Sox, batting .288. Fox was a 15-time All-Star who won the league's Most Valuable Player Award in 1959 when Chicago captured that pennant.

Aparicio was inducted into the National Baseball Hall of Fame in 1984 and the White Sox retired his No. 11 uniform jersey. The year prior to the erection of the Aparicio-Fox statue, the White Sox summoned him from Venezuela to throw out the first pitch at a Chicago World Series game. That 2005 team won the franchise's first championship in 88 years.

Aparicio, who followed his father, Luis Aparicio Sr., into the game, was the first native-born Venezuelan inducted into the baseball Hall. Some years after the statue unveiling, Aparicio did participate for a few years as a broadcaster of his home country's baseball. A handful of years ago, Aparicio became concerned with the nation's in-house politics over the unrest in society and the tensions surrounding the national government.

What Aparicio is best remembered for is not the way he swung the bat, but the way he made his legs move, both on the bases, and in getting to ground balls that should have been beyond reach.

"He's positively the greatest I've ever handled," said Aparicio's White Sox manager Al Lopez.

BRONSON ARROYO

THE SETTING

There has rarely ever been a better clubhouse guy to chat with than Bronson Arroyo. Whether it was a drive-by question, a long conversation, or simply game analysis, he was a ballplayer who was ready, willing, and happy to talk while standing by his locker. Over a few-year period when I was around the Cincinnati Reds in the early 2010s, I was able to speak with him many times.

Got a minute, Bronson? Sure. He was always accommodating and usually had something interesting, if not amusing, to say.

Although he did not play (as far as I know) in the locker room, Arroyo was just about as accomplished a musician with the electric guitar as he was throwing a baseball.

The right-handed throwing Arroyo stood 6-foot-3 and weighed 185 pounds, somewhat classic dimensions for a modern-day starting pitcher in Major League Baseball. However, despite having those measurements that usually portend a slick fastball that spins hitters around, Arroyo was about the slowest throwing big-leaguer out there who did not rely on a knuckleball.

There are definitely college pitchers deep-down-on-the-roster who throw faster than Arroyo did and maybe even civilians at carnivals knocking over dolls to win stuffed animals.

»»»»»»»»»»»» *THE STORY*

A pitch travels 60 feet, 6 inches to home plate from the pitcher's mound, and a number is almost immediately posted on the outfield scoreboard for all of those in attendance to read (and some sitting in their living rooms to watch). When Arroyo threw, onlookers would see 65, 69, or 71 miles per hour pop up on the wall rather than the 95 or 97 they were used to reading.

Pitchers throw fastballs, curves, change-ups, and split-fingered fastballs, but none of them claim to throw slowballs. Only Arroyo. The first inclination would be to believe the scoreboard was broken when it registered 67 mph next to Arroyo's name. Not so. When he was tentatively asked if that could be accurate, Arroyo candidly admitted it represented the truth.

To illustrate how dumbfounding this was, the New York Mets' R.A. Dickey was on his way to winning a National League Cy Young Award by counting on a 75-mph knuckleball. Arroyo's teammate with the Reds, reliever Aroldis Chapman, had been clocked throwing a ball at 106 mph. Was Arroyo even playing the same game? Police officers didn't even give out speeding tickets for driving 67 mph.

So, Arroyo was slower than slow, slower than the game's premier knuckleball pitcher. "I know," he said. He proceeded to relay one of his favorite stories.

Albert Pujols, still in his first go-around with the St. Louis Cardinals, reached first base one game and was talking with Cincinnati fielder Joey Votto. Votto later informed Arroyo that Pujols said this: "Bronson doesn't have good enough stuff to pitch in the big leagues, man, but I have no idea what this guy is going to throw me." When

Votto told Arroyo that, the pitcher took it as a compliment. Speed was not the name of his game, getting hitters out was. There was more than one way to fool them.

Arroyo broke into the majors at 23 in 2000 with the Pittsburgh Pirates and pitched for that team and the Boston Red Sox before landing in Cincinnati. He had an eye-catching delivery, with his left leg thrown straight out stiffly, separating the style of his windup from most other hurlers. And even if he did not possess the pure fast stuff of other pitchers, Arroyo had excellent control.

"I've always had a feel for the game," Arroyo said. "It's kind of like shooting a free throw. Guys who shoot free throws well, the John Stocktons of the world, will always be able to shoot good free throws. I've always had a feel for the game since I was a young kid. I could throw a spinning breaking ball over the plate whenever, so throwing strikes has never been a problem."

Scouts always have to take a longer look, and make more convincing arguments to their employers, if they hope to see a prospect like Arroyo drafted. Raw tools can be harnessed, it is thought, as in the theory that speed cannot be taught, but must be innate. But along come pitchers like Arroyo who can get foes out by using their heads as much as their arms.

"You find multiple ways to maximize your ability in the strike zone without being able to throw the ball by guys very often," Arroyo said.

When Arroyo threw a pitch past a hitter it was just as likely the guy would say he got a speck of dirt in his eye as to admit his swing-and-a-miss was due to Arroyo's canniness.

CAREER

During a 16-year Major League career, Arroyo compiled a record of 148 wins and 137 losses. His best season was 2010 when he finished 17-10. He won a Gold Glove that year, too. In 2006, Arroyo led the National League in innings pitched with 240 2/3 innings and made his only All-Star team.

Perhaps Arroyo's grandest single achievement on a baseball diamond occurred in the minors when he was still in the employ of the Red Sox. He pitched a perfect game for the Pawtucket AAA Red Sox in 2003 on assignment when he was still attempting to be a full-time regular in the majors.

One day in August of that year, his arm not feeling especially good, Arroyo walked to the mound and speedily and thoroughly dispatched the Buffalo Bison, tossing the perfect game that took just 101 pitches to complete. Arroyo struck out nine men and blitzed through all 27 batters at McCoy Stadium in Rhode Island. Some 73 pitches were strikes.

Whether it is Little League, American Legion, Class A, or in this case AAA, a perfect game is a rarity and Arroyo's gem was just the fourth thrown in the 120 years of the International League. Arroyo was so sharp that day, he fired a first-pitch strike to 22 hitters.

Arroyo said his arm did not feel particularly good. However, he got better and better during the 7-0 shutout, as he went along. "But after you get through three or four innings of easy work and you haven't thrown that many pitches, you kind of keep rolling and rolling," he said.

There were nearly 10,000 fans on hand and the crowd was tuned in early. Aware of what was going on, Arroyo said it was the first time in his life on the mound he was nervous for a ninth inning.

When the game ended and the perfecto was in the books, Arroyo was naturally mobbed by teammates on the field. They then dumped the contents of the water cooler over his head.

Born in 1977 in Key West, Florida, Arroyo was always a laid-back guy. His second career, evolving even as he was pitching, was as a guitar player and singer. He actually released his first CD called "Covering the Bases" in 2005, and while with the Red Sox Arroyo performed in nightclubs near Fenway Park.

Bronson was named after actor Charles Bronson by his dad, Cuban native Gus Arroyo. The funny thing when it came to heritage was that several members of Arroyo's family were more musically inclined than baseball inclined. He said he surprised them when he drifted into music, too.

When he was still playing in the majors and practicing in off-hours, Arroyo's lifestyle didn't always mesh with the sleep habits of hotel guests. After games he lowered his adrenaline by playing his guitar, typically until hotel security came banging on the door to tell him to cease and desist.

Only hours earlier his lodging neighbor may have been applauding him, but Arroyo didn't blame him for late-night booing.

HAROLD BAINES

THE SETTING

Harold Baines was always the quiet man of the Chicago White Sox during his lengthy big-league career and then as a hitting coach for the club. Baines spoke more loudly with his bat, especially in the clutch, than he did in the clubhouse. He was not the first guy you went to if you expected to hear jokes.

But Baines was always there, either by his locker as a player, serious in game preparations, or roaming around the locker room when he was teaching a younger generation of players. He did not seek the limelight, but when I approached him to sit down and do some talking about his career, background, and favorite moments, he did not duck out.

I believe the time we talked the longest we were sitting down in the dugout, instead of the clubhouse, in the hours leading up to the game. His team was ramping up as it took batting practice at what was then U.S. Cellular Field.

One of the anecdotes of Baines' life that made some chuckle related to his home area. Baines grew up in St. Michaels, Maryland. That was near Easton. By coincidence, Bill Veeck, the Hall of Fame owner, who twice operated the White Sox, had a home in that community.

It was said that Veeck, who first moved to Easton when he thought he was retiring from baseball for good due to health reasons, saw Baines play as a 12-year-old Little Leaguer and was struck by his apparent talent. Everyone knows that the stars as kids rarely mature into the stars of adulthood, but Baines did so. Veeck quietly followed Baines' progress as a teenager and when the young man turned 18 and became eligible for the Major League draft, he spoke up. The White Sox grabbed him.

"Bill Veeck discovered me," Baines said. "I just think I was in the right spot at the right time."

⟫⟫⟫⟫⟫⟫⟫⟫⟫⟫⟫⟫ THE STORY

Of the 2,830 games Harold Baines played in during 22 seasons between 1980 and 2001, the game he chose as a career highlight was actually the equivalent of almost three games. He did get his bang for the buck and his bang concluded this dramatic game story with a loud period.

The White Sox played the Milwaukee Brewers, who were still located in the American League then, on May 8, 1984. The starting pitcher for the Brewers was future Hall of Famer Don Sutton, who won 324 games during his career. The finishing, final relief pitcher, for the White Sox, was future Hall of Famer Tom Seaver, who won 311 games during his career.

Those were only a couple of the minor notable facts about the game. Although Baines was speaking about the game inside U.S. Cellular Field, the ballpark this game was played in was the original Comiskey Park, with 14,754 spectators in attendance for what they presumed would be a normal, regular-season, early-season game.

However, it turned out to be anything but.

This game turned into a 25-inning, 8-hour, 6-minute odyssey that ended with a 7-6 White Sox win on a home run by Baines. Baines was Chicago's right-fielder in the contest and came to the plate 12 times. Twelve times in one game! He walked twice, reducing his official at-bats to 10, and had two hits. His other hit was a double.

Essentially, the game was played over a two-day period and the sheer length of it always stayed in Baines' mind.

"As a player, I've been involved in nothing else close to that," Baines said.

Taking two calendar days, May 8-9, to complete one game is something else that stuck out about the experience to Baines. The White Sox and Brewers played 17 innings on the first day and umpires adjourned the activity with the score 3-3. The teams picked up on the second day and kept right on going. The Brewers, who totaled 20 hits, seemed to have things wrapped up when they scored three runs in the top of the 21st inning. However, the White Sox, who totaled 23 hits, came back to score three runs themselves, in the bottom of the 21st, kind of sending the game into extra-extra innings.

When Baines came to the plate in the bottom of the 25th inning, Chuck Porter was on the mound for Milwaukee. He pitched 7 1/3 innings in relief that game. If the White Sox had been tamed in that at-bat the game would have gone on to a 26th inning, equaling the longest Major League game ever, a 1-1 tie between the Boston Braves and Brooklyn Dodgers in 1920.

Instead, Baines concluded the proceedings with a 420-foot solo home run. Baines, as everyone knew who watched him play, never emoted strongly on the field even when a special moment occurred, and he did not celebrate this blast openly, either. However, his manager, Tony LaRusso, another future Hall of Famer, did recognize a sense of occasion and grabbed Baines' bat and shipped it to the National Baseball Hall of Fame in Cooperstown, New York.

"People in Chicago and Milwaukee remember that game," Baines said off-handedly in 2012. He knew that because he was coaching in those days and visible around the ballpark. "Because I get people all of the time who say they were at that game."

As Baines noted, and as anyone considering the eight-hours-plus that went into completing it over a two-day span might wonder, those fans do not tell the player if they sat through the whole thing or not. Attendance was taken only at the start, not as the game went on.

Post-game, after that sterling game ended, a sportswriter hoping for detailed commentary from Baines following the big home run, reportedly began his inquiry by saying it appeared he got all of that pitch.

Typical of Baines' game analysis chattiness, he famously replied, "Evidently."

CAREER

During his two-decades-plus in the majors, Baines had 11,092 official at-bats, collected 2,886 hits, smacked 384 home runs, drove in 1,628 runs, and batted .289. Baines was a six-time All-Star and his No. 3 uniform jersey is retired by the White Sox.

Baines was a member of the White Sox as a player for three different stints – traded multiple times by owner Jerry Reinsdorf despite saying Baines was his favorite player. He was also a coach for the club between 2004 and 2015, including working the clubhouse in 2005 when the Sox won the World Series title.

Baines had been out of the limelight for a few years when in what came as a surprise vote, he was elected to the Baseball Hall of Fame in the class of 2019. By then the White Sox had erected a statue of Baines at their home park.

In a surprise to no-one, Baines' Hall acceptance speech lasted less than 10 minutes, one of the shorter ones. He spoke emotionally about his wife Marla and their four children, and his father, Linwood, who worked six days a week to support the family and imparted life lessons.

"Through his words, and more importantly, his deeds, he taught me how to approach life," Baines said. "You work at it, you put your head down, you keep your mouth shut and you work at your craft day in, day out."

Baines said he believed working-class Chicago responded to him as a working-hard player and said he really enjoyed it when the White Sox' famous organist Nancy Faust played tunes igniting the home fans to begin chanting "Haaa-rold! Haaa-rold!"

Compared to his White Sox background, it is sometimes overlooked Baines played seven years for the Baltimore Orioles and was also chosen for that team's Hall of Fame. Since Baines grew up in Maryland, as did his children, that was a fitting connection, too.

Although Baines expressed thankfulness each time, he was the recipient of special honors, but at no time was he more grateful than in April of 2022 when he revealed he had undergone coronary heart and kidney transplants over the previous 11 months to save his life. The afflictions were the same diseases that killed his father.

"I'm grateful," Baines said in a video released to the public by the White Sox. "It wasn't easy."

DUSTY BAKER

⫸⫸⫸⫸⫸⫸⫸⫸⫸⫸⫸ *THE SETTING*

In 1980, when we were both much younger, Dusty Baker and I crossed paths in the world of baseball for the first time. He was an outfielder playing for the Los Angeles Dodgers. I was a sportswriter for the Philadelphia Inquirer. We collaborated on a feature story for that newspaper.

Many years later, after Baker had begun his lengthy career as a Major League manager, he was the field boss of the Chicago Cubs and I was a sportswriter for the Chicago Tribune and researching baseball books. My main role for the Tribune was outdoors-adventure writer. At the time, Baker was raising a young son, and he periodically asked where in Chicagoland he should take the boy fishing on the typical Mondays or Thursdays his team had for off days.

In the mid-2010s, Baker was managing the Cincinnati Reds and I was writing about the team for a nearby Indiana newspaper. Hours before home games, writers would gather in the manager's office to talk baseball with Baker, mostly about what was going on then and there with the team, who was injured and who was healthy. Occasionally, weightier topics were discussed.

One time, the annual Major League draft loomed the following day and Baker was asked what was going through his mind as he hoped to hear his name called to begin his own professional career years earlier.

≫≫≫≫≫≫≫≫≫≫≫ THE STORY

The night before the Major League Baseball draft was conducted in 1967, "Dusty" Baker was still better known as Johnnie B. Baker. A clearly talented baseball player, he prayed he would not be selected by the Atlanta Braves.

When he was a youngster growing up in California, Baker's favorite play spot outside regularly dirtied his clothes. His mother thought it too extreme to nickname him "Dirty" and settled for "Dusty" as a compromise. When he was 18, living in Sacramento, he wanted no part of the Deep South, where the Civil Rights battles and horror stories emanated from and spread across the nation. He preferred to keep a couple of thousand miles of distance between him and the headlines on the six o'clock network news.

Those were tumultuous times in the United States. The country was torn between Black and White more so than at any time perhaps since the Civil War ended. The nation's greatest shame was slavery, but while Abraham Lincoln announced the Emancipation Proclamation, in much of the South it was as if the world had been frozen in time and those with the ugliest of minds felt it acceptable to still discriminate against those with darker skin. It was easy to understand why a young Black man from California would prefer to steer clear of the Deep South.

By the late 1960s, as surely as the song of cicadas sounded, words of protest, of standing up for change, spread across the Deep South. Through Dr. Martin Luther King's fiery oratory and other courageous souls, the consciousness of Americans in different regions began to change.

Dusty Baker was a sports guy, not a crusader. He played football and participated in track with distinction. Baseball was not even his best sport. As we chatted while he sat in a Cincinnati manager's chair, presiding as leader of a ballclub, Baker expressed a thoughtful memory to what the younger version of himself was thinking about on that draft day. It was far away, when he harbored an early prejudice against Atlanta while sitting on the other side of the nation.

Baker may have possessed a sports-centric outlook, but he did pay attention to the news cycle in Sacramento. In 1967, the Vietnam War played out across TV screens with Walter Cronkite, the most trusted man in America telling the country he had lost faith in presidential administration policy. In the domestic war, playing out in Alabama, Mississippi, Arkansas, and their neighboring states, Baker could watch reports of lynchings, of White civil rights workers being chased back north at gunpoint. Anonymous men wearing white sheets on their heads might parade through communities bearing flaming torches to terrorize innocent hearts.

He listened to inflammatory speeches made by Alabama governor George Wallace and Georgia governor Lester Maddox. They spoke English with drawls, but spit poison like rattlesnakes. It seemed they growled from faraway planets. Assuredly, a darker complected man like himself would not be welcome in that region of the United States.

"The South wasn't the place to go in 1967," said Baker while sitting in his Reds office. "In my heart, I was a No. 1 draft choice. Everybody hopes. I knew I could play with those guys."

Draft day can be a career maker or breaker. A player learns how much his potential is loved. It is important that he be chosen by the right team, one where he can fit in and one where he will receive the coaching to raise him up to the top level.

In those days, professional sports leagues' drafts were not televised. It sounds somewhat quaint, but they were conducted in virtual secrecy and it may have even taken a few days for a player to discover if he was drafted at all and by whom. Baker was antsy to learn his future. He was ready to embrace his destiny. His mother, not so much.

"My mother wanted me to be a doctor or a lawyer," Baker said. "I said, 'Momma, that's too much school.'" None of the above for Baker. He did ponder attending college and said he would have majored in journalism, not to be a sportswriter, but to be a general interest reporter, covering hard news, the same kind of hard news of nationwide import he followed on TV growing up.

"Superman was my hero and he was Clark Kent," Baker said of the reporter for the fictional Daily Planet. "I wasn't going to be no Jimmy Olson, cub reporter."

The closest Baker came to that lifestyle was being regularly interviewed by other reporters, day after day, as a baseball player and manager. He contributed to the process of getting the news out, but not writing the news up.

On the eve of that 1960s draft, Baker may have been a top draft pick in his own mind, but not on the boards of big-league clubs. He was not drafted until the 26th round. There were some other issues. His parents, Johnnie Baker Sr., a defense industry worker, and Christine Baker, a professor, had just gone through a divorce and he worried about finances.

Plus, both his mother and father preferred he enroll in college rather than try out for a baseball team. Baker was offered a basketball scholarship to the University of California-Santa Clara. Baker's dad even told scouts from many teams not to waste a draft pick on Baker because he was going to pursue advanced education. The tip was ignored. His mother ended up co-signing his baseball contract, necessary because he was under age.

The team that called Baker's name was the Atlanta Braves, a nightmare scenario – he thought – the Deep South team he did not want to go near. But he was wrong about Atlanta and becoming part of the Braves. He was right about his ability, taking only until September of 1968 to reach the majors.

Most importantly, the lifetime lessons gained by living in what he presumed was going to be hateful Atlanta, developed him as an individual off the field more than it did on the diamond. Baker learned and matured. Thrust into the hotbed of the Civil Rights Movement, Baker got to know Andrew Young, eventually Atlanta's mayor and the U.S. Ambassador to the United Nations, and Rev. Ralph Abernathy, president of the Southern Christian Leadership Conference.

He did not mingle at all with governors Wallace and Maddox, but discovered there were other White people in the South worth knowing, people who did not all think like troglodytes.

"I met some good people," Baker said. "It made [me] a better, well-rounded person. It was one of the five best things that ever happened to me."

It all came to pass because the wrong baseball team selected Baker and God ignored his pleas. Atlanta turned out to be a blessing.

CAREER

As a player, Baker was a two-time All-Star, won two World Series rings and a Gold Glove. He played 19 seasons with the Braves, Dodgers, San Francisco Giants, and Oakland Athletics between 1968 and 1986. Baker hit 242 home runs with a lifetime .278 batting average.

Aside from actual baseball statistical production, Baker found himself in the right place at the right time periodically in big-league games. On April 8, 1974, superstar Hank Aaron, who had taken the younger Baker under his wing offering advice on baseball and race relations in Atlanta, smacked the home run that propelled him past Babe Ruth on the all-time home-run list. As Aaron blasted No. 715, Baker had a perfectly situated view waiting in the on-deck circle as the next batter scheduled to hit.

Although there are some doubters that this occasion was the genuine first-ever example, Baker is also credited among most baseball people as being an active participant in the first high-five in sports. The scenario described took place on October 2, 1977, the last day of the regular season. Although the Dodgers lost this game to the Houston Astros, 6-3, Baker ripped a sixth-inning home run to give him a notable 30th homer for the season. Greeting Baker at home plate was teammate Glenn Burke, who had entered the game the preceding inning.

Burke felt Baker's home run was worth celebrating, so as Baker trotted across the plate, he lifted his arms in the air. The gesture caught Baker off-guard and initially he did not know how to respond. Then he came up with an answer.

"His hand was up in the air and he was arching back," Baker said. "So, I reached up and hit his hand. It seemed like the thing to do." ESPN The Magazine, now defunct, wrote about the encounter in 2011 and ESPN the TV network, included it in its series of documentaries 30 for 30.

Baker first managed in the majors with the Giants in 1993 and stints followed with the Cubs, Reds, Washington Nationals and starting in 2020, the Houston Astros. The Astros cleaned house administratively after being accused by Major League Baseball of stealing signs. Baker, who had won three manager-of-the-year awards, was viewed as a winner who could maintain the team's prominence and restore a tarnished image. Despite long-term success, he also had a little bit of unfinished business in the game.

In 2022, the Astros' regular-season mark of 106-56 was the best in the American League and Baker reached one long-held goal of passing 2,000 victories. At the end of the season, the Astros blitzed the playoffs to capture the World Series over the Philadelphia Phillies in six games and Baker won his first championship ring as a manager. Television commentators repeatedly offered compliments about Baker's leadership and achievements while noting what a gentleman he is and valuable ambassador for the game. During the Series, fans in the stands held up signs reading, "Do It For Dusty." Similarly, Astros players said they were happy to win it all for Baker.

"You gotta persevere," Baker said after the deed was accomplished. "You gotta believe in yourself."

Entering the 2023 season, Baker had recorded 2,093 wins and owned a World Series title, so it was widely expected that he would be elected to the National Baseball Hall of Fame in December of 2023, when the Hall's Veteran's committee next was scheduled to meet to consider managers and administrators for inclusion. Baker ranks eighth all-time on the list of managers with the most wins and was 101 wins shy of sixth place.

Meanwhile, the man who waited so long for the ultimate triumph as a manager, and who was scheduled to turn 74 in the middle of the 2023 season, signed a one-season contract extension to lead the Astros for another year.

ERNIE BANKS

⟫⟫⟫⟫⟫⟫⟫⟫⟫⟫ THE SETTING

Ernie Banks was one of the staple stars of Major League Baseball when I was growing up, a perennial All-Star who excelled first as a shortstop and then as a first-baseman. But he had long retired and moved to the Los Angeles area before I moved to Chicago and began writing about sports there.

Although Banks did move back to Chicago during the last years of his life, most of the time when I resided in his city, he was in another. Almost all of the several conversations we had took place on the telephone and mostly in the context of historical books about his one and only team, the Chicago Cubs.

However, any time that I reached out to "Mr. Cub," as Banks was famously known as the permanent face of the franchise, he was gracious, friendly, and cooperative. He was not always all-business, either. Banks liked to make small talk and the topic could range far from the baseball diamond. He was also seemingly perpetually cheerful in the sense that he used the phrase with me, "That's wonderful," almost as a punctuation mark.

You never wanted to call Ernie Banks for one of those baseball talks if you were in a hurry, for example a sports newspaper writer on deadline. Two conversations, preambles, essentially stand out as fun beginnings of interviews we conducted.

"Ernie Banks here. How are you feeling?" That was how Ernie answered the telephone in Marina del Rey, California. He immediately conveyed the mood that he was still ready to "play two" as the immortal phrase he was tagged with expressing his desire to play a double-header any day, every day.

One of those occasions took place during the winter in the early 2000s. Banks, who was married more than once, often inquired about the love life of anyone he spoke with – hoping they were all happily in a loving relationship. Gravely, he wanted to know what I had bought my wife for the soon-arriving Valentine's Day. I told him I had not yet done my shopping, but planned to obtain a card and a gift. "Chocolates," he said. I should buy chocolates for my wife. Which was not an outrageous suggestion, but my wife does not eat chocolate. I hated to break that fact to him.

On another occasion, the topic veered far from the diamond. During that stage of his life, Banks was wearing bow ties as his formal dress-up wear. It gave him a dapper look. This time Banks told me I should start wearing bow ties. For anyone who knew me this would be a ludicrous suggestion since I am practically allergic to any semblance of fancy dress. "Ernie," I said, "bow ties look good on you, but they wouldn't look good on me."

I didn't really believe that bow ties would become me, especially not accompanying jeans and a Hawaiian shirt.

》》》》》》》》》》》》》 *THE STORY*

Infamously, the Cubs were a team spinning its wheels in the sand for most of the many years Ernie Banks represented them in uniform. He was one of the finest players of all time, but a Hall of Famer who never was a member of a pennant-winning team, or had the pleasure of competing in a World Series.

That failure to go all of the way with his beloved club, or even come close enough to sniff the roses, was one thing that frustrated Banks between 1953 and 1971.

Not even when he hoisted the weight of an entire club on his shoulders could the power enable Banks to lift the Cubs to a single championship during the nearly two-decades-long playing connection with his favorite team. Instead, for the most part, Banks had to settle for statistical greatness. One of the aspects of the game Banks became known for was hitting home runs, a production that was almost alien for those playing shortstop during the 1950s and 1960s.

It was a given that shortstops were rangy, usually shorter in height and lighter in weight than almost everyone else in the lineup. They were often tagged with the "good field, no hit" appellation. Banks pretty much broke the mold and shattered that image.

Five times Banks hit more than 40 home runs in a single season and twice led the National League in circuit clouts. Not only did his sparkling performance at the plate win him two Most Valuable Player awards while competing for a team finishing deep in the second division, an almost unheard-of event at all, Banks exceeded 500 home runs during his career when it was a rarer achievement. Banks finished with 512 blasts.

Reaching 500 home runs – and the way he was celebrated – was a special moment for Banks and perhaps his favorite of all on-field personal happenings.

The all-time disappointment for Banks, the Cubs, and fans, was represented by the waning days of the 1969 season. Chicago played terrific ball much of the summer, but as the so-called "Miracle Mets" charged, the Cubs faded. In the end, it was the Mets, not the Cubs, experiencing glory that October.

It was a crushing blow to the team's psyche and even as manager Leo Durocher defended his handling of the players, he sought to force an aging Banks into retirement. Attempting to win a public relations war with Banks in Chicago was futile and silly.

And it was Banks in the early 1970s who gave the team a renewed sense of excitement. On May 12, when the Atlanta Braves were visiting Wrigley Field, a poor crowd of 5,264 fans drifted into the ballpark. Banks stepped to the plate in the second inning and creamed a pitch off hurler Pat Jarvis.

The ball sailed out of play for Banks' 500th career home run in a 4-3, 11-inning victory. The crowd was small, but the noise it made was mighty. As he circled the bases, and his people cheered him, Banks tipped his cap.

Although many more sluggers have since joined the club, the shot made Banks the ninth player in big-league history to reach the milestone total and 500 is still an enviable total to reach.

"The pitch was a fastball inside and up," Banks said of the toss he hit so hard.

In the context of it being the closing period of his career, and the often less-than-subtle reminders from Durocher that he wasn't getting any younger, Banks had the presence of mind to note (and repeat later), that since it was a Tuesday, it was Senior Citizens' Day at Wrigley Field. It was, for sure, as it almost always was, Ernie Banks Day at Wrigley Field.

⫸⫸⫸⫸⫸⫸ CAREER

Banks never got into a verbal war with Durocher. Only whenever he got a chance to play, he did his job, coming through with a big hit. After that game Banks did say he hoped to play for 20 years, all in a Cubs uniform. This was his 18th season and he did play for 19, retiring following the 1971 campaign.

Lifetime, Banks played in 2,528 games, ending up with those 512 homers, 1,636 runs batted in, and a .274 average. A 14-time All-Star, Banks' No. 14 jersey was retired by the Cubs. He was elected to the National Baseball Hall of Fame in 1977.

Not bad, overall, for a guy who grew up in Dallas, Texas playing softball, not baseball. One of Banks' early proponents was one-time

Negro Leagues star Buck O'Neil, who managed him with the Kansas City Monarchs and then as the first African-American coach in the majors tutored Banks with the Cubs.

O'Neil, who was known for his savvy but also positive disposition, influenced Banks in that way, too. Banks said he got his sunny attitude about baseball and life from O'Neil.

For all his accomplishments, once when Banks was asked to name his most memorable game, he chose his Major League debut of September 17, 1953. That was only a half-dozen years after Jackie Robinson broke the color barrier in the National Pastime with the Brooklyn Dodgers. Although he quickly teamed with another Black player, Gene Baker, being in the lineup that day made Banks the first player of color to appear in a game for the Chicago Cubs.

It was a milestone occurrence, but Banks later said he thought only this: "That is the way it is supposed to be." And of course, he was right.

Banks said he had no desire to manage a big-league team, but he did some coaching for the Cubs. For years, in addition to his community service work and efforts in business, he was affiliated with the team's front office. There was no more popular a spokesman for a team that had difficulty putting a winner on the field than Banks.

In 2008, the Cubs unveiled a statue in front of Wrigley Field honoring Banks in bronze. In 2013, President Barrack Obama named Banks the recipient of the Presidential Medal of Freedom.

Banks died of a heart attack in 2015 at the age of 84 and he was buried at Graceland Cemetery, which is only a short distance from Wrigley Field.

During the last years of his life, Banks cast about for a way to make a bigger lasting contribution to American life. Originally, some believed Banks was only kidding when he said the one worldwide honor he coveted was winning the Nobel Peace Prize. Banks never did find a niche that would have the world bowing at his feet in gratitude once more, though. He had to be content with baseball immortality.

CHAD BENTZ

》》》》》》》》》》》》》 *THE SETTING*

Chad Bentz is not as famous as he should be. Every baseball fan remembers Jim Abbott, who became a long-shot, unlikely hero for succeeding in Major League Baseball between 1989 and 1999 despite a disability that would have benched almost anyone else.

Abbott, who won 87 games in the majors in stints mainly with the California Angels and New York Yankees, plus the Chicago White Sox, and finally the Milwaukee Brewers, was a left-handed pitcher. It was never going to be any other way, because he was born with a deformed right arm, so he had no fully shaped right hand to throw with.

Abbott, who also threw a big-league no-hitter, starred in college at the University of Michigan and for the United States national team. He was also an inspiration to and a role model for Chad Bentz, who followed the trail blazed by Abbott.

Like Abbott, Bentz's birth defect was being born without the use of a right hand. He was also a left-handed pitcher who after he wound up and threw the ball, slipped his glove onto that hand to field.

If Abbott was one-in-a-million, Bentz made it two-in-a-million. Call him Jim Abbott II, but Bentz was also unique. Growing up in Juneau, Alaska, Bentz had less attention early on than Abbott did. Bentz also faced the reality that Alaska may be the best place in the world to be a dog musher, but it is not a haven for future Major League baseball players.

Alaska is the largest state in the union, but with a population that hovered in the 500,000 range when he was growing up in the 1980s, and harsh weather patterns that essentially wiped-out spring baseball, Bentz had little chance to gain notice.

For those of us working in sports journalism in Alaska, Bentz was a known and impressive quantity, as well as someone to be admired, rooted for, and followed. He was drafted by the Yankees in 1999, after he played summer Connie Mack League ball in Michigan. Instead, he opted for college at Cal-State Long Beach, then was drafted again by the Montreal Expos.

At 6-foot-2, 215 pounds, Bentz had size, as well as a 90-mph fastball when they were a little less common. There were big-league clubs willing to take a look at the guy from Alaska.

⋙⋙⋙⋙⋙⋙⋙ *THE STORY*

For most of his life, when Bentz competed in sports, he was the object of curiosity and he was impossible not to notice on the playing field. He might have been shorted in the dispersal of all body parts, but he certainly knew how to use what he had to his utmost advantage.

In the summer of 1999, as part of his journey of hope, as he was beginning to understand the challenges that lay ahead at each higher level of the sport, Bentz suited up for the Anchorage Glacier Pilots of the Alaska Baseball League. Since the 1960s, the ABL has been one of the premier summer stops for college players seeking more experience. Typically, the handful or so of Alaska teams that played under the Midnight Sun recruited the finest college players to compete from June to August.

Bentz was a rarity in being from Alaska, even if not from Anchorage, 800 miles from Juneau, and he brought a local name with him for fans, even at just 19. Unfortunately, whether he just wasn't ready for the limelight or pressure, he had a rocky summer, going 1-3 with a 9.50 earned run average while pitching 18 innings. It was a little bit like having a birthday cake explode in your face.

Bentz said he became intimidated early on when the public address announcer would tell the crowd at Mulcahy Stadium what school the hitter represented as he stepped to the plate. It was somewhat like the "Wizard of Oz" comment by Dorothy that when things happened so quickly, she realized she wasn't in Kansas anymore. Bentz recognized the batters weren't high school foes coming up against Juneau-Douglas.

"I heard the schools," Bentz said of College World Series participants and the like, "and I went, 'Oh, man.' These guys have been playing at good programs a year or two. They're older and stronger."

Bentz's self-assurance definitely took a bruising.

"I've learned every single time I've been out there," Bentz said that season. "I've learned I've got to master two or three more pitches. My curveball used to be great."

Statistics compiled in summer ball for the most part don't follow a player. The ABL is supposed to be an educational and development tool as well as an opportunity to play extra games and gain experience, and maybe go fishing in a player's free time.

"If you look at my stats," Bentz said, "it's been a bad summer. But this summer's been great. I had a lot of fun. My confidence is not very high, but at the same time it is high. I think it will help me in the long run."

After a freshman year of college ball, Bentz was back with the Glacier Pilots in 2000 for another run and he definitely seemed sharper, more mature and renewed. One of his solid outings was a five-inning, one-run relief appearance.

"I built my arm strength and changed my leg kick," Bentz said of what coaches did for him during the intervening year. "They were just fine-tuning me a little bit."

He did put the swerve back in his curveball and worked on improving his change-up.

From there, Bentz only got better, about to earn a different kind of evaluation in the college game and again in the pros. He became Mercedes Bentz.

CAREER

After Bentz was drafted by a Major League club for a second time, he signed, joining the Montreal Expos' organization. He spent time with minor-league teams in Harrisburg, Pennsylvania, Edmonton, Albuquerque and Louisville, among other stops.

Teammates marveled at his ability to field with one fully functional hand and even erupted in cheers when he speared a line drive back to the mound.

Bentz met Abbott – probably the only true relevant role model for him -- and they spoke about their mutual disability. He said Abbott basically told him to keep working hard and not to change what he was doing.

As he progressed and gained attention, Bentz said he tried to respond to any contact from a youngster or anyone else who flattered him by referring to him as inspirational. As someone who was once insulted by other youths for being different, Bentz embraced locker room banter, making jokes about his right hand, laughing when teammates called him the "One-Armed Bandit" or "Sebastian the Claw."

He kept flirting with sticking with the Expos and finally did for a bit in 2004, though going just 0-3 with a 5.86 earned run average as a reliever in 36 games. After that, he had a short connection with the Florida Marlins, going 0-0, but being hit hard in limited innings.

A couple of tastes of Major League play. However, that was as far as his baseball talent took him. Bentz retired without an elusive Major League victory, but he advanced farther in the game than 99.9

percent of the boys who grow up with big baseball dreams.

Intriguingly, when he was in high school, Bentz had been re-cruited to play NCAA Division I football and when he stepped back from baseball, he re-enrolled in school at Division III Castleton State College in Vermont. He played one season there and worked as the baseball team's pitching coach for the 2013 season, too.

Bentz, married with a family, returned to Juneau, Alaska and then became the athletic director at his old high school.

In an appropriate icing-on-the-cake moment honoring his ath-letic career, in April of 2019 Bentz was inducted into the Alaska Sports Hall of Fame. During his acceptance speech, Bentz praised Abbott for being a role model to him and said when he was playing professionally, he was conscious of filling that slot for many who approached him.

"I was able to meet a ton of people that were disabled in some way," Bentz said. "I could see they were looking at me like I looked at Abbott."

TOM BROWNING

〉〉〉〉〉〉〉〉〉〉〉〉〉〉 *THE SETTING*

A left-handed hurler who was a native of Casper, Wyoming, Tom Browning was a member of one of the most elite clubs of throwers who ever played in the majors. He is one of 23 pitchers in history to hurl a perfect game.

Dating to the origins of the National League in 1876, with more than 235,000 games recorded, the perfect game is indeed one of the rarest of all accomplishments. No pitcher has thrown more than one perfect game and the task has eluded even the extraordinary resumes of most of the finest pitchers in the Hall of Fame.

Throwing a perfect game – 27 men up, 27 men retired over nine innings, no walks, no hits, no base runners allowed – is somewhat akin to a lightning strike. It is basically unpredictable and comes out of nowhere.

The first two recognized perfect games took place in 1880 when hurlers Lee Richmond and John Montgomery Ward pulled off the feat within five days of one another in June of that year. Then there were no more for a long time, something which has periodically happened throughout baseball history.

Cy Young, the winningest pitcher of all-time with 511 victories, and for whom the annual award for pitching excellence is given to the best in the National League and American League each year, followed in 1904.

Addie Joss, Sandy Koufax, Jim Bunning, Jim "Catfish" Hunter, Randy Johnson, and Roy Halladay are the other Hall of Famers who were perfect for a day. A few others, such as Mark Buerhle and Dennis Martinez, had exemplary careers. And some others put together the greatest day of their professional lives as an aberration compared to the remainder of their performances.

Tom Browning fit into the middle, essentially. He was a top-notch pitcher in a few seasons, winning 123 games in 12 Major-League seasons, all but one with the Cincinnati Reds. And he was perfect once.

I first met Browning in connection with an event for the Reds Hall-of-Fame, of which he is a member, but we spent our longest time talking via telephone in 2013 during a brief period when I was the sports editor of his hometown newspaper in Casper, Wyoming, a place where he always retained ties, and a city which remembered him fondly.

⟫⟫⟫⟫⟫⟫⟫⟫⟫⟫⟫⟫ *THE STORY*

By the time I was in Wyoming, Browning was making his year-round home in Kentucky, but venturing out for assignments wherever the Reds might deploy him. One such job was coaching rookie league ball in Billings, Montana, which is just down the road from Casper. Or he might be sent to a slightly different environment, coaching in the Arizona Instructional League.

Browning lived in Casper the first 14 years of his life, but he seemed in tune with the sagebrush forever. Indeed, Casper, a city of

60,000 or so, is a Western place where a pedestrian might be struck by wind-driven tumbleweeds.

"The wind blows," Browning said succinctly of the old homestead area.

Browning learned the game in Casper, played Little League and Babe Ruth there and in his early teens played in Wyoming tournaments everywhere from Sheridan, Powell, or Rock Springs, any of the towns where Buffalo Bill Cody might have ridden, as well.

"Anywhere in the state," Browning said.

His own family was filled with a dad and uncles who played plenty of fast-pitch softball well into adulthood.

Browning fell in love with baseball in Casper and the place also shaped his view of the world, instilling in him appreciation for the outdoors and a joy for fishing.

"It's beautiful country," he said.

Demonstrating that sports rooting allegiances can be ingrained early, Browning said his favorite college athletic program was the University of Wyoming Cowboys. Using the local vernacular, he said, "I do pull for the 'Pokes."

When he began getting serious about baseball, Browning tried Tennessee Wesleyan for a little while and then LeMoyne College in Syracuse, New York. Even though those were small schools, in locations far different from Casper, he did well enough for the Reds to draft the 6-foot-1, 190-pounder.

His first minor-league assignment was in Billings in 1982 with the same Mustangs he returned to coach years later. Browning was a rookie at 24 in Cincinnati, or really an unofficial rookie, going 1-0 in three outings.

That minimal big-league exposure retained his rookie status for 1985 when he burst on the NL scene with a 20-9 record that left him runner-up for Rookie of the Year. That turned out to be the best year of Browning's career. He made one All-Star team, in 1991, but won between 14 and 18 games for Cincinnati five other times. He was a workhorse and led the National League in games started four times and was a member of the 1990 Reds team that won a World Series championship.

Browning tossed his perfecto on September 16, 1988 against the Los Angeles Dodgers during an 18-5 season. It was a home game when the Reds were still playing in Riverfront Stadium and Pete Rose was the manager. The game was over in 1 hour, 51 minutes. Once it started.

The first pitch time was actually just after 10 p.m. because of a rain delay of 2 hours and 27 minutes. The 1-0 victory over L.A. starter Tim Belcher, who also threw a complete game while allowing just three hits and striking out seven, was a bona fide treat for the 16,591 fans. That was paid attendance. Imagine having walked out on the night's events early because of the showers falling and being left with a ticket stub, but no memories attached to it that were not of a soggy nature.

Browning had taken a no-hitter into the ninth inning in June of that summer against the San Diego Padres, but Hall of Fame batting wiz Tony Gwynn broke that one up with a single. Browning settled for a one-hitter at Jack Murphy Stadium in a 12-0 win.

While teammates almost unanimously refuse to mention a budding no-hitter to a pitcher in the middle of a game, Browning was quite self-aware in the perfect game, talking to himself.

"I was laughing by the seventh inning," Browning said as he recalled his demeanor on the mound at Riverfront. "I was also thinking, 'It ain't happening.'"

"It" was the perfect game result and it did happen. At the time, Browning's gem was the 12th perfect game in history and it had been 23 years since a southpaw (Koufax, in 1965) had thrown one.

Some years later, in the 2000s, when some other perfect games had been notched, Browning was invited to participate in a get-together of the living perfect-game throwers.

"It was really cool," he said. "It was awesome. When you break it down, it's a very small club."

⟫⟫⟫⟫⟫⟫⟫⟫⟫⟫⟫ *CAREER*

Browning pitched for the Reds between 1984 and 1994 and at age 35 in 1995 he appeared in a couple of games for the Kansas City Royals. He retired that season with a mark of 123-90. He was selected as a member of the Reds team Hall of Fame in 2006.

Clearly, the perfect game was the ultimate high in the sport for Browning, but he was also known for a colorful, unusual stunt during a 1993 Reds game against the Cubs at Wrigley Field in Chicago. In the middle of the game, while in uniform, Browning slipped out of the ballpark and joined some fans in the famous rooftop seating across the street. The Reds may have laughed, but also felt compelled to fine him $500.

Browning had already once departed a park in uniform, mid-game, though for a completely different reason – and it was Game 2 of the World Series in 1990. His wife Debbie was going into labor and Browning neglected to inform manager Lou Piniella he was splitting to join her at a hospital. When the game, ultimately won by the Reds over the Oakland A's, 8-3, was going into extra innings, Piniella put out an SOS radio bulletin summoning the AWOL Browning back to the ballpark.

After retiring from playing, mostly due to nagging injuries, Browning was a spring training instructor for the Reds, handled those minor-league jobs, did some broadcasting, and co-authored a book called *Tom Browning's Tales from the Reds Dugout*. A son, Logan, pitched in the Boston Red Sox minor-league organization.

Tom Browning fans were shocked in late 2022 when he was found dead in his Union, Kentucky home on December 19 at age 62.

There were many heartfelt tributes issued in Browning's memory upon his sudden death.

"RIP, my friend, Mr. Perfect, Tom Browning," said Hall of Fame shortstop Barry Larkin on Twitter.

MARK BUEHRLE

THE SETTING

Most of Mark Buehrle's career played out with the Chicago White Sox. During much of that time, I was living in Chicago and attending White Sox games both as a spectator and a sportswriter, depending on the occasion.

He was always a cooperative locker room interview and a serious competitor on the mound as he built a resume about as good as anyone's in the American League. As someone who covered the outdoors for the Chicago Tribune, talking to Buehrle about non-related baseball topics related to the outdoors, especially hunting, was also a treat. He had his own ranch in Missouri.

The southpaw was a notable regular in the Sox rotation from the time he was in his early 20s and was also a highly regarded fielding pitcher.

The 6-foot-2 and 240-pound Buehrle was one of the rare pitchers who have thrown a perfect game in the majors, but he also threw an additional no-hitter, an even rarer combination achievement. Being the author of both pitching accomplishments is not something many have done.

Buehrle could do just about anything he was asked to do on the baseball diamond – except hit. As someone who spent the first 12 years of his career in the American League, nobody asked him to hit for quite some time because of the designated hitter rule.

Then Buehrle became a free agent and signed with the Miami Marlins of the National League. That led to a most amusing conversation with a man I had never before seen swing a bat. In the Marlins locker room one day in 2012 we talked about his hitting prowess, or lack of such.

»»»»»»»»»» *THE STORY*

While spending those dozen years in the employ of the White Sox, Buehrle almost never came to the plate. Basically he had about a half-dozen plate appearances per season and his successful hitting rate was almost non-existent. Six times he went oh-for-the-season for a batting average of .000. He never had more than one hit in a season, though one year when he was 1-for-4 he batted .250. The other years his average was .167.

So, when I sidled up to Buehrle in the Marlins' clubhouse at the start of the new season of 2012 and asked how his hitting was going in the new league, he not only smiled, but held out his hands to show off the callouses he had developed by practicing his hitting in spring training.

"I never batted in Chicago," Buerhle said.

Which was not quite literally true since he came to the plate those periodic handful of times when the White Sox were engaged in interleague games at a National League home park. He said he never did come to bat at the then-home field U.S. Cellular Field.

As it turned out, Buerhle, who had just turned 33, said he had not really batted for real, with intent for about 15 years. That took him all the way back to high school in Missouri. At Jefferson College in Missouri, he had one at-bat. In the minors, with Burlington in the Midwest League and Birmingham in the Southern League, his job did not involve swinging away. Each time he came to the plate in the majors except for the interleague stuff, it was almost an accident. To say he was out of form would be putting it mildly. But now he was playing in a league with no DH rule, so he was going to have to take his at-bats in every start.

Miami did not recruit Buerhle to hit home runs, or hit at all. The Marlins wanted him to throw complete games, or at least a large number of innings, something Buerhle was good at in his AL days, twice leading the league in innings pitched.

Much of Buerhle's time in Chicago, Ozzie Guillen was his manager. When he joined Miami, Guillen was his manager there, as well. Guillen was asked about the new man's hitting, but he danced around the question in a general way.

"The only thing I care about my pitchers is that they get three at-bats," Guillen said. "I don't care if they go oh-for-three." What Guillen meant was that he wanted his throwers to go deep enough into their starts to come up in the order three times, not worrying so much about how they fared swinging the bat. "I know this kid for many years. I know what I'm going to get from him."

That meant he knew Buerhle was not going to be confused with Mickey Mantle, nor even old Chicago Cubs pitcher Ferguson Jenkins, who was a hurler dangerous enough to hit homers.

Buerhle as a pitcher was never going to throw fastballs as fast as he was going to see in the batter's box. His tosses sometimes paralyzed the radar gun at 72 or 75 mph, not 95 or 100. Yet he knew how to pitch.

"Location, that's all it's ever been," he said.

The Marlins were paying him millions of dollars to pitch, not to hit.

As it so happened, coming to the plate regularly for Miami was only a short-term aggravation. He finished that season 13-13 with a 3.74 earned run average. No matter how much practice he put in wielding the bat, it did not pay off, though. That season Buerhle had 71 plate appearances, 67 official at-bats, and struck out 29 times. He safely struck just three hits for a batting average of .045.

Oh, Buerhle once participated in a true-or-false quiz where one item on the list was whether or not the designated hitter rule was created by the devil. Appropriately, for a guy who benefited so much from it, he said, "False."

⟫⟫⟫⟫⟫⟫⟫⟫⟫⟫⟫⟫⟫ CAREER

Buerhle's National League vacation lasted just that one season. In November, after the season, the Marlins swapped him to the Toronto Blue Jays, back to the American League, as part of a 12-player trade.

From a hitting standpoint that was marvelous. But as a dog lover who was extremely close to his pet American Staffordshire terrier/pit bull mix, Buerhle was stymied by Canadian authorities as he sought to bring his dog with him to his new place of employment. Ontario had a ban on pit bulls, so Buerhle had to rely on the kindness of other family members to take care of his pal.

Buerhle pitched the last three seasons of his Major League career in Toronto, retiring at 36 in 2015 with a pitching mark of 214-160 and an earned run average of 3.81. He was a five-time All-Star and a four-time Gold Glove winner. He pitched at least 200 innings in a season for 15 years in a row.

During those last three years with the Blue Jays, Buerhle was back to his infrequent plate appearances, batting just 13 times total, zero in 2014. His lifetime batting average ended up an anemic .072. He will not be remembered for wielding a big stick.

Buerhle will be well-remembered for his mound demeanor and exploits. He won 19 games in 2002 and went 16-8 in 2005 when the White Sox won their only World Series crown since 1917.

The lefty hurled his first no-hitter on April 18, 2007 in a home game against the Texas Rangers. It was the White Sox's first no-hitter in 16 years and first no-hitter in the new version of the old Comiskey Park. Buerhle came close to firing a perfect game that day, too, a walk to Sammy Sosa being the only opposition base runner.

It was difficult to improve on that effort with any day on the mound, but Buerhle somehow did so on July 23, 2009 when he became one of 23 major leaguers to pitch a perfect game. Buerhle bested the Tampa Bay Rays in that effort. Chicago won 5-0 in a game that took just 2 hours, 3 minutes with 28,036 fans present for the afternoon contest. Buerhle struck out six.

There was one notable threat to the perfect game, a blast to deep center field by Gabe Kapler in the ninth inning. But the Sox's Dewayne Wise ran down the bash for an outstanding grab. Afterwards, someone asked Buerhle if he owed Wise a steak dinner and he replied, "I think I owe him a lot more than that."

Funny thing, President Barack Obama, White Sox Fan No. 1, phoned Buerhle from Air Force One to congratulate him and yes, he said Buerhle should reward Wise with a steak dinner.

Celebrating Buerhle's Perfect Game

STEVE CARLTON

THE SETTING

It was an of-all-people, in an of-all-places scenario when Hall of Fame pitcher Steve Carlton visited Alaska and provided baseball instruction to some Little Leaguers in Anchorage.

What were the odds? This was the same Steve Carlton who spent many of his pre- and post-game work days on the mound with the Philadelphia Phillies ducking out of sight in the trainer's room rather than speaking with sportswriters. Tim McCarver, or some other catcher, acted as his verbal ghost-writer, explaining what Carlton was up to when he fired that fastball on the 3-2 count, or something like that.

For years during his lengthy Major League career, one of the greatest by any pitcher, Carlton was a semi-recluse from the public, not uttering a single word. He had developed a grudge against the media and zipped his lips for years at a time, even when he was the finest pitcher in the game, even when he helped pitch the Phillies to the 1980 World Series championship. He didn't even celebrate in the locker room with his teammates after they clinched the title.

The sudden appearance of Carlton a few thousand miles north of the baseball world he inhabited, providing friendly, graceful, charming advice to little kids who could only dream of accomplishing one-tenth as much as he did on a baseball diamond, seemed stunning. He and some others traveled to Alaska to participate in a charity golf tournament.

The reason I was so surprised, was because during part of Carlton's Philadelphia heyday, I was a sportswriter for the Philadelphia Inquirer, a member of the particular media he despised (although I was not around at the beginning of the feud and didn't really know what jump-started it).

Now here I was as a sports reporter in a different place, at a different time (long after Carlton's retirement) being invited to cover his vacation/baseball visit to the Far North. Up until that moment in 1995, I had never actually met Carlton because whenever I was assigned to coverage of a Phillies game, he was in his hideout. I was one of those sportswriters who quizzed Phillies catchers and got them to interpret how the fastball and slider were working that day off the arm of the big lefty, aka Lefty, as if he was the only one in the sport.

A part of me struggled to hold in chuckles throughout our interview, pondering the incongruity of the situation and me by no means about to tell Carlton I was once upon a time a member of the bad-guy Philadelphia media when he was pitching there. I was just the stranger, the innocent sports editor of the Anchorage Daily News.

》》》》》》》》》》》》》》 *THE STORY*

The clinic for kids had about 35 participants and most, if not all, were under 12. They were young enough they hadn't even seen Steve Carlton throw on television because he was out of the game. Reluctantly, Carlton only went into retirement grudgingly in 1988 at age

43 after 24 seasons in the big leagues. Even seven years later, Carlton seemed tempted to make a comeback. He was living in Colorado and the Rockies needed pitching.

Carlton played at 6-foot-4 and 210 pounds, could whip a fastball past anyone and baffled everyone else with a slider. He looked younger than his age and in conversation did seem a little bit open (if questionably serious) about taking another spin around the block with a Major League team. At that time, that summer, the Rockies' team earned run average was nearly five runs per game. That was kind of an embarrassment. Could Carlton help lower that mark?

"I could do it," he said. "I could commute."

He was making a joke, really. That was something many of the sportswriters he had met in the past didn't think he had in him.

Speaking off-the-cuff was never a strong point for Carlton. Often enough in retirement, on the few occasions he had granted interview access, he had felt burned by what came out in print, stories that made him sound like a whack-job attributing statements to him that he later denied.

Some of them were nasty, talking about a conspiracy of Jewish bankers in Switzerland running the world, about such prominent international organizations such as the World Health Organization and International Monetary Fund conspiring to run the world, and suggesting that the AIDS virus was concocted in a Maryland laboratory with the aim of killing off Blacks and gays. These days that almost sounds like the Republican Party platform – just kidding – but Carlton was painted unkindly by those quoting him.

The Little Leaguers were a safer audience, some of them as young as seven. One of the oldsters, 12, admitted barely knowing who Carlton was, but said, "I know he's good."

Statistically, in the baseball world, that was absolute fact. The guy won a lot and he struck out more guys than anyone in history besides Nolan Ryan, Randy Johnson, and Roger Clemens, more than 4,000 would-be hitters overpowered.

A southpaw with a big leg kick that probably alone frightened a share of scheduled batters, Carlton was talking to kids who barely stood above his waist, but at least he passed on the thought that if they grew and wanted to develop their pitching motion, they could take advantage of a stretch-to-the-sky leg kick.

"There's more potential for velocity the higher the knee," Carlton said.

»»»»»»»»»»»»»» *CAREER*

One thing Carlton spoke about during his Hall of Fame induction speech in 1994 was how the biggest break in his career actually occurred during a trip to the same small upstate Cooperstown, New York town.

Carlton made fun of himself in his speech, taking note of his nickname as "Silent Steve" and added, "This will probably be the most talking I've done in quite a while."

Spoofing that image in another way, Carlton implied that not saying much caused some awkwardness. He said in 1987, when the Twins won the World Series and President Ronald Reagan visited the World Series, a photo caption in a Minnesota newspaper called Carlton "an unidentified Secret Service agent."

In Anchorage, Carlton admitted he was nervous about being required to give a speech at the Hall of Fame event.

"There was pressure," Carlton said. "Making a speech is not my bailiwick."

In 1966, Carlton was property of the St. Louis Cardinals, was in the minors, but was given a trial in an exhibition game against the Minnesota Twins at Doubleday Field. Carlton said he struck out 10 men and revived his career.

Carlton was a first-ballot Hall of Famer, voted in with more than 95 percent of the vote. Noting baseball writers whom he was often at odds with did the honors, Carlton said he appreciated that. Most closely linked to the Phillies, despite switching teams, Carlton entered the hall representing that club.

"Philly is a tremendous sports town and Philadelphia was very good to me," Carlton said.

Over his 24 seasons with the Cardinals, Phillies, Giants, White Sox, Cleveland Indians, and Twins, Carlton won 329 games and struck out 4,136 men in 5,217 2/3 innings. He won four Cy Young Awards and was a 10-time All-Star.

It is probable that in his last-gasp efforts to stick in the majors, even some die-hard baseball fans don't recall Carlton's brief stays with some of those teams. In his Hall of Fame speech, Carlton alluded to that, commenting, the game pretty much "ripped the uniform off my back, which is how I ended my career."

He also spoke about focus and concentration and had previously said those mental attributes were his strengths and contributors to his success.

Once, in an interview with television personality Roy Firestone, the host asked Carlton, "Why do you think you were put on this earth?" As the fact succinctly summarized his mindset while pitching and perhaps illustrated the root of his success, Carlton said, "To teach the world how to throw a slider."

TONY CONIGLIARO

THE SETTING

It helps to be from the Boston area of that era, to have lived and groaned, to have experienced the glory and the tragedy of the star-crossed life of the local superstar cut down in his prime, but even now, going on 60 years after it all began, Tony Conigliaro's name evokes strong emotions among Boston Red Sox fans.

First of all, he was local, born in 1945, in Revere, the Atlantic Ocean town on the outskirts of Boston. He graduated high school from St. Mary's in nearby Lynn. He was only 17 when he signed with the Sox and right away he was a can't-miss guy, hitting .363 in the minors. Just like that he was promoted to the big club and as a rookie in 1964, "Tony C.," as he was routinely known, batted .290 with 24 homers in 111 games.

It was an instant star turn. In 1965, when Tony C. was 20, he led the American League in home runs with 32, the youngest league leader in that category of all time. He was no longer just a Boston phenom. All of baseball knew about Tony C. and what a great young player he was, set to partner in the outfield at Fenway Park with Carl Yastrzemski for years.

By 1967 at only 22 years old, Conigliaro surpassed 100 career homers, the youngest to that milestone of anyone in AL history. The 1967 season is well-remembered in Boston baseball for several reasons, mostly for the good. The team which had finished 9th in a then-10-team American League the year before, won the pennant in what was labeled "The Impossible Dream." Yaz won the Triple Crown by hoisting the entire franchise on his shoulders in September.

But the black cloud of remembrance is what happened to Tony C. in the midst of this energizing season. On August 18, Conigliaro was hit in the head by a pitched ball thrown by Jack Hamilton of the California Angels. He was carried off the field on a stretcher and hospitalized.

This began a years-long saga of health recovery and subsequent deteriorating, of bouncing back well enough to play at a big-league level again and then seeing the skills slip away once more. Conigliaro was traded to the Angels, where he lived in a development next door to actress Raquel Welch. Then he retired, unretired, retired, and tried to make comebacks.

After word spread that Tony C. was going to chase one last comeback with the Red Sox in spring training, in January of 1975, I met with the ballplayer at snow-covered Fenway Park, where he was doing indoor workouts before departing for Florida.

⟫⟫⟫⟫⟫⟫⟫⟫⟫ THE STORY

Tony C. sat on a training table in the bowels of the ballpark as a winter wind ripped outside. He was doing everything he could to get his body ready for a last-chance opportunity to write a new ending to his baseball career.

When Conigliaro was first hit by the pitch, it gave him an incredibly bruised black eye, memorialized in photography while he lay in the hospital. The problem that ensued as his body mostly healed, was that he could not see with the same degree of sharpness he possessed before the injury. His eyesight came and went. Excellent eyesight is a critical component of what he was in being able to spot the pitch traveling towards the plate. Only a minor adjustment downward in capability meant the difference between being an All-Star batter and a guy who couldn't hit his way out of the minors.

Now, after even more rest and time passing, Conigliaro believed his vision was back to full strength and all he was asking of the Red Sox was a look-see in spring training. A million Bostonians were rooting for him.

Tony C. was loosening up his right shoulder with heat packs so he would be ready to go when he could find someone to play catch with on this day. The young sensation had morphed into a 30-year-old who should have been in the prime days of his career, not preparing for a wing-and-a-prayer tryout. He was emboldened by a recent examination at the Massachusetts Eye and Ear Infirmary, the results of which were stunning.

What had been a gradually growing, interfering spot on his left eye, the cause of so much of his heartache, had vanished.

"The doctor was amazed the spot had disappeared altogether," Conigliaro said of the handicap that had been caused by the force of the infamous pitch. "My eyesight is now 20-15 in both eyes. As soon as he said it, I started thinking about coming back."

The report lifted his outlook from hopelessness to hope. Tony C. had been optimistic about what he might hear from medical experts already because the previous year he spent time in the Arizona winter league and he had batted about .300.

"That was against players of about AA or AAA caliber," he said, "but I was seeing the ball well."

That effort was a revival of baseball wistfulness in itself. He had become convinced he could no longer cling to the sport he loved. He did not play it and hardly watched it on TV or attended games in person.

"Put it this way," Tony C. said, "if you've been a ballet dancer all your life and put your all into it and you broke your leg and couldn't dance anymore, then you wouldn't enjoy watching it either."

People asked him why he persisted in the face of so much disappointment, but it was not hard to understand, he said. The itch was still there, however, so he gave the Arizona fling a chance. Now this.

He was watching the previous World Series on television with a friend when his buddy turned to him and asked, "'Hey, don't you think you can play as well as those guys?'" He hoped he could. He thought he might be able to. So, he contacted the Red Sox general manager Dick O'Connell asking for one last opportunity to make the team for 1975. For one thing, there was this new thing called the designated hitter and for a guy who could always hit, he might be well-suited for such a position.

The one glitch was that Conigliaro's rights were still owned by California, but it was not difficult to obtain his release. The Angels weren't expecting him to give it another go with them.

"I never expected to hear back from Mr. O'Connell," Conigliaro said. "I'm not worried about money. I'll probably sign something so I'll be Red Sox property when I'm down there. But then if I make it, they'll give me a real contract. I'm not looking to make money."

Mostly, he was seeking to fill the hole in his soul, though of course if all went well, the Red Sox would pay him well, too.

Although Conigliaro would prefer to play the field, being a DH would be fine, and hitting would carry him. A few months earlier, he said, he had taken nearly 4,000 swings with a lead bat, about half-and-half with live pitching and with a pitching machine.

"I've been working on my strength," Conigliaro said. "I want to stay a power hitter."

Tony C. out-lasted winter and joined the Red Sox in spring training in Winter Haven, Florida. His months-long build-up paid off and to the delight of Boston fans, he made the team. But the good news didn't last. His vision began clouding up again and after appearing in 21 games with two homers and a demoralizing batting average of .123 Conigliaro admitted his comeback was over and he retired. This time it was for good.

>>>>>>>>>>>>>>>>>>>>> **CAREER**

In the middle of all the ups and downs following Tony C.'s breakout start to his career, his injury, recovery, trade, and comebacks, he recorded one other spectacular season in 1970. He slammed 36 home runs with 116 runs batted in that year.

Lifetime, Conigliaro hit 166 homers with 516 runs batted in and a .264 average spread over parts of eight seasons. His younger brother, Billy also reached the majors. Billy was a lifetime .256 hitter in five seasons.

Tony C., who was 6-foot-3 and weighed 185 pounds, had movie star looks and was a heartthrob for female fans in Boston, especially after he also appeared around town as a singer and released a record. He was often tabbed as a playboy.

After baseball, although it took some time, Conigliaro found a niche in sportscasting, something he enjoyed very much and another career he was advancing in. He became an on-air personality in nearby Providence, Rhode Island and then in San Francisco.

In early 1982, Conigliaro, then 37, was in Boston where he was interviewing for a broadcast job that would have brought him home. On his way to catch a flight back to the West Coast, while being driven to the airport by brother Billy, he suffered a serious heart attack. Subsequently, Conigliaro endured a stroke that left him in a coma with some brain damage.

His last years were ruled by poor health. Conigliaro eventually died of pneumonia and kidney failure at 45 in February of 1990. Ever since, the Red Sox have given out a Tony Conigliaro Award in his memory to a Major League player who overcomes adversity with Tony C.'s spirit and determination.

The National Baseball Hall of Fame in Cooperstown, New York includes a research library containing a file folder for every player who has appeared in a big-league game. Inside Conigliaro's folder there is a xeroxed copy of a piece of paper on Boston Red Sox stationary that can only be termed nostalgic.

It is a questionnaire the team handed to young prospects to fill out, listing their home address and phone number, information about their high school days and the like. The date on Conigliaro's form is September 20, 1963, after he had already played a season in the New York-Penn League where he was named rookie-of-the-year for batting .363.

All of Conigliaro's responses were hand-printed and the one item that stands out as humorous came in answer to whether or not he had a nickname. The nickname he admitted to? "Choo Choo. I was given the name because of good speed in the Little League."

Choo Choo? Say that aloud in Boston these days, or even when he was wearing a Sox uniform and no one would know whom you were talking about. There was really only one nickname for Conigliaro: Tony C.

TONY GWYNN

⟫⟫⟫⟫⟫⟫⟫⟫⟫⟫
THE SETTING

During Hall of Fame weekend of 2012, Tony Gwynn traveled to Cooperstown, New York to mingle with his fellow members of baseball's shrine to the game's greats. It was a well-received appearance, a demonstration that one of the greatest hitters of all-time was alive – and well.

This was a good thing for Gwynn, for baseball, the Hall, and fans. Only a few months earlier, most of those observers of the sport had been blindsided upon hearing Gwynn, the greatest of all players in the history of the San Diego Padres, was battling cancer.

It was a worrisome time. Gwynn was not an old man, in his early fifties, so the news was particularly hard-hitting. It also struck many quite hard because Gwynn was a personable, well-liked individual across the board in the game.

Gwynn, an eight-time National League batting champion, with a lifetime average of .338, had resumed his connection to baseball, returning to San Diego State University where he had played both college baseball and basketball, as the baseball coach.

Then he was forced to take a leave of absence to undergo cancer surgery for a tumor on the left side of his face. For years, Gwynn had been somewhat of a typical old-school baseball guy as a regular tobacco chewer. He had tried hard to break the habit, but couldn't, and ended up becoming one of the players paying an exorbitant price for his habit.

Now, in July of 2012, Gwynn appeared to have made a complete recovery. One of the side effects of his surgery was a fear that he would lose the power of speech and be unable to deliver talks in public.

On this occasion, however, Gwynn was proving people wrong. Inside the Hall of Fame building, inside one of the theaters, Gwynn came to talk in connection with a popular event connected to the hall ceremonies. The U.S. Postal Service was unveiling stamps of four baseball stars honoring some of them who were members of the hall.

I was a member of the crowd in the auditorium and got to speak one-on-one with Gwynn after his public talk. It was an encouraging performance, showing us that he was well despite being scarred by the experience.

That was scarred, as in literally, from his operation. Surgeons digging out the tumor left a scar on the left side of his face that ran down to his neck, though it was not a wide one and was more easily viewed up close than it would have been if Gwynn wore a button-up shirt, tie, and sport coat.

⟫⟫⟫⟫⟫⟫⟫⟫⟫⟫⟫ *THE STORY*

The scar, it was noted, was on the left side. This marked the third time Gwynn had undergone a related operation stemming from the cancer provoked by his tobacco chewing.

A year before, a procedure on the right side left him with the inability to smile. For those who knew the man, saw the man on television, or in the flesh, that was a harsh sentence, because smiling was a natural condition for him.

There were two almost automatic pictures coming to mind when the name Tony Gwynn was mentioned: A ballplayer stroking a single to the outfield and a man with a wide smile on his face.

As therapy, Gwynn was required to chew gum as often as possible to strengthen those mouth muscles. Compared to a sentence of walking after knee surgery, lifting weights or doing 1,000 push-ups, the gum-chewing method seemed like lighter work.

Smiling, which he was at the time, Gwynn projected the presence of a cured man in the Cooperstown theatre. "Believe me, I'm happy to be here," Gwynn said at the event. "I'm doing really good."

The words provided relief from anyone who doubted Gwynn's status. His usual high-pitched voice was back in place and he seemed healthy, full-bodied, not like someone who had lost considerable weight due to a medical ordeal.

The cancer was an ordeal. Gwynn did not expect the problem, was startled by the diagnosis, and it disrupted both his college coaching and family life – more than once. He underwent a 14-hour operation to remove a malignant tumor about six months before this public appearance at the hall. To fix Gwynn's problem, doctors transplanted a nerve from Gwynn's right shoulder into his face.

The first two times doctors checked out Gwynn, he was informed that the tumor they found was benign. The third time around it was malignant and that frightened Gwynn. Besides the gum chewing, Gwynn also underwent surgery, radiation therapy, and chemotherapy, so things weren't all as simple as just munching on Juicy Fruit.

Gwynn was so hooked on chewing tobacco that he did not even stop biting down on it after the first check-up. He finally willed himself to give it up when he heard the word "malignant." By then he was equating the word malignant with cancer and cancer with death. The motivation to stop chewing at last overtook the habit of continuing.

One topic Gwynn touched on was one of the more fascinating baseball relationships he developed late in his career and late in the life of Ted Williams. Williams, the man many call the greatest hitter who ever lived, who reduced batting to a science and even used that word in the title of a book he co-wrote about it, won six American League batting titles and smashed 521 home runs. Appropriately enough, Gwynn and Williams hit it off and wherever they over-lapped they talked about hitting a pitched ball, which some say is the most demanding task in sports. They had a mutual respect and a shared interest in the intricacies of hitting well.

"He was always giving me advice to make me a better player," said Gwynn of Williams, who died at 83 in 2002 with a .344 lifetime batting average.

Gwynn's presence highlighted the Postal Services release of new baseball stamps featuring Larry Doby, Joe DiMaggio, Willie Stargell, and Gwynn's friend Ted Williams.

"I hope one day they make a decision that I'm worthy to be on a stamp," Gwynn said.

At that moment, though, Gwynn was more grateful for having good health again. "Right now, I'm glad to be standing here," he said.

⫸⫸⫸⫸⫸⫸⫸⫸⫸⫸⫸⫸ CAREER

Fans and baseball people left Cooperstown that summer day in 2012 feeling good about Gwynn's long-term prognosis, believing he was cured and would have plenty of time left to be anointed as a popular figure on a stamp.

Yet Gwynn, his wife Alicia, who was in the audience, friends, and others were shocked when the player soon endured another bout of cancer and this time he did not get well. They were greeted by stunning news when Gwynn passed away in June of 2014 at age 54.

The 5-foot-11, 185-pound left-handed batter was never a power hitter, but always a man who disrupted pitchers' rhythms with his uncanny manner of hitting anything they threw at him. During his 20 Major-League seasons ending in 2000, in addition to his .338 average, Gwynn collected 3,141 hits.

His eight times leading the NL in batting equaled the mark set by Honus Wagner of the Pittsburgh Pirates and they are tied for second all-time behind Ty Cobb's 12 American League titles established during his stay with the Detroit Tigers.

Known in San Diego as "Mr. Padre," Gwynn was a 15-time All-Star who won five Gold Glove Awards, and seven times led the National League in hits.

One of the more fascinating accomplishments of Gwynn's career took place during the strike-shortened season of 1994. Gwynn batted .394 in 110 games and many have ruminated over the years whether he could have become the first player since Williams in 1941 to top .400. Gwynn's was the highest average by a National League player since 1930 when the Giants' Bill Terry became that league's last .400 hitter at .401.

"I never really new how difficult hitting .400 would be," Gwynn said after that season ended. "If you're under .400 you just about have to get three hits a day to do it. That can get mentally wearing on you. Physically, I felt fine. But you can get crushed by the pressure of trying to hit .400. In my mind, I could have handled it."

The opportunity never came around again and neither has anyone else ever come close to the magic number in the years since. If he had done it, Gwynn would have burnished an already-glowing legacy.

When Gwynn died, the outpouring of sentiment about his abilities and character was monumental.

"Tony was an icon and one of San Diego's greatest sports legends. He was beloved by so many for his passion for life, his generosity, and, of course, his laugh." And that did not even come from a baseball person, but the then-president of the San Diego Chargers football team, Dean Spanos.

REGGIE JACKSON

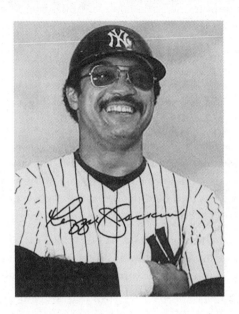

》》》》》》》》》》 ## *THE SETTING*

The 1981 Major League baseball playoffs were weird. They were played in the shadow of a mid-season players strike when competitors and owners were battling over a labor contract. The game shut down between June 12 and July 31. Then players were given until August 10 to get back in shape to play once more.

To make up for the lost games in the ordinarily set 162-game schedule, baseball reorganized the manner in which it chose teams for the playoffs, splitting the season into two halves, with teams from the American League and National League each earning a mini-pennant of sorts.

The situation ended up with teams competing in between 103 and 111 regular-season games before a round of playoffs. In the American League East, the New York Yankees won the first-half standings and the Milwaukee Brewers (before they transferred to the NL), winning the second half. The Oakland Athletics and the Kansas City Royals did likewise. In the National League, the split playoff spots went to the Philadelphia Phillies, the Montreal Expos, Los Angeles Dodgers and Houston Astros.

The Yankees faced the Milwaukee Brewers for the right to continue in the playoffs. At this stage of his playing days, future Hall of Famer, the slugger Reggie Jackson, was in the prime of his career, having already starred in Oakland and moved on to New York in free agency.

Jackson was seemingly always in the news, if not for hitting prodigious home runs, then for bickering with in-and-out Yankees manager Billy Martin and owner George Steinbrenner. Jackson was made for Broadway and the big city's bright lights, an incandescent personality who backed up big words with big deeds.

He had earned the accolade of "Mr. October" for bashing important game-changing hits in the World Series and the Yankees were on the cusp of another opportunity to play fall baseball.

Jackson attracted sportswriters from all over the country to his locker within the clubhouse, or when he stepped into the batting cage for warm-up swings. No one knew what he might say on a given day, but it was sure to be entertaining, if not newsworthy. He lured in the same kind of attention at Yankee Stadium or Milwaukee's County Stadium.

In those days, before indoor batting cages, fans used to come through the turnstiles early to watch batting practice, their eyes especially on the prominent power hitters like Jackson, hoping they would get a bonus homer show, even if it did not show up on the scoreboard.

When Jackson stepped into the batter's box for his turn at BP at County Stadium, the small number of early arrivals noticed and shouted his name. "Hey, Reggie!" rang out. Jackson took his time settling in, positioning his muscular body into a comfortable hitting stance, then easing into his swings. It took until the ninth and 10th pitches of batting practice for him to smack home runs, belting two consecutive shots beyond the fences, into the bleachers. He smiled after those balls flew far.

>>>>>>>>>>>>>>>>>>>> THE STORY

Jackson helped make his teams into winners. He was part of three World Series champions with Oakland and two more with the Yankees. Both teams won other division titles and pennants. The California Angels with Reggie won division titles.

The man had a sense of occasion, and sure enough, in the Milwaukee series, Jackson hit a two-run homer in the series-clinching 7-3 contest, sending the Yankees ahead to the next round of the playoffs.

Sitting in the dugout pre-game during the Milwaukee playoffs, Jackson was looking ahead, annunciating what he knew was expected of him at the plate. "I know I'm being counted on heavily to produce," he said. "I'm going to be, hopefully... very motivated."

Up until that mid-season players strike, Jackson had been hitting like an old man, batting an uncharacteristic .199. Of course, Steinbrenner, the man with no patience, was not willing to let the circumstances ride out without bombastically weighing in. He said Jackson must have something wrong with him and he should be examined mentally and physically by doctors.

Things improved after the strike ended and the Yankees moved on to the post-season. Jackson was one-for-four in Game 1 versus Milwaukee. He was one-for-four in Game 2, the hit being a home run. He went oh-for-four in Game 3 in New York and the fans weren't happy.

Jackson actually grinned when talking about home fans who were so demanding and impatient. They booed him if he didn't hit a home run in every game.

"I've been booed for about six consecutive years," Jackson said. "If I didn't get booed, I'd get riled. It doesn't really bother me. I try to turn it around and make it a positive thing. I try to say they're booing me because I'm good."

There was truth to that. He raised expectations so high with his own chatter that when he failed with a strikeout or fly-out, it was his own fault for letting everyone think he would always come to the rescue.

Of course, there were some people who would never be satisfied. Some didn't like Reggie Jackson simply because he said what he thought. He was another in a line of outstanding athletes, such as boxer Muhammad Ali and football star Joe Namath, who told everyone how good they were and why they were going to win the big ones.

When he retorted to Steinbrenner's criticism – the man who made his fortune in the ship-building business – as "the little kid with the boats," Jackson made the milk run out of some fans' noses with snorts. There was not that much sympathy out there for the other zillionaire.

There was no doubt Jackson had an ego about the size of the Empire State Building and any suggestion his personality did not feed into his image was just silly. Jackson collected millions of dollars to help the New York Yankees win championships. At no time did he do it better than during the 1977 World Series when he ripped home runs in three consecutive at-bats in the deciding contest over the Los Angeles Dodgers.

In his own way, Jackson was a baseball philosopher, once saying, "Hit the ball over the wall and everything takes care of itself."

Indeed, that was an accurate description of Reggie Jackson's career.

CAREER

After establishing himself as a star of the first magnitude with Oakland, Jackson boasted that if he signed a contract with the Yankees in free agency, he would become so famous, someone would name a candy bar after him. It was an amusing comment, but it came true. There was a Reggie Bar. For that matter, when the New York tabloid newspapers ran a headline and referred to him simply as "Reggie," there was no confusion over who they were talking about.

During a 21-season Major League career between 1967 and 1987 when he retired at age 41, the native of Pennsylvania cracked 563 home runs. Jackson drove in 1,702 runs and batted .262. He also struck out a lot, a huge amount, 2,597 times, the most in big-league history.

Yet Jackson was a 14-time All-Star, led the American League in homers four times, was a member of five World Series champs, won an AL Most Valuable Player Award and was a two-time World Series MVP.

Over time, besides the candy bar thing, Jackson endorsed cameras, televisions, radios, eyeglasses, toys, and sports shoes. He did a stint as a sports broadcaster. Always in the spotlight as a player, in his later years Jackson has receded somewhat from the public eye. In some ways he has become an elder statesman of the game.

When enshrined in the Hall of Fame in Cooperstown, New York, Jackson delivered a humbling speech that impressed listeners with its sincerity and wisdom about the sport that made him famous.

In part, Jackson said, "I'm just a link in the chain that makes the whole world go around. And so are today's players and those in the baseball community. So, whether you're the Babe, Stan the Man, the Say Hey Kid, or Mr. October. You're just part of a long tradition of baseball and the game is owed our respect and gratitude. We all borrow from it, exploit it, cling to it, and need it."

Also, during the speech, when singling out family, friends, and baseball people to thank for his success, Jackson did acknowledge Steinbrenner, his one-time loud quarreling partner.

"Thanks for the pinstripes, George," Jackson said.

FERGUSON JENKINS

Photo courtesy of BASEBALL HALL OF FAME

▶▶▶▶▶▶▶▶▶▶▶▶▶ *THE SETTING*

I first met Ferguson Jenkins in Fairbanks, Alaska, at the annual Alaska Goldpanners' Midnight Sun game. He was traveling with Greg Harris, then a vice-president of the National Baseball Hall of Fame and later president of the Rock and Roll Hall of Fame.

Harris loved taking Hall of Famers on tour to the northern reaches of Alaska to see a unique game. The Midnight Sun game is always played on the longest day of the year in the third week in June and the trick is for the hometown Alaska Goldpanners to play against a visiting team without turning on the stadium lights for a night game.

Sometime after that, Jenkins and I collaborated on a book about his life in general and life in the sport. We talked and interviewed in many locations. His chief baseball affiliation was with the Chicago

Cubs, but he did not reside in Chicago. He returned several times a year and once we met for dinner at Gibson's, the famous steak house. Another time, Jenkins and his wife came to dinner at my home in the Chicago suburbs. Other times we met in a hotel lobby. And we spoke on the telephone.

An outgoing man who was the only Canadian in the Baseball Hall of Fame for many years until joined by Larry Walker in 2020, Jenkins also made frequent trips to his home area in Ontario for baseball functions, banquets, and other appearances.

On that trip to Alaska (I did not witness it happening), but later heard how Jenkins caught a 50-pound king salmon, a prized catch in the angling world. Jenkins was an outdoorsman and I recall him once telling me how he hunted regularly with Bill Buckner, the former Cub and Red Sox hitter who resided in Idaho.

While no one keeps track of such things, Jenkins makes so many appearances, many of them for charity, that it must be said there will never be a shortage of Ferguson Jenkins autographs in the sports memorabilia world.

Besides making appearances together for the book we worked on called *Fergie: My Life From The Cubs To Cooperstown*, I once accompanied Fergie to a sports card store in Aurora, Illinois in the Chicago suburbs, where he signed autographs. A line of more than 100 people formed seeking his signature.

One youngster, a four-year-old named Jeffrey, was quite shy as he put down two Jenkins baseball cards on a table that he hoped to have signed. "Hey, big fella, how are you?" said Jenkins, who towered over the boy at 6-foot-5.

A teenaged boy in the line requested that Fergie write "Hall of Famer" on a ball next to his name. In the sports memorabilia world, that enhances the stature of the item and makes it more valuable. Most Hall of Famers almost automatically pen in "HOF" in pride after their election to the Cooperstown museum.

Jenkins laughed out loud at the request. "Young man," he said, "I put that on everything but checks."

》》》》》》》》》》》》》》 *THE STORY*

Chicago Cubs fans who relished the team winning a World Series title in 2016 for the first time in 108 years had waited generations to celebrate. The Cubs had been situated in the bowels of the National League standings for decades, a ballclub that regularly won pennants in the 1930s and into the 1940s, but then stopped winning altogether.

Fergie, who broke into the majors with the Philadelphia Phillies, came to the Cubs in 1967 and that year represented a breakthrough in optimism. In the late 1960s, the star-studded group seemed certain to win a pennant.

Jenkins was the ace of the pitching staff. Ernie Banks, perhaps the greatest Cub of them all, was still in the lineup. Hall of Famers Billy Williams and Ron Santo were on the roster. Other top-notch starters on the field included Randy Hundley, Glenn Beckert, and Don Kessinger and the bunch was managed by Hall of Famer Leo Durocher. In limited action, 21-year-old Ken Holtzman made his impact felt on the mound. Owner P.K. Wrigley was sick of losing and he thought he had finally assembled the team to be the difference-maker.

The 1967 season was the first of six years in a row that Jenkins won at least 20 games. It represented his emergence as an All-Star. The Cubs had gone from finishing 44 games below .500 to 13 games above in one year.

"The players came out of the 1967 season believing the organization was putting together a Cubs team that could contend for a pennant," Jenkins said. "We were not the National League doormat anymore. I won my 20th game at the very end of the season. I won it and two days later I was driving back to Canada. There was no champagne in the clubhouse. Everybody shook hands and everybody was pretty happy about what we had done that season."

The preceding three seasons, Jenkins had experienced mixed results on the mound as he was maturing as a pitcher with the Phillies and then with the Cubs. In 1967, his performance represented potential fulfilled, though he could hardly have imagined that one good year would translate into a stretch of many.

"I acquired the goal of winning 20 games," Jenkins said. "Every pitcher wants to do that. It is something permanent, something that stays with you when people talk about your career and ask what you accomplished. I can say, 'I was a 20-game winner in the big leagues.' I liked the sound of that. It gave me a secure feeling. I had no way of knowing that that was going to be the first of six straight seasons of winning at least 20 games with the Cubs."

Rather than entering the off-season in a gloomy mood as so many recent Cubs teams had, this team thought its future looked just grand. The players felt, "What's next?" Jenkins said.

The team was ahead of itself, however, and won three fewer games in 1968 than it had in 1967. Not Jenkins, though, who again won 20 games and started a league-leading 40 times.

All of that set the stage for the 1969 season, one which was supposed to bring redemption, but which ended in heartache and haunted the players and fans seemingly forever. The Cubs took command in the NL's East Division early and, as the pennant race turned for the home stretch, seemed certain to take first place in a new-fangled divisional race.

Then everything fell apart in September and the Cubs were caught and passed by the New York Mets, the so-called Miracle Mets led by Tom Seaver, the team which ended up winning the World Series.

"Even before the 1969 season began, we expected it to be a big year for the Cubs," Jenkins said. "We knew we had the talent to contend for the National League pennant. And his eminence, 'Mr. Cub,' Ernie Banks, announced, 'The Cubs will shine in '69.'"

Jenkins won 21 games and the entire Cubs infield, catcher included, and around the horn, was selected for the NL All-Star team, Hundley behind the plate, Banks at first, Beckert at second, Kessinger at third, and Santo at third.

"I really did have something going," Jenkins said. "The Cubs had something going, too."

The team was rolling and ended up winning 92 games, but just faded completely in the waning days of September.

"That was a bittersweet year," Jenkins said. "It did feel like [the] one that got away. It could have been us in the Series instead of the Mets. We just didn't get it done at the end of the season. There was a lot of feeling that if we had won it in 1969, we would have kept on winning and probably won in 1970, too. I thought we had an even better team in 1970."

Instead, the Cubs and their fans, had to wait until 2016 to claim that so very elusive World Series crown.

≫≫≫≫≫≫≫ CAREER

Ferguson Jenkins, who is from Chatham, Ontario, was born in 1942. He won 284 games in a 19-year Major League career, his most distinguished years with the Cubs. But Fergie, who won the 1971 National League Cy Young Award, also pitched for the Phillies, the Boston Red Sox, and Texas Rangers.

During his skein of six straight 20-game-winning seasons, Jenkins won 24 times in 1971. But he won 25 games for the Rangers in 1974. He is a member of Texas' team Hall of Fame. The Cubs retired his number, 31, in a special ceremony in 2009. It so happened that another Hall of Famer, Greg Maddux, also wore No. 31 for the Cubs. During the event, the team raised one number 31 for Jenkins and one for Maddux, using the flag poles on the right-field line and left-field line to display them.

That was a sweet day for both stars, with sustained standing ovations being delivered by fans at Wrigley Field.

Jenkins also had his face displayed on a bottle of wine in his home territory of Ontario, where he regularly hosted a charity golf tournament. The Rockway Glen Estate Winery appreciated Jenkins' roots – he is a member of the Order of Canada for his accomplishments.

"It's kind of unique," Jenkins said, "but fun to see. I like wine. Give me a nice Cabernet or Merlot and I'll love it."

Naturally, growing up in Canada in the shadow of the national game of hockey, Jenkins first aspired to become a player good enough to make it to the National Hockey League. Instead, baseball became his sport, but he also had a brief sojourn with the Harlem Globetrotters basketball team.

Jenkins was approached to be a part-time member of the touring, entertainment-oriented basketball team in 1967, originally just to appear in some games in Canada. He ended up playing for the world-famous team for parts of two baseball off-seasons.

"I had a blast," Jenkins said. "I was a pretty good player in high school." Nonetheless, even if he was most sought for name recognition, the Globetrotters put Jenkins through the paces of a tryout in Chicago. He passed the tests.

Jenkins said he was paid $150 a game and that included his efforts doing public relations for the contests. The Cubs were worried about Fergie incurring an injury. "They did tell me I'd better not get hurt," he said.

Playing such games in Ontario, when his mother and father and other members of the extended Jenkins family could attend, provided the most fun he gleaned from the tours. Jenkins acted with famed Globetrotters Meadowlark Lemon and Curly Neal, among others.

Jenkins sat on the bench the first half, then at the beginning of the third quarter, he was inserted as part of a specially designed routine before he played real basketball for the rest of the third quarter.

The comedy skit the Globetrotters devised around Jenkins was a role as a pitcher who gave up home runs every night he pitched. It was a good thing Fergie had a sense of humor.

TOMMY JOHN

THE SETTING

The context for chatting with long-time left-handed pitcher Tommy John were his ties to Indiana. John is a member of the Indiana Baseball Hall of Fame, a topic I was focused on in a feature story for the Seymour, Indiana, newspaper.

John grew up in Terre Haute, a few hours north of Seymour, and is one of the more prominent living members of the Indiana hall, which is located in the community of Jasper. Among some of the other highlighted Hoosiers in that hall are Don Mattingly: 98-year-old former Brooklyn Dodger Carl Erskine; and Scott Rolen, recently selected for inclusion in the National Baseball Hall of Fame in Cooperstown, New York.

Others in the Indiana hall who are also honored in the Cooperstown hall are: Mordecai "Three-Finger" Brown, Gil Hodges, Judge Kenesaw Mountain Landis, Sam Rice, Edd Roush, Amos Rusie, Chuck Klein, Oscar Charleston, Sam Thompson, and Max Carey.

Some other well-known Indiana contributors in the Indiana hall who did not reach the status of the national museum are: Kenny Lofton, Ron Kittle, Lloyd McClendon, Dizzy Trout, Andy Benes, Don Larsen, George Crowe, Steve Hamilton, Fred Fitzsimmons, Bob Friend, and Everett Scott.

John, who lives in Sarasota, Florida, was born May 22, 1943. When he was a youngster, he was more interested in playing basketball than baseball. Naismith Basketball Hall of Famer Bob Leonard, also from Terre Haute, remembers John being the ball boy for his high school team.

Probably the most astonishing aspect of John's lengthy and excellent Major League pitching career is that he is better known for an injury he suffered and its related medical procedure cure than almost anything else. Arguably, John's arm is better known than his life since even non-baseball fans are not only acquainted with "Tommy John surgery," but have undergone it to fix their own health problems.

>>>>>>>>>>>>>>> THE STORY

For all his identification with baseball and his early start and success in the game going back as far as high school, some 60 years later, John admits that his first sporting love was basketball. He said no one should be surprised about that, either, because basketball is essentially the state sport of Indiana.

"I had to," John said of playing basketball and loving it so much. "I grew up in Indiana. I would have been looked at as a Communist if I didn't."

John might well have been given the Red Scare of the early Fifties promulgated by Wisconsin Senator Joseph McCarthy, or at the least seen as un-American. Didn't matter. John well could have taken a different path to athletic achievement. It turned out that baseball, and his trusty, strong left arm, was the way to go. The 6-foot-3 John was also good at that game and said he had about 50 scholarship offers to pursue hoops in college.

Along the way, John did have one baseball offer he could refuse. When he was 17 and playing for an American Legion team, the squad made an appearance playing a ballgame behind the walls at the Terre Haute Federal Correctional Institution. The youthful John was not only the starting pitcher for the teenagers, he pitched a complete game that won him an invitation to extend his stay and stick around.

"I struck out 23 batters," John recalled, and their (the inmates') coach asked, 'Do you think you could stay longer?'" A spot in the behind-bars prison team rotation was not on a list of long-term goals for John as he sorted out his life choices between baseball and basketball.

John's serious basketball career ended when his serious baseball career began. John was just 18 years old when he pitched in his first professional games for the Dubuque, Iowa minor-league team, a Class D club in the Midwest League. He was property of the Cleveland Indians, which promoted him quickly through other ranks of the minors with stays in Jacksonville, Florida and Charleston, West Virginia.

By most standards, especially for a pitcher with no college ball on his resume, John was a prodigy, making his first big-league appearances with the Indians when he was just 20. Still, it took a little bit longer to record successes. The Indians gave up on John too early, but by the time he was 22 in 1965 he had won 14 games for the Chicago White Sox. John remained with the Sox through the 1971 season.

His best years lay ahead of him, however, first with the Los Angeles Dodgers and then the New York Yankees. Not without an interruption, though. In 1974, John was clipping right along with a 13-3 record and a 2.59 earned run average after 22 outings, leading the National League with an .813 winning percentage. Then life took an unmarked, sharp left turn.

On the day he disappointingly was left off the NL All-Star team roster, John suffered an elbow injury pitching against the Montreal Expos. The sudden rupture, explosion, snapping, or just what exactly, left John groping for an explanation as to what just happened. He made damage done to his ulnar collateral ligament in his left, pitching arm almost sound as if was an out-of-body experience. Doctors examined the elbow and a lot of tut-tutting took place.

The legendary follow-up to remember what seemed to be a hopeless situation became world famous. Dr. Frank Jobe, the Dodgers' team physician, operated on John with a new, experimental surgery in hopes of rescuing his career. Jobe transplanted a tendon from John's right arm to fix the problem. Jobe even admitted the odds were 100-to-1 against the operation being successful enough for John to return as a big-league pitcher.

Discouraged, but in no way prepared to give up, John went to work with a rehabilitation regimen. He did not pitch for the Dodgers at all the next season. He later said in an interview that he was going to pour everything he had into getting his arm back to its former capability within two seasons. His main weapons were a curveball and a sinker.

In a little-known belief (perhaps because John rarely uttered the plan and didn't need it) the pitcher said though he wanted to return to his old self, but if he could not, he harbored a Plan B.

"I wanted to pitch again," John said. "If I couldn't do it my way, I was going to try the knuckleball."

Only a tiny fraction of pitchers have success with the knuckleball, which is thrown with little stress on the arm at a slower-than-average speed. John had been teammates on the White Sox with Hoyt Wilhelm, whose expertise with the knuckler earned him a spot in the National Baseball Hall of Fame.

John said if he could not do things his way, he was going to head to spring training and mimic Wilhelm's routine of throwing the knuckler every day in the outfield, playing catch, working on the technique.

"I had given myself two years to come back," John said, "then I was going to go down to Sarasota and spend time with Hoyt and learn the knuckleball."

In the end, however, John did not need a knuckler to return to the majors.

To almost everyone's shock, John resumed his career with the Dodgers in 1976, going 10-10 in 31 games at age 33. The next season, with his rebuilt left arm, John was better than ever. He finished 20-7 with a 2.78 earned run average, was the runner-up for the NL Cy Young Award and turned in some of the most satisfying pitching performances of his career.

Most meaningful and most memorable to John was his victory in Game 4 of the 1977 National League Championship Series when the Dodgers clinched the pennant, 4-1, over the Philadelphia Phillies and John topped the East Division champ's ace Steve Carlton.

"It was the first playoff win for Tommy Lasorda (the Hall of Fame manager)," John said. "It was probably the best baseball game I ever pitched."

John is perhaps most identified closely with his time spent with the Dodgers and he said Lasorda made going to the park fun. Once, Lasorda told the players he had hired a psychologist who would help out their mental game. John said everyone in the clubhouse groaned.

"Everyone went, 'Oh, god,'" John said. "Then the door opens and in walks Don Rickles."

The insult comedian was a pal of Lasorda's and he cracked up the house, loosened up the players with humor. It was not the kind of scene repeated in dugouts farther away from Hollywood.

CAREER

John ended up pitching longer after his career-threatening injury than before it and can only laugh over how the phrase "Tommy John surgery" has entered the common lexicon.

It was 1963 when John first pitched in the majors at 20 and it was 1989 when he was 46, when he threw his final games. In-between, John twice won more than 20 games in a season for the Yankees and finished his career with a record of 288-231, accompanied by a 3.34 ERA. He won 164 games after the operation.

A four-time All-Star, John is pretty much a walking miracle as the guinea pig who took the risk of undergoing the dramatic surgery that has helped save the careers of numerous big-league pitchers and helped others.

In 1985, John and his wife Sally co-authored a book about the parental torture they underwent helping to nurse a son, Travis John, back to health after a life-threatening injury following a fall through a window to pavement as the baseball world and others rooted for them. After two weeks in a coma and brain surgery, the boy did recover.

John never did shake his relationship with the arm surgery. In

1978, he spoke at a Philadelphia sports dinner with 1,100 people giving him a Most Courageous Athlete Award. He said at the time that was roughly 1,096 more people who ever thought he'd pitch again after the injury.

The four were John, his wife, Lasorda, and the Dodgers' farm director Ben Wade. Not even Jobe, the medical man, believed John would throw such high-caliber pitches.

"Dr. Jobe told me, as a friend, that I should go look for another line of work," John said. "He said I'd never throw a ball again, let alone get out major leaguers."

John won the 1976 National League Comeback Player of the Year Award and he was also awarded baseball's Fred Hutchinson Award for overcoming adversity. But one can say he has maintained a sense of perspective about Tommy John surgery.

In 2012, John had a check-up in an Indianapolis medical facility for a shoulder problem. While he was there, MRIs were taken of his elbow to look it over, something that had not been done previously. John ended up purchasing 100 copies of the MRI's and had Jobe sign them.

In the spring of 2014, John put up for sale four MRIs of his once-damaged elbow autographed by John and Dr. Jobe, who passed a couple of months earlier. The money was scheduled to go to the "Let's Do It Foundation." The organization is dedicated to keeping the planet clean.

SPIDER JORGENSEN

THE SETTING

Sitting on the hard wood seats behind home plate at Anchorage's Mulcahy Stadium in 2000, then-80-year-old Spider Jorgensen shared some baseball thoughts from his 60 years connected to professional baseball, though there was time out in the 1940s due to World War II.

In his current role, Jorgensen was doing what he began doing in 1970: scouting. He had been employed in that role since 1970 for the Kansas City Royals, Philadelphia Phillies, and Chicago Cubs and was present in Alaska on this trip on behalf of the Cubs. He was doing what he always did, bringing his instinctive feelings about identifying talent to the ballpark. This represented Jorgensen's sixth year of spending part of the summer watching the young collegiate athletes at play in the Alaska Baseball League. He made the trips with his wife Scotty.

Jorgensen had been working the West Coast for the Cubs since 1983 and Alaska fit the geographic model. Jorgensen had previously recommended the signing of Mark Grace who had played for the defunct North Pole Nicks in the Alaska league, a team that sold T-shirts picturing Santa Claus swinging a bat as souvenirs. During his 16-year Major League career, Grace made three All-Star teams and won four Gold Gloves and batted .303.

On this occasion, Jorgensen staked out a good seat behind the plate in the grandstand to watch the multi-day Anchorage Bucs Wood Bat Tournament play out. Several teams were involved, competing in several games, giving him multiple opportunities to see the same players in different circumstances. Ordinarily, the ABL used the more cost-friendly aluminum bats, so this also gave Jorgensen and other scouts the chance to watch players swing away with the wood bats they would use as pros.

Jorgensen was also the Cubs scout who first eyed future Hall of Famer Greg Maddux and recognized that he could become a special pitcher. Maddux won 355 games during his long career, becoming one of the greatest of all time by emphasizing control and location and not a super-speed fastball. He was just 17 when Jorgensen saw him throw with brilliance.

"He can tell them what he's throwing and they still can't hit it," Jorgensen said.

⟫⟫⟫⟫⟫⟫⟫⟫ THE STORY

John Donald Jorgensen picked up his colorful nickname of "Spider" when he was in high school in Folsom, California. It was not because he was awkward, all arms and legs, or a superb fielder grabbing every ball hit to him. The nickname had nothing to do with baseball.

After wearing black shorts with orange markings on them, a teacher teased Jorgensen in front of other students, saying the teen reminded him of a black widow spider he had just killed in his woodshed.

No one remembers the teacher's name, but the nickname stuck and followed Jorgensen for a lifetime.

Setting out to play professional baseball, Jorgensen was 21 in 1941 when he broke in with Santa Barbara in the California League and batted an excellent .332. However, his career then went on a long hiatus, because he was busy serving the United States in World War II.

Jorgensen was 26 in 1946 when he returned to the game with the Brooklyn Dodgers' top minor-league affiliate, the Montreal Royals. It was there Jorgensen made the acquaintance of another young player about to make history. His teammate, then, and with the Dodgers, was Jackie Robinson, signed by team operator Branch Rickey with the express goal of cracking baseball's longstanding color barrier banning Black men from playing in the majors.

Jorgensen was a ringside witness to many of the challenges of racist behavior experienced by Robinson and for a man who had an average, five-year, big-league career, is better remembered today for being in the picture with Robinson on many occasions, whether that meant on the field, in spring training, traveling on the road, or having conversations. There is a Jorgensen character in the movie *42* and his name can be read in books about Robinson's struggles and career.

"Some of them resented him," Jorgensen said while in Anchorage of how even some players reacted poorly to having Robinson as a teammate.

There was a lot of racist verbiage tossed Robinson's way from fans and opposing players and Jorgensen heard much that, too. "He took a lot of crap," Jorgensen said.

It was a different time and a different, much harsher, world, and while the teams in the AAA International League were located in big cities, Baltimore seemed as much a southern community as if it had been situated in Arkansas or Mississippi.

One time in Baltimore, Robinson did not even play in a game for the Royals because of injury, but the game had a controversial ending with a fight and fans flooded the field as Montreal players hurried into the clubhouse. As the team sat indoors, the unruliest fans gathered outside the locker room and some shouts were heard such as "We know you're up there, you Black SOB!"

On this trip to the park, there had been no Montreal team bus. The players took taxi cabs from the hotel. One by one players on the Royals took their chances and slipped away, returning to the team hotel. Certainly, in this day, there would have been a strong law enforcement presence on hand to disperse the fans and escort the visiting players out. But not then and it wasn't always clear whose side those uniformed men would be on.

"Nobody called the police and said, 'Hey, let's break this bunch up,'" Jorgensen said.

So, he, Robinson, Marv Rackley, and another player named Tommy Tatum, patiently or impatiently, sat around on their own in the clubhouse, truly, as the cliché goes, waiting until the coast was clear.

"We stayed until the clubhouse boy looked out and said they were all gone," Jorgensen said.

Robinson excelled with Montreal, batting .349, and was earmarked for the Dodgers and a place in history. Not many of those other Royals made much of a splash in the majors. Jorgensen batted .293 with 71 runs batted in in 117 games.

Still, at the end of spring training in 1947, Jorgensen did not expect to make the final cut to stay with the Dodgers. He was so certain he was headed back to AAA Montreal for Brooklyn, he shipped out all of his equipment, gloves and bats included, to Syracuse, New York, where the Royals were scheduled to open.

Only he then surprisingly learned, because of injuries to other players, he was going to be with the Dodgers at the start of the season. Jorgensen happily went one way, even as his gear inconveniently went another way.

 ## CAREER

April 15, 1947 saw the Dodgers open the new season at Ebbets Field, hosting the Boston Braves in front of 26,623. The historical significance of Robinson joining the team as the first Black player in Major League Baseball since Moses Fleetwood Walker and his brother Weldy Walker in 1884, has made the date memorable and etched in lore.

Joe Hatten was the starting pitcher for Brooklyn and Johnny Sain for the Braves. The Dodgers won the game, 5-3, with the victory going to reliever Hal Gregg.

In more recent recognition of the pioneering stature of Jackie Robinson, who is a member of the Hall of Fame, all teams have retired his uniform jersey number of 42. Also, every season on April 15, all members of all big-league clubs wear the number 42 for their games that day.

Robinson went oh-for-three in his debut, though he scored a run. At the end of that season, Robinson won the rookie-of-the-year award. It is a given that the coincidental major league-debut of Spider Jorgensen in that same game did not garner nearly as much attention from newspapers and broadcast outlets as Robinson's.

The fact that Jorgensen was even present had already caught him off-guard. Then he learned he was going to be in the starting lineup, playing third base. Somewhat panicked, Jorgensen was worried, because he had farmed out all of that equipment and it had not turned up yet.

Jorgensen said he was "scared to death" as a rookie making the start. But because Robinson was playing first base, his usual infielder's glove was available and he lent it to Jorgensen, who also scrounged up a borrowed pair of spikes. Jorgensen went oh-for-three that day, too, though he knocked in a single run. A couple of other former Royals teammates from the bomb shelter hideout, Tatum and Rackley, both made appearances in the game.

There was a two-day break before the next game and this time, as the Dodgers clobbered the Braves, 12-6, Jorgensen played a major role at the plate. He hit his first big-league home run, slashed three hits, scored two runs, and drove in six runs. It was the best game of his career.

Simultaneously, Jorgensen said, the performance by him as a rookie – most of whom were viewed with skepticism by veterans in those days – gained him quick acceptance.

"Then I became one of the boys," Jorgensen said. "I was not an outcast."

Jorgengen's big-league playing career lasted just five seasons, through 1951. He never played more than his 129 games, or showed better, batting .274, than he did in 1947. By 1950, Jorgensen was a member of the New York Giants.

Overall, Jorgensen's lifetime batting average was .266 in 267 games. He played in two World Series for Brooklyn in 1947 and 1949, appearing in 11 post-season games. After retirement, Jorgensen did some coaching and then began his long journey as a big-league scout. He died in 2003 at 84 – while still doing some scouting for the Cubs.

JIM KAAT

>>>>>>>>>>>>>>>>>>>>> *THE SETTING*

In late March of 1979 while employed by the Florida Times-Union, the larger of two daily newspapers in Jacksonville, Florida, I made my only journey to spring training. I roamed around various camps within a tight radius in the state and visited with well-known baseball figures for a series of stories. It was a blast.

At that time, southpaw Jim Kaat was a member of the Philadelphia Phillies. A player who made his first appearance in the majors in 1959, Kaat was already an old-timer who had been around as long as almost any competitor in the sport.

Kaat could not read the tea leaves, but he knew his own heart and desires. Although so many others in the baseball world believed he was close to the end of the line, he was determined to continue pitching. And he did so, not retiring until after the 1983 season when he was 44 years old and had pitched for 25 years in the big leagues. That was not the longest of anyone in history, but Kaat was right up there on the list.

At a time when weight-room work was either non-existent or at a premium, Kaat's vital statistics were 6-foot-4 and just 205 pounds. These days he probably would have had another 15 or 20 pounds of muscle packed on him.

Kaat had been around the game so long, he made his first pitching appearances with his original franchise when it was called the Washington Senators. That was before the old Senators transferred to Minnesota to become the Twins.

Much of the meat of Kaat's career was spent with the Twins, but he also had a couple of excellent seasons with the Chicago White Sox and at this time had been a member of the Philadelphia Phillies for a few years.

Kaat and I spoke in Clearwater, Florida, the long-time spring training home of the Phillies.

⟫⟫⟫⟫⟫⟫⟫⟫⟫⟫ *THE STORY*

At the time, Kaat, who was born in Zeeland, Michigan in 1938, was 40 years old. By that time, the ageless legendary pitcher Satchel Paige had published his biography, Maybe I'll Pitch Forever. It seemed as if Kaat was poised to author volume two. At the least he had the mentality to keep on chuckin'.

Much like any athlete watching the calendar in any professional sport, Kaat was busy denying the aging process. As far back as 1973, his trusty Twins were giving up on him, only to watch him win at least 20 games twice for the opposing White Sox. That had to sting.

In Clearwater, Kaat was starting to get similar vibes from the Phillies' management team, that maybe they would be happier if he retired and went on to do other things with his life. Kaat's presence was almost a gesture of defiance. He wanted to stick around with the Phillies a little bit longer and he definitely retained the belief that he had the skill to stay in the sport.

"I feel very good," said Kaat, who was enjoying the strong Florida sun on his freckle face and as the author of 261 victories at the time wanted to remain in the game long enough to reach the coveted milestone of 300 wins.

By that point in his career, Kaat had won the Gold Glove as the best fielder at his position in the American League 16 times, an astounding number. That is a lot of gold. Whether he felt that proved he was still spry enough coming off the mound to grab bunts or just what, Kaat was proud of that skill. He just wasn't sure how many times making a praiseworthy play in the field outright helped him win games.

"I made a few plays that are the best I've ever made," Kaat said of the 1978 season, one year he did not win the award. "But there were other years I made four or five errors and still won, so I guess it evens up."

Pitchers who stay in the majors for a long time as they age through their late thirties and into their forties often are forced to make adjustments to survive. Sometimes their arm strength slips a little bit, their youthful vigor declines. By 40, Kaat had made those types of adjustments, a better word than sacrifices, to remain gainfully employed by a big-league club.

When he was younger, starting out, Kaat threw faster than he did two decades later. He had more of a big, sweeping delivery, but one of those strategy switches involved him altering the delivery to make pitches in more of a hurry.

"Once I went to that style, I wanted to stay in the proper rhythm," Kaat issued as an answer to batters who complained he was quick-pitching them. "I think it's helped me. It's easier to concentrate." He would have loved the new hurry-up pitch clock introduced to the majors for the 2023 season.

Kaat was a member of the Phillies when they were a powerhouse in the National League, winning division titles, but not able to get over the top and win the National League Championship Series to make it into the World Series.

"It's like a horse race," said Kaat, who wanted to be part of a Phillies Series team. "Ability is not our problem. We have as much as any team. But the team with the most talent doesn't always win."

As it so happened, Kaat was not with the Phillies much longer after that March spring training. He was with Philadelphia when the team broke camp and went 1-0 in three games before being sold to the New York Yankees, where he spent the rest of the 1979 season and part of the 1980 season. There the perpetual member of starting rotations became a reliever for the first time.

Unfortunately for Kaat, it was in 1980, a year after he departed for other pastures, that the Phillies won their long-coveted World Series championship.

>>>>>>>>>>>>>>>> *CAREER*

Kaat had pitched in the World Series with the Twins and he was lucky at 43 to be a member of the St. Louis Cardinals when that ballclub made it to the Series and he got another chance. The 1982 club won the title and it was Kaat's only world championship.

Things ended on the field for Kaat when the Cardinals released him in July of 1983, a move that shocked him. After recovering from the initial jolt, he said he could not complain because, "I had a 25-year vacation."

Overall, Kaat won 283 games, falling a bit short of his goal of 300, with a 3.45 earned average. He had remarkable longevity, appearing in 898 games over a quarter of a century of pitching. He won 25 games during the 1966 season, and all of those 16 Gold Gloves, while three times being named to All-Star teams. By breaking into the majors in 1959 and lasting until the early 1980s, Kaat was one of the unusual players whose career spanned four decades.

Kaat said the toughest hitter for him to face over the years was Detroit Tiger Hall of Famer Al Kaline and the baseball coaches and managers he learned the most from were legendary pitching coach Johnny Sain and Jack McKeon.

A pitching coach for the Cincinnati Reds in 1984 and 1985, Kaat had such a long broadcasting career it sometimes eclipsed his playing career. For a later generation, he was a different kind of baseball figure. He started broadcasting locally in Minnesota in 1965. He spent time handling Yankees games and then Twins games and worked for NBC in varying capacities, including covering the College World Series and Olympic Games baseball.

He then moved to CBS and worked on "Baseball Tonight" for ESPN. He also later broadcast for the MLB Network. For a while it seemed possible Kaat was going to match his Gold Glove haul with Emmy Awards, but he only won seven.

Kaat received his greatest honor in 2021, at the age of 83, when the National Baseball Hall of Fame's Golden Era Committee selected him for enshrinement. In 2022, the same year he was inducted, Kaat co-authored a book about his baseball life called, *Good As Gold: My Eight Decades In Baseball.*

It should not be a surprise given his last name that the pitcher's nickname during his playing days was "Kitty." Some said "Kitty Kat." It was much later, when he lasted in the majors for 25 years with those several teams, and had the same type of well-traveled broadcasting career, that the Kitty part was given a double meaning in describing Kaat as a cat with nine lives.

"There's no question I was running out of time," Kaat said of his Hall of Fame selection as an octogenarian. "It's been worth the wait."

JERRY KOOSMAN

⫸⫸⫸⫸⫸⫸⫸ *THE SETTING*

The guest of honor did have a terrific summer in Auburn, New York once upon a time early in his baseball career when he was still trying to find a spot on a Major League roster. It was 1966 and after going 12-7, Jerry Koosman got his first taste of the big leagues.

During the winter of 1977, Koosman received another taste of Auburn, this time as a sports banquet speaker in the small town in upstate New York near Syracuse.

By then he was an established star, a key figure in the 1969 New York Mets run to the World Series title. Though he could not know what was on the horizon, Koosman was about to have the worst season of his big-league career. He may not have been invited if the event took place a year later.

Or perhaps that would not have been the case since Koosman

truly shined in Auburn with a 1.38 earned run average and as a pivotal player in the club's run to a championship as winners of the New York-Penn League's Governor's Cup. Fans were always going to remember Koosman's good times with the then-Auburn Mets who finished with an 80-49 record.

The southpaw from Minnesota did enough to endear himself to Auburn fans to be remembered a decade later and provide a speech entertaining them all over again.

As a humorous personal aside to the event, I was covering as a reporter for the nearby Syracuse Herald-Journal. Even as Koosman was signing autographs post-dessert, this marked the first time in my life I was asked to script my own signature for someone.

More than 600 people attended the Sacred Heart Parish Sports Dinner and there seemed to be an endless line of 12-, 13- and 14-year-old boys seeking Koosman's autograph. He signed personal messages, good-luck notes, and the like with affability.

The aside began as a joke on me. A photographer snapping pictures of Koosman exercising his pitching arm, took advantage of the slow-moving kids to whisper to those waiting. He told them that the guy (me) sitting close by watching was really such a big-name sportswriter that they would be remiss if they did not also ask me for my autograph.

The youngsters fell for the sales pitch and all of a sudden I was being surrounded and asked to write my name. Initially perplexed, I then realized what was going on. I was kind of embarrassed to be plunked into the circumstance and repeatedly told the kids that they really didn't want my autograph. It was not a collectible they would want to save. But they looked at me with disappointment in their eyes, as if I was merely blowing them off.

Gradually, I slipped into the role, asking the seekers for their first names so I could personalize the autographs. Periodically, I glanced up and Koosman was making out just fine, so I plodded on. The kids just followed the leader in my line, not asking who I was, or anything like that.

After telling one youngster I wrote for the Syracuse newspaper, he said he used to be a delivery boy carrier, "But I stopped because they got too heavy."

When the last supplicant appeared before me, I once again asked why he wanted my autograph. He said his mother and he used to like me. I wondered if this meant they liked my writing.

"Do you read the Herald-Journal every night?" I asked, grinning at him. He said, "I mean when you used to be on television." Which was, of course, never.

>>>>>>>>>>>>>>>>>>>>>>> *THE STORY*

Not every baseball player comes from wealth. Koosman grew up on a farm in Northern Minnesota and he didn't always have the ready-made sporting goods equipment he wanted or needed to develop the pitching arm that would take him to the majors.

For Koosman, he could not always line up on a diamond with a catcher to throw to any time he wanted to practice. Instead, he built his left arm up by throwing as often as possible, just not always a baseball.

"I threw rocks," Koosman told his audience in Auburn, New York. "I threw corn cobs. Whatever was available."

There was no indication that like George Washington, the father of the country, that he threw silver dollars anywhere, such as across the Delaware River. If Koosman had silver dollars to spend he would have bought more baseball equipment.

Koosman did not play for very long in Auburn because the New York-Penn League was a Class A short-season rookie league operation. His stay in Central New York lasted just two months. But there were many highlights. As part of the show at the banquet, someone had dug out a recording of Koosman polishing off the Binghamton Triplets in the ninth inning of the championship contest from 1966. Koosman blushed while the radio description was played aloud for the crowd.

After Koosman struck out the last batter – for a second time, just a bit later – he said, "Wasn't that terrific?" Those in the house thought so. Even if it took 11 years to relive it. Koosman, teammates for several years with Hall of Famer pitcher Tom Seaver with the Mets, joked about the ending.

"That's the difference between Tom Seaver and myself," Koosman said. "He strikes out three guys in two minutes and I give the folks their money's worth."

Koosman was coming off a 21-victory season and was under contract with the Mets for three more years. That didn't stop the young people in the audience from asking during a Q & A session if he would rather play for the New York Yankees.

"I'm too old to play out my option," said Koosman, 33 at the time. Playing for the other New York team "wouldn't be any fun. They've got all the money in the world. They went out and bought every-body – and they're still not going to win."

At that time, it was felt the Mets needed some off-season shopping themselves to add some power hitting, but as spring training loomed around the corner, management had not yet done so. Koosman figured out how the players could cope.

"We'll just have to win games 1-0 again this year," he said. "The Mets are not competitive with the team they have right now. We'll finish third unless we get more hitting, or unless some of the other teams lose something."

Diplomatically, Koosman called Auburn, "the best town I ever played in," praised Seaver as a good friend and Gil Hodges as the best manager in his experience. When someone asked about the controversial topic of throwing at batters, Koosman spoke protec-tively, but added a theatrical gesture, perhaps offering a good lesson for young players while also sending a message to their parents.

"Very seldom do you ever hit anyone on purpose," Koosman said. "If you do, it's an accident." And then he winked.

The Mets of 1977 were even worse than Koosman predicted. They finished 64-98. He had his worst season, going 8-20. The Yankees of 1977, with all their money, won the World Series. Koosman's prog-nostications were far off the mark, but the young players probably didn't remember them months later.

>>>>>>>>>>>>>>>>> *CAREER*

Overall, the 6-foot-2, 205-pound Koosman compiled a 222-209 Major League record with a 3.36 earned run average across 19 seasons. He was 42 when he retired in 1985. Twice a 20-game-winner, Koosman was twice chosen for All-Star teams. The Mets retired Koosman's No. 36 and he is a member of the team's Hall of Fame.

As time passed in his career, Koosman was asked how he could still throw as well as he did at 40.

"I don't know if you can put your finger on it," he said, "but I was lucky enough to be born and reared on a farm. I think the hard labor had a lot to do with developing a strong body at a young age. Because of that, maybe I'm less prone to injuries."

Over the course of his career, Koosman adapted to situations, too, in the late 1960s dropping his slider and favoring a curveball. Inevitably, as his birthdays passed the 40 mark, the speed of Koosman's pitches slowed down traveling from mound to plate.

After a game when he defeated the Kansas City Royals and was praised for his talent to change speeds, Koosman joked about himself.

"That was my hard curveball," he said. "It may have been slow to you, but it was hard to me."

BARRY LARKIN

THE SETTING

Barry Larkin was already retired from baseball by the time I started covering the Cincinnati Reds. However, the star shortstop made appearances at Reds team events periodically and I first met him in connection with those.

Then, fulfilling his dream, in 2012, the native of Cincinnati who made his mark in the game with the Cincinnati ballclub, was voted into the National Baseball Hall of Fame.

Over 19 seasons, all with his hometown team, Larkin won a Most Valuable Player Award, was part of a World Series champion in 1990, and was selected to All-Star teams 12 times. It was a special time for Larkin, his family (including basketball-playing brother Byron who starred at Cincinnati's Xavier University) when he was honored by being voted into the Hall of Fame.

Entering the vote that season, Larkin had been a leading contender, already the recipient of more than 62 percent of the past percentage of voters when it takes 75 percent to be elected. His off-field image was also sparkling, an aspect considered to be enhancing his chances. One thing noted about Larkin that is virtually unheard of: At a time of growing influence in baseball by Latin Americans he learned to speak Spanish in order to better communicate with his fellow Reds.

Larkin was the winner of baseball's Roberto Clemente Award in 1993. That award honors an individual whose efforts exemplify sportsmanship and community service, as well as a high-level of on-field performance. It is regarded as the most honorable award a player can earn that is most focused on off-the-field service.

Looking back, Larkin said he continued to live his life according to principles of giving back to the community as evidenced by fellow Hall of Famer Clemente of Puerto Rico, who died in a plane crash on a mission of mercy delivering needed emergency supplies to earthquake victims in Nicaragua in 1972.

"I just thought what a great story and great man," Larkin said 50 years after Clemente's death. "He was somebody that I truly respected for his play on the field as well as what he did off the field."

Larkin was inducted into the Hall of Fame in July of 2012, along with the late Ron Santo, the former Chicago Cubs third baseman and Ford Frick Award winner Tim McCarver, who had a long career as a catcher, but was chosen for his work in broadcasting.

The announcement of the new class for the Hall of Fame becomes public during the winter, months ahead of the induction event in July. This gives those selected time to react and process the honor and prepare an acceptance speech.

Larkin embraced the role of holding press conferences prior to the enshrinement and giving interviews.

"I'm incredibly, incredibly moved by this experience," Larkin said, "so humbled by being the newest member of the Hall of Fame."

THE STORY

In the early days of Hall of Fame inductions, the ceremonies took place in downtown Cooperstown, New York, right outside the front door of the museum on Main Street. However, long before 2012, the biggest occasion of the year in the town had outgrown that location.

Instead, seats were arranged and a stage set up a couple of miles away from traffic on a grassy field to accommodate ever-growing crowds. Although this was not one of the largest groups to gather on that field behind the Clark Sports Center, there were still an estimated 18,000 people present.

At that time there were 65 living Hall of Famers and 45 of them were present on the stage to support Larkin when he began his induction speech. Larkin was one of the younger honorees, still only 48 when he was inducted.

It is quite common for the baseball individuals who are chosen for the Hall to cry, or at least tear up when they begin to reminisce about their past, their experiences, their families, and all of those who helped get them to this hallowed place. Larkin was no exception. It took only a few moments of speaking for him to tear up as he stood at the microphone.

Given his lifelong connection to the city where he played his entire career, and Cincinnati's long history in the sport – back to its professional beginnings – there was much to feast upon for Reds fans who made the trek to upstate New York.

Among those whom Larkin thanked for their advice and guidance through the Reds were Buddy Bell, Tony Perez, and Pete Rose. Present on the stage as Reds Hall of Famers were also Johnny Bench, Joe Morgan, and Frank Robinson.

Rose, the sport's all-time hits leader, is a pariah at the Hall of Fame. Due to a lifetime suspension from the sport for gambling, Rose has never been allowed to have his name appear on the Hall of Fame selection ballot. Thank-yous like this one might be as close as he gets to enshrinement in the near future.

When Larkin was brought up from the minors to join the Reds in 1986 at 22, Rose was the player-manager. It was a hurry-up call, Larkin summoned from Denver, which was still a minor-league outfit. His plane connections were delayed. Larkin barely made it for game time, but his luggage trailed behind in some airport.

"Larkin, it's your first day in the big leagues and you're already late," Rose teased Larkin when he greeted him at the ballpark.

Given the baggage woes, Rose asked Larkin if he could play and the young player had to admit he had no bat, glove, or shoes, items considered essential to taking the field. Rose provided the necessary items and Larkin made his Major League debut August 13, 1986. That day Larkin pinch hit in the fifth inning at Riverfront Stadium and made an out, but the grounder drove in a run. The Reds beat the San Francisco Giants, 8-6, that day.

After the game, as Larkin changed back into street clothes, he gathered up the gear with plans to keep them as souvenirs of his first contest. That was a thrill in itself, but they had also come from Rose, one of his boyhood Reds heroes.

"They were going in the car," Larkin said of his plans to store them at home. "They weren't going to see the light of day."

Rose approached and asked Larkin if all of the utensils had worked out for him on the field. Larkin said yes, they did, thank you.

"Awesome," Rose said. "Good. Give them back. Your stuff will be here tomorrow."

With such a long allegiance to the Reds and special connection to the fan base of the Ohio River city, it would have been an oversight if Larkin hadn't expressly mentioned Cincinnati supporters. As it so happened, he was given easy entrée to do so.

After Larkin had been speaking on the stage for some time someone in crowd shouted, "We love you, Barry!" Larkin immediately responded, saying, "We love you, too, my man!"

»»»»»»»»»»»» CAREER

Larkin appeared in 41 games for the Reds after his 1986 call-up from Denver, batting .283. Then he stepped in as Cincinnati's regular shortstop. Lifetime, Larkin batted .295 with 198 home runs and 960 RBIs.

He won three Gold Glove Awards and nine times was singled out for the Silver Slugger Award naming him the best hitter at his position.

Those weren't bad accomplishments for someone coming out of high school who initially attended the University of Michigan to play football.

The year before he was inducted at Cooperstown, Larkin found himself in an intriguing position, sent to South Korea as part of a diplomacy effort to conduct baseball clinics.

Larkin may have once before negotiated such tricky diplomatic channels – when he had to tell Michigan's iconic football coach Bo Schembechler that his recruit was giving up that sport for baseball after a red-shirt freshman year in the early 1980's.

In anticipation of the volatile meeting after he made his sport decision, Larkin called his mother and asked her to telephone Schembechler and tell him her son was leaving football. She said, Uh-uh, he had to do it himself.

Larkin described Schembechler as a multi-tasker, who didn't make eye contact with a player when he arrived for his appointment. Schembechler had his head bent, writing something.

"I don't walk into his office like I normally do and sit down at the desk right in front of him," Larkin said. "I kind of stand in the doorway and I don't enter his office."

Schembechler began rambling about the possibility of the 6-foot, 185-pound athlete running back punts. Eventually, the coach sensed something was up and asked if there was a problem. Finally, Larkin squeezed out his desire to switch to playing baseball full-time.

As expected, Mount Schembechler exploded like a volcano, going, "Larkin this is The University of Michigan! No one comes to the University of Michigan and plays stinkin' baseball!"

Schembechler wouldn't accept the decision initially and made Larkin return to his office the next day to tell him all over again.

Throughout the baseball season, Schembechler showed up about once a week on the sidelines to heckle Larkin, the player said, shouting such things as "Larkin! Come hit a man who can hit you back instead of that sissy baseball!"

While at Michigan, Larkin did represent the Wolverines in the College World Series twice and twice was chosen All-American, so the baseball thing worked out, even in Ann Arbor. Larkin said he told his Schembechler-football story to other Michigan folks over time. They were all amused. Schembechler was not.

"But Bo hated it," Larkin said.

DON LARSEN

>>>>>>>>>>>>>>>>>> *THE SETTING*

It was World Series time, October of 1993. Although I was in Anchorage, Alaska and not able to come any closer to that year's Series between the Toronto Blue Jays and the Philadelphia Phillies, I mentally cast about for a subject that would be dear to the baseball readership of a sports page.

The idea that came to me was tracking down and trying to interview Don Larsen on the telephone. The only pitcher ever to hurl a perfect game in baseball's showcase event was long into retirement.

Larsen's perfecto, which can never be improved upon, and has yet to be equaled by any other pitcher in a championship round, took place on October 8, 1956 when his New York Yankees met the Brooklyn Dodgers at Yankee Stadium. On that day, Larsen gained a certain type of immortality.

Larsen otherwise had an average pitching career, with some highs and some lows, but his signature achievement made him the subject of countless articles over the following decades. If he had grown weary of talking about the perfect game, no one could blame him.

Sometime later, when the sports memorabilia boom came along and Larsen emerged from his somewhat remote living area in Idaho, he was again in the public eye and as he signed autographs he chatted about the highlight of his career. However, at this particular time he was pretty much on a hiatus from hanging out, living somewhat reclusively.

When I reached Larsen via telephone, though, he chose to talk baseball with me. The main reason was that I was calling from Alaska and that intrigued him. In fact, he said, "I wouldn't be talking with you if you weren't from Alaska."

It was World Series time, too, and perhaps that jump-started his thoughts about the greatest, most important game ever pitched.

⫸⫸⫸⫸⫸⫸⫸⫸⫸⫸⫸ THE STORY

Born in Michigan City, Indiana in 1929, Larsen was a good-sized pitcher for his era, standing 6-foot-4 and weighing 215 pounds. He spent time with several teams without winning big. Yet during his stint with the Yankees, Larsen was productive and manager Casey Stengel relied on him to take the mound in some big, pressure-packed situations.

At that point in the 1956 Series, the Yankees and Dodgers, bitter opponents trying to share the New York market, engaged in one of their so-called "Subway Series" where all it took to travel between home ballparks was hopping a subway car. The World Series was knotted at 2-2 when Larsen took the mound for Game 5.

The Yankees were the supreme juggernaut in the game in the 1950s, considered a very buttoned-down organization. Ironically, Larsen's nickname was "Gooney Bird" because his personality was anything but buttoned down. He was regarded as someone who enjoyed staying out late and partying.

There were 64,519 paying customers in the house, so Larsen's feat was not accomplished in obscurity, but under the bright lights. His opponent on the mound was Sal "The Barber" Maglie, so nicknamed because of his propensity to throw inside to hitters digging in too deeply in the batter's box.

Baseball games play out in any number of manners, slugfests, pitcher's duels, over the scheduled nine innings, in extra innings, with comebacks, with one-sided, blown-up scores. Although no one remembers it, Maglie actually pitched very well. The right-hander went eight innings, allowed five hits and two runs and struck out five. On any other day those would have been satisfactory box score numbers worthy of discussion. Instead, Maglie's effort was practically reduced to the level of a trivia question under the shadow of Larsen's monumental performance.

Perfect games of 300 are rolled much more frequently in bowling than they are pitched in baseball. They are so rare in baseball that even lifetime fans would be terribly fortunate to buck the 1,000-to-1 (or something like that) odds to ever be present for one.

As of the beginning of the 2023 Major League Baseball season, there had been 23 perfect games thrown. At the time Larsen pitched his perfect game of 27 men up and 27 down, it was just the sixth ever.

In the majors, pitchers and their fielders don't even think about perfect games until the very late innings. Ditto for no-hitters. Everyone knows that things can change in a hurry and often do, so why expend the energy worrying early? There have been many more one-hitters than no-hitters in baseball history, dozens more close calls than perfect games.

"Every pitcher knows when the first hit happens," Larsen said. He said they are lying if they don't admit that.

Of course, often enough the first hit occurs in the first inning, the third or the fourth, not so late that anyone would be thinking about the prospect of a no-hitter. Still, there is a commonly held superstition that neither a pitcher nor his teammates in the dugout speak of the no-hit opportunity as if the mere mention of it might jinx it.

Larsen himself violated that precept during the Series game. It was later recounted by outfielder Mickey Mantle that during the fifth inning, a casual Larsen waltzed up to him and said, "Hey, Slick, wouldn't it be funny if I pitched a no-hitter?" Supposedly, the startled Mantle replied, "Get the hell out of here."

By mid-game, the Yankees had built a small lead. Mantle hit a solo homer in the fourth inning and the lead was extended to the final score of 2-0 in the sixth when outfielder Hank Bauer drove in third-baseman Andy Carey with a single. Mantle also helped in the field, hauling in a Gil Hodges 400-foot fly ball to left-center after a long run and later referring to that grab as the best catch he ever made.

Meanwhile, this was a stacked Dodgers lineup Larsen was facing, filled with menacing hitters such as Hodges, Jackie Robinson, Roy Campanella, Duke Snider and Pee Wee Reese, all of whom ended up in the Hall of Fame. This was no tip-toe through the tulips.

"My control was excellent," Larsen recalled. "I only had three balls on one batter, Reese."

The game lasted just 2 hours, 6 minutes and the final out came on a called third strike to pinch-hitter Dale Mitchell. Once that third out of the ninth was recorded, Yankee catcher Yogi Berra sprinted to the mound and jumped on Larsen with a big-league hug that was preserved for prosperity by photographers.

Larsen said he was glad this was a close game. "If I'd had a big lead, like 10-0," he said, "maybe I wouldn't have come close. This way you bear down on every pitch."

This was a major achievement, regularly revisited in the baseball world, and especially at World Series time. Larsen always had the perfect game in the forefront of his mind.

"It's a long time ago," he said in that 1993 phone call. "Where does the time go? But it's an everyday thing that I think of it. The stadium. The guys. How wonderful it was just to be in the Series."

Since it is difficult to improve on perfection, or even match it, as the years and decades pass, Larsen's gem has solidified its place as the best game ever pitched, the ante upped because of the magnitude of the circumstances during the World Series.

Somewhat surprisingly, in 1993, Larsen did not make that claim outright.

"That's not for me to say," Larsen said. "There's been a lot of great games. I know it was a great game. I'm just glad it happened to me and to the Yankees."

⟫⟫⟫⟫⟫⟫⟫⟫⟫⟫ CAREER

During his 14 years in the majors, Don Larsen had the misfortune of playing for the horrible St. Louis Browns, balanced by also playing for the terrific New York Yankees. His lifetime record was 81 wins against 91 losses, with an earned run average of 3.78.

As a 24-year-old, second-year man with the Baltimore Orioles in 1954, Larsen somehow survived a 3-21 season (most losses in the American League that year). The Orioles were being transformed from the horrible St. Louis Browns and hadn't quite made the adjustment yet. It was a welcome trade being part of a 17-player swap to New York.

He never won more than 11 games in a season, but in the mid-1950s, Larsen put together some solid, useful seasons for the Yankees, going 11-5, 10-4, and 9-6. His career spanned 1953 to 1967.

Other times fans wondered what his bosses saw in Larsen, especially after he cracked up a car in spring training in Florida at 5 o'clock in the morning, helping to develop another nickname as "a night leaguer." Others referred to him as "a night rider."

In a famous lead sentence to its game story, the day after the big Series game, the New York Daily News' Joe Trimble wrote, "The imperfect man pitched a perfect game yesterday." The story called Larsen "a free soul who loves the gay life."

It was later revealed that the day before the perfect game, Larsen had a premonition that he was going to have a super game against the Dodgers. "I got one of those crazy feelings I'm gonna pitch a no-hitter tomorrow," he told an acquaintance. He did not say perfect game. Apparently, the crystal ball did not delve deep enough.

As the impact of Larsen's accomplishment sunk in, a man named Dave McEnery wrote a song about Larsen, including biographical details and material from the game itself, called "The Ballad of Don Larsen." The chorus went like this: "Don Larsen was his name and he won enduring fame; When he pitched perfect baseball at the great World Series game."

While living in Hayden Lake, Idaho, where he passed away at 90 in 2020, Larsen was an active fisherman. He sold his perfect game uniform for $765,000 to pay for his grandsons' educations. He also had a unique license plate for his automobile: "DL000." As in Don Larsen, no hits, no runs, no errors. In other words, perfect.

BOB LEMON

>>>>>>>>>>>>>>>>>> **THE SETTING**

Low-key greatness is one way to describe Bob Lemon, who it seemed gained more notoriety managing the New York Yankees in the spotlight under owner George Steinbrenner than he did during a Hall of Fame pitching career with the Cleveland Indians.

Lemon, born in 1920 in San Bernadino, California, was a high school phenom of a baseball player whose entire career was almost sidetracked by World War II. His participation in the service of the United States as a member of the Navy meant that he did not break into the majors as a rookie until he was 25 in 1946.

And until then he wasn't even a pitcher. In 1946, Lemon, who had always been a fielder, was in Cleveland's starting lineup for opening day as the club's centerfielder. It wasn't for two more seasons that he began new life as a full-time hurler. Before that he was an infielder, but his biggest flaw was being unable to hit good big-league pitching. The switch to throwing was enhanced by the time Lemon spent in the service used as a pitcher. He was technically out of the game during the war, but was improving his game.

As crazy as his late start in the big leagues made it, Lemon promptly became a wizard on the mound, winning 20 games per season and playing catch-up for missed time he won recognition as a seven-time All-Star in the late 1940s and early 1950s.

Following that, after retiring in 1958 at 37, baseball people began appreciating Lemon's acumen in other ways. In 1970, he became manager of the Kansas City Royals. Then he led the Chicago White Sox.

Somewhat surprisingly, given his placid demeanor and habit of putting losses behind him quickly, sometimes by washing them down with a beer, by the late 1970s Lemon was a figure in Steinbrenner's rotating cast of managers. They were managers who he generally mistreated equally, haranguing them, calling them to make lineup suggestions and firing them.

This was the height of the constant soap opera activity between Steinbrenner and Billy Martin. Lemon took over the Yankees for the first time part-way through the 1978 season, guiding New York to a 48-20 record, the American League pennant and the World Series title.

After the 1979 season, Lemon was kicked upstairs to general manager as Martin reclaimed the job. Then Lemon returned to the dugout in 1981, a season mixed up because of a player's strike with 50 scheduled games lost. However, the Yankees captured what was deemed a first-half-of-the season pennant and the right to compete in the odd playoffs.

That meant Lemon was at the helm in October and leading the Yankees against the Oakland Athletics. It was during that series that Lemon and I overlapped as his team eliminated the A's.

⟫⟫⟫⟫⟫⟫⟫⟫⟫ THE STORY

As terrific as Lemon was as a pitcher, he was overshadowed in

Cleveland by Bob Feller and then blended into a dominant starting staff also featuring Early Wynn and Mike Garcia. As a manager with the Yankees, Lemon seemed to be overshadowed by the Steinbrenner-Martin fiddling and the tabloid media speculation about when Steinbrenner would fire him and bring Martin back.

Meanwhile, Lemon mostly spent his time winning with the Yankee roster he was handed. Martin's style of winning with pitching, defense, and running the bases, so-called "small ball," picked up the nickname "Billy Ball." In 1981, the Yankees took the A's apart in the American League Championship Series, sweeping three games by scores of 3-1, 13-3, and 4-0. The new style, with a tip of the hat to Bob Lemon, was "Bobby Ball." Under any definition, it got the Yankees to the World Series. Ironically, at that particular time, Martin was inhabiting the Oakland dugout, representing the losing side of the series.

"Maybe I pushed the right buttons," Lemon said. "But it helps to have a good ballclub. And I have one here."

Lemon was managing Yankee talent like Reggie Jackson, Graig Nettles, Dave Winfield, Lou Piniella, Bobby Murcer, Ron Guidry, Tommy John, and Rich Gossage.

"We have a little more depth in our bullpen and, when we're afforded an opportunity to get ahead, it's cut and dried what we're going to do," Lemon said.

That meant calling for relief, which is quite commonplace in the modern game, but less likely to happen for starters more than 40 years ago.

Lemon didn't even deploy Jackson, aka "Mr. October," in the deciding game because he was bothered by a slightly strained hamstring. Jackson himself, and his teammates, didn't even imbibe champagne after winning this Oakland series, though they did pour down some beers.

"This is a formality," Jackson said. "Just part of the itinerary on the way to the World Series."

Lemon said that thinking ahead to the World Series, Jackson only rested as a precautionary measure.

"He'll be ready," the manager said.

Only the Yankees really weren't this time, losing to the Los Angeles Dodgers, 4-2.

CAREER

Bob Lemon last managed in 1982, when Steinbrenner swooped in to make another change.

"When you get fired, it's always hard to take," Lemon said. "Nobody goes out laughing and giggling. I'd like to have stayed around, but it's George's ship. He's the captain and he can do whatever he has to do."

Although a second career as a manager, a World Series championship, and two pennants, was a nice perk to have on his resume, Bob Lemon was not voted into the Hall of Fame in 1976 because of his work in the dugout.

He was honored because of his pitching prowess. That included a 207-128 overall record despite his late start as a thrower, with a 3.23 earned run average. He led the league in complete games five times.

Lemon was a member of the last Cleveland team to win a World Series in 1948 and was on the 1954 team that returned to the Series, but lost.

That same year, Lemon hurled a no-hitter on June 30, 1948, beating the Detroit Tigers 2-0. Lemon led the American League in victories in 1950, 1954 and 1955. Twice, he won as many as 23 games in a season as part of his hot streak of winning at least 20 games seven times.

Maybe it was because he won more often than he lost during his career, but Lemon liked to say that he never let the defeats linger in his mind. When Lemon delivered his Hall of Fame induction speech in Cooperstown, New York in 1976, Lemon explained how he did that. "I never took my defeats home with me," Lemon said. "I left them in the bar on the way home."

Lemon was light-hearted in general and could approach stand-up comic status at times. In the movie *Bull Durham*, the catcher character played by Kevin Costner frequently calls the young pitcher character Tim Robbins "Meat," as a minor insult, though perhaps as a term of endearment. The script may have borrowed from Lemon's lexicon since he regularly hailed people he recognized with "Hey, Meat, what's going on?" In return they called him "Meat," too.

In 1998, Lemon's old Indians club beckoned him back to town to retire his No. 21 uniform jersey and he spoke briefly to the crowd, saying, "It's a great honor. Now let's get on with the game, throw out the first pitch, or whatever the hell we do, and let the good times roll."

Lemon was 79 years old when he died in Long Beach, California in 2000.

JIM MALONEY

THE SETTING

It is inescapable to examine Jim Maloney's fine pitching career without reviewing the three no-hitters he hurled for the Cincinnati Reds that were later downgraded to two no-hitters because of Major League Baseball rules changes.

Maloney and I met when I was covering the Reds for a time in the 2010s and he was attending team functions such as club Hall of Fame events, or the team's winter convention. We also spoke on the telephone for interviews over time.

The combination of Maloney's cusp-of-brilliance career being cut short by injuries when he was challenging such other throwers as Sandy Koufax, Juan Marichal, Bob Gibson, and Don Drysdale for pre-eminence in the National League and the passage of time, have cost Maloney in reputation. Everywhere but in Cincinnati, where he remains an honored figure from 60 years ago when he was mowing down batters with the best of them.

A fastball that crackles has always been a weapon of dominance over the history of baseball. If a pitcher can throw faster than a batter can catalogue the time of the ball's arrival at home plate, he always has an advantage. When Maloney was on his game in the 1960s, he could reach 99 mph. Not many others could at that time and that speed is still the backbone stuff of careers in the 2020s.

Maloney was a right-hander who had some of the best stuff of anyone around during his heyday. The native of Fresno, California was every bit the threat to overpower hitters on any fourth day he took the mound as a starting pitcher. Even though he finished his 12-year career abruptly in 1971, Maloney is often-remembered whenever the topic of the no-hit game comes up in discussion.

On June 14, 1965, Maloney pitched a no-hitter against the New York Mets. He struck out 18 batters and gave up one walk, but lost the game, 1-0, in 11 innings when New York's Johnny Lewis hit a solo homer. This game was hailed as a no-hitter at the time, but due to revisionist history was later taken away from Maloney.

Later that same summer, on August 19, Maloney threw another no-hitter against the Chicago Cubs that also went into extra innings. But he won the contest, 1-0, in 10 innings.

The third time around – and there was nothing close about this one – Maloney was victorious in a 10-0 game against the Houston Astros on April 30, 1969. Still another no-hitter.

In 1991, though, MLB issued a new definition of what constitutes a no-hitter and it was applied retroactively. The administration of the sport examined all of the credited no-hitters throughout history and exiled some from the list. One of the no-hitters excommunicated was Maloney's 1965 no-hitter versus the Mets.

Maloney was tripped up by the part of the revised definition saying the no-hitter had to be a complete game and even though he had held the Mets without a hit for more than nine innings, he ran afoul of the rule by losing it in extra innings.

The pitcher was not happy about the new version of history.

>>>>>>>>>>>>>>>>>>>>> ***THE STORY***

"How do you think I feel?" Maloney said years after the change was made that disqualified part of his achievement. "I'm glad I threw two others. I got credit for three for a long time. My (Reds team) Hall of Fame plaque said I had three no-hitters."

Indeed, if one was on the field, or present in the stands, you went home from the game at Crosley Field believing you witnessed a no-hitter and you thought that was fact for the next 26 years. Never mind just Maloney.

"It's history," Maloney said with a sigh.

Interestingly, on another occasion when Maloney and I spoke and I asked him to choose the game of his life, he selected none of the no-hitters as a favorite.

Instead, he picked a September 2, 1963 contest, though it was also against the Mets. This was yet another 1-0 game, but what made it so special was that it gave Maloney his first 20-win season. He established himself as an elite pitcher that year, going 23-7 with a 2.77 earned run average after winning just nine games the previous year. That was also the first time he topped 200 strikeouts in a season with a career-high 265.

"I had a lot of breaks," Malone said of that year. "I pitched a lot of good games and I had good team support. So that was a memorable year for me. I had a few 1-0 games, but my dad always told me that if nobody's scoring a run, you go up there and hit a home run and shut them out. That's a pretty good philosophy."

No-hitters are always special and memorable, too, but winning 20 games is a season-long sign of excellence and something that sticks on the record forever, as well.

"Every starting pitcher has goals," Maloney said, "and one of those goals is to win 20 games at the Major League level. In 1963, everything clicked into place. Every year you try to win 20 games. You try."

The goal is to win 20 games in a season every year, especially after a pitcher has done so once. Maloney was able to do so two years later, the season when he tossed two no-hitters (he thought).

"I was fortunate in 1965 to have another 20-game season," Maloney said. "That year was probably my best year, even though I won three games less than I did in 1963."

His thinking on maybe 1965 being better than 1963 was the two no-hitters going up on the board in a single season.

It was easy for Maloney to feel cheated by the baseball rules change taking away a no-hitter, but he could feel even worse because of the way his starry career terminated. He ruptured an Achilles tendon in 1970 and except for essentially a three-game cameo with the California Angels in 1971 that didn't go well, he was unable to pitch again, resulting in his retirement at 31.

⟫⟫⟫⟫⟫⟫⟫⟫⟫⟫⟫ CAREER

After the loss of his big-league career, Maloney struggled with personal problems, drinking too heavily, and it took some time and work to shake his addiction.

"I really had a hard time sliding back into society," Maloney said of his readjustment from his professional sports life. A former teammate, Jim Merritt, reached out and got him help and later Maloney became an alcoholism counselor and ran the Fresno City Alcoholism and Drug Abuse Council in his hometown, where he still lives.

"Someone helped me," a thankful Maloney said.

Between 1960 and 1971, Maloney compiled a pitching record of 134-84, a .615 win-percentage with a 3.19 earned run average. He struck out more than 200 batters in a season four times and threw more than 200 innings in a season five times.

In 1973, Reds fans voted Maloney into the team's Hall of Fame, which is located in Great American Ball Park.

Going back to the no-hitter that never was, if anyone wants to watch the tape of how fans reacted or read up on what it was like to allow zero hits for 10 innings, it makes it difficult to swallow that it never counted.

When that game ended, Maloney was quoted by a sportswriter covering the game as saying, "My arm got tired from tipping my cap to all of those standing ovations I was getting after each inning."

The moment seemed awfully real to Jim Maloney.

JUAN MARICHAL

》》》》》》》》》》》》 *THE SETTING*

Hanging out with Juan Marichal in Santo Domingo, Dominican Republic for several days was one of the most pleasurable baseball-related experiences of my life.

We got together to collaborate on a book about the right-handed, Hall of Fame pitcher's life. While most of our time was spent talking in the equivalent of his home's man cave, decorated with baseball souvenirs and keepsakes, we also moved about town.

I flew into Santo Domingo, the capital of the island country with a population of about 1.3 million. Juan had told me not to rent a car to drive on the strange-to-me geographical streets and that he would have me picked up each time at my hotel. So, when I landed, I climbed into a taxi cab to carry me to the hotel.

Almost immediately, I got a chuckle as the car exited the airport and I noticed a street sign reading "Sammy Sosa Boulevard." As if there had been any doubt the Dominican was perpetually infatuated with baseball, I saw the love exhibited right away.

Much of the time Juan and I spent talking was spent inside his home. But we also attended a Dominican winter league ballgame at a stadium in the intervening years has been named after Marichal. The short walk to the ballpark from where the car was parked was illuminating, offering the constant reminder that Marichal remains a national hero. Every few steps someone stopped him and asked to take a photograph together.

Inside the park, accompanied by Juan's son, we sat in first-rate grandstand seats close to the home team's dugout. At that time the squad was being managed by Moises Alou, not so long before a player for the Chicago Cubs. More importantly, though, he was a member of the famous Alou family, part of the younger generation of three brothers who had played on the San Francisco Giants with Marichal. Juan and Moises chatted over the fencing.

Once it became knowledge Marichal was in the house, fans began to slip down from their own seats to hail him and ask for autographs. Fairly swiftly, a security cordon formed to keep them away so Juan could actually watch the game. Still, ESPN Desportes, broadcasting the game, sent word from high above in the press box asking if Juan would go on the air for a short while, which he did.

Afterwards, we found our way to a late dinner for steak at a place named "Davy Crockett." Only one other table was occupied, by about six men. Of course, they also recognized Juan Marichal and he glided over to talk with them before he and I ate dinner.

The next year, we had a biography of Juan appear called, Juan Marichal: My Journey from the Dominican Republic to Cooperstown.

>>>>>>>>>>>>>>>> *THE STORY*

Born in 1937, Marichal worked his way into the majors by the time he was 22 and in an era featuring several future Hall of Famers, "the Dominican Dandy" won more games (191) in the 1960s than any other thrower.

Marichal came from hard beginnings, growing up in farming country without his father who died when the future pitcher was three years old. The farm produced all the food the family needed, but as a youth he lived without electricity. He and his friends played as much baseball as they could, but they couldn't afford up-to-date proper equipment and improvised, making their own baseball utensils.

One of Juan's brothers, Gonzalo, was a major influence in baseball. A very good player, he taught Juan rudiments of the game and Juan tagged along to watch him play in his own games.

"Whenever I wasn't working on the farm," said Marichal, who covered considerable territory on the land via horseback, "I tried to play baseball. We always played baseball on Saturday and Sunday and whenever we could sneak away from school."

Marichal said he was only six or seven years old when he began telling his mother he was going to become a professional baseball player. She was not happy, however, when his teacher came to the house to report on his truancy.

His friends being in similar financial straits, Marichal said, they made their own balls to throw and hit. They came up with lost golf balls, then wrapped cloth around them to expand their size. Then they raised a single peso in the group, brought the in-progress ball to a shoemaker and paid him to make a covering. They made their own gloves from the tarp material taken from trucks.

Juan's mother was not terribly keen on his career choice, wondering how he would support a family since the Dominican Republic's best players had not yet made a splash in the majors. He told her not to worry and replied, "Mother, you're going to be so proud when you hear my name on the radio."

Marichal's dreams did come true, of course, and his exploits were reported on radio, TV, and in newspapers as he became an All-Star and a member of the Baseball Hall of Fame. His style of hurling, mixing a variety of pitches, his left leg kicked so very high, helped him win 243 games, pitch a no-hitter, and be chosen for 10 All-Star teams.

He made a mark right from the start in his 16-year Major League career. Called up from the minors mid-season, Marichal made his big-league debut on July 19, 1960 against the Philadelphia Phillies and won 2-0. He pitched a complete-game, one-hitter with 12 strikeouts, stunning the opponents, teammates, and fans.

Back-up Phils catcher Clay Dalrymple broke up the no-hit bid in the eighth inning with a pinch-hit single. Marichal was so new to the National League and so raw he didn't even know all the names of the Philadelphia hitters. It sounded humorous, but was true. When a sportswriter asked Juan what he said to Dalrymple when he got his big hit, Marichal said, "Nothing. I do not know him."

Players around the NL swiftly got to know Marichal and his stuff, even if they couldn't hit it. He became so good and the gentlemanly Juan became so popular, in the Dominican, in San Francisco, and across baseball, that he appeared on the cover of Time magazine.

"I used to sign autographs everywhere in San Francisco," Marichal said. "Even now, years after I finished playing, whenever I go to San Francisco, people ask me for autographs. I never said no to an autograph because I know what it means."

He said when he was a youth and he attended soccer games in the Dominican, those players were heroes to him the way he was in baseball for others. He believes all ballplayers should sign. "Let the kid be happy," Marichal said.

The more he pitched, the better he got, throughout the 1960s.

"When you are winning 75 percent of the time, everything is great," Marichal said. "It looked like I was in a groove in those years. You get out to the mound, you feel comfortable, and you know you can do it. In 1968, I won 26 games and lost nine. I felt I could have won 35 games."

CAREER

Marichal retired in 1975 at 37, partially due to chronic back problems. His won-loss record was 243-142, a winning percentage of .631 and his earned run average was a superb 2.89. He won at least 20 games six times.

He also threw 244 complete games, a performance that can't even be imagined in the modern game. In one of his most famous games, Marichal went head-to-head with another Hall of Famer, Warren Spahn, in a game that lasted 16 innings. Both men went the distance after refusing to be removed when their managers asked them if they were tired.

The July 2, 1963 game featured Marichal, then 25, for the Giants, and Spahn, 42, for the then-Milwaukee Braves in an astounding effort of pitching stamina and excellence at Candlestick Park. The game lasted four hours, 15 minutes. The Giants and Marichal prevailed, 1-0. Willie Mays hit a solo homer to end it.

Spahn reportedly said he was not going to come out of the game as long as the young whippersnapper was still hurling. Marichal issued a similar comment, saying he wasn't coming out of the epic game as long as the old-timer was still pitching. In a remarkable demonstration of stamina, each man threw more than 200 pitches that day (Spahn 201, Marichal 227), which today would be viewed as borderline insanity.

After his playing days, Marichal, who turned 85 in 2022, participated in several ventures, including acting as minister of sports for his country. He was elected to the Hall of Fame in 1983.

"I hugged Alma (his wife) and told her how happy I was," said Marichal, who was the first player of Latin heritage to be elected to the Hall through its regular process after Roberto Clemente had been inducted by acclamation after his early death.

"I thanked God. So many players go through the game and never have the experiences I did. I was one of the lucky players, a small number, who reach the Hall of Fame."

WILLIE MAYS

Photo courtesy of BASEBALL HALL OF FAME

>>>>>>>>>>>>>>>>>>>> **THE SETTING**

There were two occasions when I had Willie Mays to myself for private conversations about baseball. To be honest, because it was Willie Mays, and I was of the youth generation that watched him closely growing up, the situations took on tinges of unreality, as a voice whispering in my head said, "I'm talking to the Willie Mays."

During the 1980s, when professional boxing was at one of its apexes in the United States, when millions of fans knew the names of the champions by weight class, and Atlantic City was vying to become the major American city staging big-time fights, I covered boxing as a beat for the Philadelphia Inquirer.

Philadelphia was always one of the biggest fight towns in America and Philadelphia produced many world-ranked fighters across all weight classes. What changed, though, was an influx of fresh money into the sport funneled to casinos to host fights on the Jersey Shore. For promoters, it became less about selling tickets to fill larger arenas such as the Spectrum in Philadelphia than about high rollers attending the bouts and then dropping big bucks at the tables.

The casinos were competing with one another and sought new ways to woo those high rollers. One of those casinos on the boardwalk where families had frolicked on the sand and in the Atlantic Ocean for decades, was Bally's Park Place. A marketing genius for that outfit convinced the bosses to hire Willie Mays as a greeter.

Mays was retired from playing and not coaching or managing. Bally's made him a great offer and he took it. Indeed, Mickey Mantle likewise took advantage of a similar offer from the Claridge Hotel and Casino down the street. Both icons of baseball filled roles as community representatives at public charity events and the like. Mantle was more often seen at golf events. Mays showed up when boxing cards were scheduled. Only baseball Commissioner Bowie Kuhn considered their connections to gambling institutions to be a taint on the game and suspended them from baseball.

I never met Mantle, in Atlantic City, or elsewhere, but began seeing Mays regularly at the fights. He did not figure into the events I covered and so I once, after careful thought, somewhat violated journalistic integrity rules by bringing along a baseball to a fight card and asking him to autograph it for me.

A few years later, much to my amazement, after I moved to Alaska, becoming first assistant sports editor of the Anchorage Daily News, and then sports editor, I was informed Willie Mays was coming to town to make a public appearance at the local ballpark used as a home field by two Anchorage teams in the Alaska Baseball League. I had never expected to see him close-up again. I re-introduced myself to Mays and did a column about Willie Mays being in Alaska. That was the last time I ever saw him in person.

⟫⟫⟫⟫⟫⟫⟫ *THE STORY*

It is difficult to believe there was a time when Willie Mays was suspended from Major League Baseball. Forced out of the game. Punished for actions claimed to be detrimental to the game.

This was not when Mays was starring for the New York or San Francisco Giants, but when he was 49 years old, long into retirement from his Hall of Fame career that astonished and delighted fans in so many ways that he is considered by many to be the best pure talent ever to wear spikes on a diamond. Nicknamed "Say Hey," because that was a greeting he used to others, Mays was also greatly admired for the joy he brought to his play.

A latter-day Willie Mays was on baseball's negative hit list because he chose to accept a $100,000 deal to be himself as an ambassador for an Atlantic City casino. Mays did well in the salary wars as a player, but in his era being at the top of the heap did not bring in millions of dollars a year.

So, Mays accepted an offer from Bally's Park Place Casino to appear as a friendly face 10 days a month. Mays was a 24-time All-Star and was regarded as just about the perfect do-everything player from hitting, hitting with power, running, and throwing as well as anyone who ever played.

As famous and revered as any player of his time with the possible exception of the New York Yankees' Mickey Mantle, who found himself in a similar predicament, Mays did what Mantle did and accepted a casino job. Then-commissioner Bowie Kuhn said that neither man could coach or take a job in baseball while employed by a gambling house. Clearly, the sport's attitude towards gambling and sports betting has changed since, but at the time it was essentially viewed as the original sin.

At that time, late 1979 and 1980, I was the boxing beat writer for the Philadelphia Inquirer. Much of the biggest action in boxing shifted to Atlantic City as casinos battled for customers based on who put on the biggest matches with the most prominent fighters. I saw Mays almost as often as I would have if I had been the Giants beat writer for a major newspaper during his prime playing years.

He was no average spectator at the fights. He was a draw to the fights. When working at the casino, Mays wore a Bally's blazer and his picture ID read, "Say Hey, Willie Mays," as if he would not be recognized otherwise.

This was a time when I regularly said hello to Willie Mays and Willie Mays said hello back to me. Once, we sat down in a couple of chairs and just talked baseball for a while, a discussion that included him emotionally stating that he believed his situation of being banned from the sport was absurd given his stature in the game.

"I think I should be in baseball doing something," Mays said. And probably everyone else on the planet besides Kuhn would have agreed.

That was a firm enough statement for him, but Mays, who brought such obvious pleasure to his play in the game as a younger man, exhibited the same type of cheerful demeanor about a career that spanned 1951 to 1973 in the majors, counting his last stop back in New York where he was so loved, with the New York Mets.

Mays answered one of those questions characterized as softball questions when he was asked who were the toughest pitchers for him to hit. His answer did take a swerve, or a curve, one might say. He listed Sandy Koufax and Don Drysdale of the Dodgers and Bob Gibson of the Cardinals – the trio all recognized as huge stars in the sport -- and Bob Rush.

Bob Rush? The right-hander spent 13 years in the majors, and did make two All-Star teams, but he finished with a 127-152 record. Bob Rush?

"Well, yeah," Mays said, smiling at the inclusion of a somewhat average hurler on a list with all-time greats. The reason Rush bothered him, Mays said, was his really thick glasses which made the Hall of Famer wonder where the fastball was going. Mays said Rush's vision was so bad he didn't even look in at catcher's signs, they "just flapped their hands." Then he burst out laughing at the whole cartoon-like image and his being intimidated by a pitcher who rarely posted a season-long winning record.

Mays the player ran with abandon on the bases, was a fly-catcher of supreme ability, sometimes grabbing the ball over his shoulder like a football wide receiver, and was renowned for his baseball cap appealingly popping off his head as he ran.

"I played for the people," Mays said. Only a week prior to the conversation, Mays had collapsed from fatigue while speaking to a group of junior high students in Atlantic City and then being taken to a hospital. Americans reacted powerfully, inundating him with good wishes and get-well cards. "That's love. People saying. 'We're very concerned about you.' It's a very good feeling." Luckily for him, he was feeling good soon after.

Usually, when Mays was at hospitals it was to visit sick kids, not as an in-patient. In retirement, he spent even more time working with charitable causes.

For two years, after 1973, Mays was out of the game. Then he went to work as a special assistant in the Mets' front office and made public appearances on behalf of the team. Mays said no one offered him a Major League managing job and he didn't really want one. He said he preferred the kind of life Bally's provided, where he met people all the time.

Those ties with the Mets were terminated at Kuhn's behest when Mays signed on with Bally's. Mays met with Kuhn to try to prove his job with the casino was no different than most other public relations jobs and that he had nothing to do with gambling.

Before making that appeal, Mays said baseball had made him feel a little bit ashamed through its ban, even though he felt he had done nothing wrong. Imagine baseball making Willie Mays feel ashamed. That sounded more wrong than anything Mays was doing.

Mays said when his ban was lifted, he wanted another job in baseball – working directly for the commissioner's office.

"They go to special events like the All-Star Game and World Series," Mays said. "I could do that. That's what I'm doing now. And that way they could keep an eye on me."

Made perfect sense, being a presence at the heavyweight championship of baseball. Mays did have a twinkle in his eye when he made that sly comment of a suggestion.

It took until 1985, after Kuhn was out of office and Peter Ueberroth succeeded him as commissioner, for Mays to be reinstated to baseball.

That was a long time ago and fans who came along later likely don't remember Mays working for a casino and being shunned by baseball. But it is a certainty that they remember Willie Mays better than they remember Bowie Kuhn.

It was only three years after that meeting in Atlantic City that I was working in Anchorage, Alaska when Willie Mays showed up in town, signing autographs during a lunch-time appearance at Mulcahy Stadium, the downtown ballpark.

If anyone thought Willie Mays seemed out of place wearing a Bally's blazer, they would also have had difficulty picturing him in Alaska, 3,000 miles north of just about anywhere. Not that his legend was unappreciated on the Last Frontier. Mays was playing in the International Rotary Golf Tournament in town and at times between gazing at the snow-capped mountains, he made other appearances.

When a man in his twenties waiting in line for a signature was asked why he had dropped by in the middle of his work day for a financial institution, he looked shocked anyone would ask. "Because he's Willie Mays," the man said. It was that simple. Absolutely. Because he's Willie Mays you show up. Because he's Willie Mays you take advantage of the moment. Because he's Willie Mays and you never know when the opportunity to shake hands with greatness will come up again, especially in Alaska.

Mays worked the autograph line hard, but didn't kibbitz much with the fans, many of whom were too young to have seen him play. It could be wondered how many autographs Mays had signed given that he probably had been writing his name on pictures and baseballs for two-thirds of his life.

There was an undercurrent of resentment towards the commissioner when he said, "I was put out of baseball." Mays appealed his suspension once, but not again. He said, "I asked one time. I don't [care] to be embarrassed again. If he (Kuhn) said, 'I'd love to have you come in, I'd love that.'"

It was not long after – the next year – when Kuhn was replaced by the next commissioner Peter Ueberroth, that baseball said to Mays that it would love to have him back in. Mantle, too.

CAREER

Over 22 seasons of Major League baseball, Willie Mays batted .302 with 660 home runs and 1,903 runs batted in. He collected 3,283 hits, won 12 Gold Gloves, and was inducted into the Baseball Hall of Fame in 1979.

Before reaching the majors, Mays, a native of Alabama, played parts of three seasons with the Birmingham Black Barons in the Negro National League as a teenager. Among other honors he received, Mays was given the Presidential Medal of Freedom by president Barrack Obama in 2015.

Scouts recruiting talent for their teams referred to a five-tool player, one who could hit, hit with power, throw, field, and run. Mays was the ultimate example of the rare ballplayer who excelled at all five skills.

His most famous catch, one that lives on in lore, came in the eighth inning of the first game of the 1954 World Series when his Giants were playing the Cleveland Indians in the Polo Grounds.

The score was tied 2-2 when Cleveland first-baseman Vic Wertz belted a deep fly. Yet Mays tracked it down, making an over-the-shoulder highlight-film catch for the ages. Two lesser-remembered aspects of the brilliant catch play itself are more subtle. After Mays made the catch, he spun around and unleashed a fantastic throw to the infield to prevent a runner advancing on a sacrifice fly.

Also, while trotting off the field with fellow outfielder Monte Irvin who praised the grab, Mays said he knew he had the ball all of the way.

As of 2023, at 92 years of age, Mays was the oldest living member of the Hall of Fame.

TIM MCCARVER

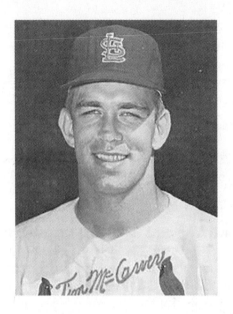

⟫⟫⟫⟫⟫⟫⟫⟫⟫ *THE SETTING*

Everywhere. For a period of years, it seemed that Tim McCarver and I bumped into one another regularly. I first spoke to the long-time Major League catcher as the end of his career approached and he was catching Steve Carlton with the Philadelphia Phillies.

Other times we ran into one another at ballparks. Once, when I was visiting Seattle, where I made stopping in at the famed Elliott Bay bookstore a priority, McCarver was inside the store when I entered. That same night we also overlapped at a game the Seattle Mariners were playing when their home field was still The Kingdome.

I also interviewed McCarver for a book project for his perspective on his St. Louis Cardinals days when he was teaming with Ken Boyer. But the most significant setting was at the National Baseball Hall of Fame in Cooperstown, New York in 2012. That year,

McCarver, who had played 21 seasons in the majors, the rare player touching on four decades of participation (starting in 1959 and finishing in 1980), was honored with the Ford Frick Award for his broadcasting work.

In the days leading up to the annual public induction ceremony, individuals being honored that year conducted press conferences and were available for interviews with sportswriters. It was in this context McCarver and I spoke the lengthiest and in the most meaningful fashion.

≫≫≫≫≫≫≫≫≫≫ THE STORY

McCarver, who grew up in Memphis, Tennessee, was actually still only 17 years old when he appeared in eight games for the Cardinals in 1959 and he did not retire until he was 38 and affiliated with the Phillies.

A savvy player, respected for his fielding and leadership behind the plate, McCarver batted .271 lifetime in 1,909 games. He was a two-time All-Star. After retiring as a player, McCarver went into broadcasting and distinguished himself for decades, particularly as a high-profile member of the Fox World Series announcing team with Joe Buck. McCarver was the color analyst for 24 World Series before stepping away from the microphone.

The question arose, though not in precisely those exact words, but was McCarver a better baseball player or baseball broadcaster? More specifically, McCarver was queried about whether he would rather have made it into the Hall of Fame for hitting and fielding or for talking.

He dismissed the suggestion out of hand. Even though there were numerous on-field highlight moments and fond memories of success, it never would have happened and his fantasies did not run in that direction.

"No," he said quite bluntly. "I wasn't good enough."

McCarver had always earned respect as a wise man of the game, someone whose opinion was respected, and who understood the sport. A noted member of the Cardinals' World Series championship squads of 1964 and 1967, McCarver was briefly a member of the 1980 Phillies for the final handful of his games, but was not with the team by the time it concluded the year as champions.

For extra credit, so to speak, McCarver was the regular catcher with the Cardinals and then the Phillies when Hall of Fame hurler Steve Carlton was the starter. He was described as Carlton's "personal catcher."

When time was running out on his playing career, McCarver knew he wanted to stay in baseball. Many players take the winding road through the minors as a coach and manager in small towns before being named to a big-league staff, or have a team turned over to them to lead. McCarver was not opposed to managing as an idea. Of course, everyone wants to go directly to a big-league managing job, an event that happens only in rare instances. And there was no sound of knuckles being pounded against McCarver's door, either.

"No one offered me a job to manage," he said.

Although he had no background whatsoever with electronics in the broadcast booth, Bill Giles, who was running the Phillies saw, or heard, something in McCarver's voice that did lead to an offer as an announcer. He was a hurry-up success in the booth, handling the Game of the Week for NBC before the end of the 1980 season.

His national work and profile expanded steadily and dramatically, but he kept one foot in local markets, becoming one of the main broadcasters for the New York Mets. At the time, the lead guy on Mets broadcasts was Ralph Kiner, the one-time Pittsburgh Pirates slugger who became a Hall of Famer as a player, but who was renowned for his malaprops and humor on the air that endeared him to fans.

Hanging with and working with Kiner, McCarver said, was "priceless." Both the fun of it and the learning experience. McCarver was associated with the Mets for 15 years. "It was the most exciting time in my professional life," McCarver said of his connection to the Mets as a broadcaster.

Along the way, McCarver did receive interview invitations from big-league teams when they had managerial vacancies, notably the

Minnesota Twins. Also, when his old Cardinals teammate Joe Torre was managing the New York Yankees, he asked McCarver if he was interested in becoming a coach. By then, though, McCarver was entrenched in the broadcasting world, which had become a passion as well as a profession, and kept him in baseball, anyway.

Looking back and viewing the experience in a certain light, probably the funniest aspect of McCarver's time acting as Carlton's catcher, was his role as a post-game stand-in interpreting what the reclusive hurler did on the diamond. Carlton refused to speak with reporters and retreated to the off-limits trainer's room. Sportswriters could not obtain the perspective of someone who was regularly one of the most important figures in the contest, so they turned to McCarver for help.

Suddenly, though sitting by his locker, not behind a microphone, McCarver assumed the role of, if not United Nations interpreter, at least an analyst, a prelude to his next career. "Doing that with Steve Carlton helped train me," McCarver said.

While there are no college broadcast courses offered requiring such roles for credit, things worked out quite well for McCarver. He won three Emmy Awards.

⟫⟫⟫⟫⟫⟫⟫⟫⟫⟫⟫⟫ CAREER

McCarver's highest profile partnership with the Cardinals was with Hall of Fame pitcher Bob Gibson. Gibson, who was Black, and McCarver, a White man from the South, made for an interesting tandem. McCarver always said the fiery pitcher taught him quite a bit about race relations.

As a broadcaster, McCarver and Joe Buck teamed up for 18 World Series telecasts. By the time McCarver stepped aside in 2013, he had talked for the Phillies, Mets, Yankees, and San Francisco Giants, too. He worked part-time broadcasting for his old Cardinals after that and from 2000 to 2017 handled "The Tim McCarver Show."

One on-the-field highlight occurred during the 1964 World Series for the Cardinals when McCarver hit an extra-inning homer to help win Game 5. Along the way, McCarver caught no-hitters thrown by Rick Wise and Bill Stoneman.

Although it is impossible to speak a million-or-so words on the air without a gaffe. McCarver's biggest baseball mistake turned wine into water, in a manner of speaking. On July 4, 1976, McCarver belted a grand slam, but because he passed teammate Garry Maddox on the basepaths, his hit was converted to a single. The Phillies still easily beat the Pittsburgh Pirates that day and McCarver joked about his own basic lack of speed in trying to explain the error. "I didn't pass him, he lapped me," McCarver said.

At one point during his broadcasting days, trying something completely different, McCarver released an album of himself singing jazz songs.

McCarver, who did not officially announce his retirement from broadcasting until 2022, died at 81 in February of 2023 from heart failure.

TUG MCGRAW

Tug McGraw (left) with Jerry Koosman (right)

Photo courtesy of BASEBALL HALL OF FAME

>>>>>>>>>>>>>>>>>>>> **THE SETTING**

The left-handed relief pitcher who made believers out of fans in two cities was as open and forthright as a baseball player could be during his splendid career coming out of bullpens to put out fires.

Tug McGraw helped the New York Mets to glory in 1973 and the Philadelphia Phillies to a similar World Series championship in 1980. With the Mets, McGraw coined the phrase, "Ya Gotta Believe" and teammates and fans followed his lead and made it into a battle cry.

Born Frank Edwin McGraw Jr. in 1944, humorously, the pitcher gained his nickname as a youth because he was said to be such an aggressive breast feeder. His father's nickname was "Big Mac," presumably so named before the hamburger became as well-known.

Tug McGraw spent just about the entirety of his 20s with the

Mets, but became a Phillie in 1975. He was the team's ace reliever in 1980 when Philadelphia won its first world title ever and spent just about the entirety of his thirties with the Phillies, in all playing 19 years in the majors.

The Phillies of 1980 are remembered in the city as an iconic team, but due to tensions between players and manager Dallas Green, they are often remembered as a group (with exceptions) for being unpopular with the sports reporters who covered them.

McGraw stood out for his sense of humor, his friendliness, and his expressions of joy when playing baseball.

At the time, as the Phillies were heating up and making a run at the National League pennant, I got to see McGraw in the locker room while working on the Philadelphia Inquirer sports staff. But we also adjourned to his home in the Philadelphia suburbs for a lengthy feature. The headline that ran above the story said much about McGraw. It read, "Forever Young." The sub-head said as much, as well, reading, "McGraw enjoys his life, his job, himself."

What more can one ask out of life?

THE STORY

As befitting a well-paid professional athlete, McGraw owned a mansion-like 15-bedroom house in the community of Media in the Philadelphia suburbs. Instead of having the manicured appearance of cleaning lady visits with regularity, its contents seemed a trifle disheveled, like McGraw on occasion.

We spent most of our time in the expansive backyard, sitting in the considerable shadow of his 22-foot-long barbecue, which had yet to roast its first meal, but was nearly ready for action. It was so colossal it could have been an entry on the National Monuments list.

McGraw, his wife, his daughter and son, and his mother-in-law, were inhabitants, but there was plenty of room to go around. He joked that they had been living on the premises for two years, but had never quite stopped moving in, hence the sense hinted of change-in-motion all over the place.

A man with great appeal to fans, at least partly because he said what he thought and what he thought was often light-hearted, McGraw said he never acquired a filter on his tongue. "It's just that I never learned to hide my feelings," McGraw said. "And I'm not trying to, either. I have a lot of fun being myself."

Imagine, candor. Of course, he was also a guy who was somewhat of a rarity, or oddity, depending on the point of view, whose fastball, curve, and slider were supplemented by a screwball.

A screwball was felt to be an appropriate weapon for someone who was often described that way and didn't mind one bit. Indeed, McGraw exploited it. When he toiled for the Mets and became a chief cheerleader with that "Ya Gotta Believe" slogan, it did not hurt to be in the middle of the marketing capital of the world. He ended up producing a comic strip for one of the local newspapers that was called "Scroogie." The thinly disguised main baseball character was him.

McGraw was infused with the enthusiasm gene at birth, it seems. He was demonstrative, not low-key or business-like on the mound. Whether it was a nervous habit or just a routine, he regularly tapped

his glove against his thigh. When he finished off an important strikeout, he might leap and thrust arms in the air in celebration. Some thought he was showing up hitters. McGraw was offended by the suggestion.

"It's a shame they don't enjoy me as much as I enjoy me," McGraw said of his critics.

At the time, well into summer, as the Phillies were making it obvious they might do something special that season, McGraw was a key factor in success. He had made 31 appearances with 10 saves and his earned run average was sitting at 2.36.

It is not a word often used in the modern game, but forty-plus years ago a player who deviated from the norm and was seen as a jokester or too fun-loving, could be described as a flake. McGraw wanted to explore his heritage on a trip to Ireland after he retired. Rather than speak with an Irish brogue, McGraw was described as being an Irish rogue. He also did have an affinity for potatoes, as if that taste was in his genes, as well.

"I have a lifetime of being a show-off guy, but that doesn't make me a bad guy," McGraw said.

A funny guy, a guy with a certain lack of seriousness, maybe, but a bad guy, no. McGraw served on the board of the Muscular Dystrophy Foundation, made speeches at Little League banquets, and visited sick children in hospitals. When a fan club was organized to root for him, McGraw accepted under the one condition that all of the dues be given to a needy Native American family in New Mexico.

Why did he spend so much time giving time to honorable causes? It was simple for McGraw. "That's part of the responsibility of being lucky," McGraw said, "good and healthy, trying to help other people who aren't blessed with one of those things."

McGraw was also wealthy by basic American standards and he indulged in a bit of opulence, with a backyard pool, driving a Mercedes with a "Tug45" license plate, and the large house. As he enjoyed himself, he seemed to enjoy his opportunities.

Blond-haired with an impish grin, one of those stereotype glints in the eye of a kid who had just raided the cookie jar, McGraw was having fun. He may have been making up for lack of fun as a youth when his parents divorced and he had little confidence. That trait is a must in professional sports and not displaying it can sink an athlete. McGraw said he was in the majors for about four years before he thought he actually belonged there.

The aha moment occurred in the 1969 post-season – yes, he was a member of that favorite Mets team, too – when he was on the mound in a critical situation. "I got a hitter out exactly as I pre-planned it," McGraw said. "I needed a strikeout and I got it. It didn't hurt the ego or confidence any that the victim was Hank Aaron.

McGraw said he was mostly misunderstood because he was a person who, like Cyndi Lauper, just wanted to have fun. But he didn't get in trouble off the field, worked hard at his craft (catcher Bob Boone supported that), and was a baseball fanatic.

He also could get hitters out under pressure in pennant races and playoffs when a team needed him to do the job.

CAREER

A couple of months later, McGraw was on the mound at Veterans Stadium when the Phillies defeated the Kansas City Royals to claim the franchise's first World Series title in history, obtaining the final out.

As was his style, he jumped in the air, arms upthrust to the sky, and cameras clicked at this precious moment, preserving it for Mc-Graw, the Phillies, and fans. It was a magical moment come to life and one that symbolized the delight of Tug McGraw and the glee he brought to the game.

That season, at age 35, McGraw's final record was 5-4 with a 1.46 earned run average and 20 saves. He spent the rest of his playing days with the Phillies, through the age of 39, finishing with a record of 96-92 and 180 saves. He was a two-time All-Star.

Always appreciated in Philadelphia, twice McGraw made re-markable news in later years. It became widely known that he was the father of famed country singer Tim McGraw, a fact the pitcher didn't even know for many years. His son was the product of a brief, minor-league fling many years earlier that ended abruptly. Eventu-ally, the grown-up singer and the retired pitcher became close.

More tragically, in the early 2000s, McGraw suddenly became se-riously ill. In March of 2003, McGraw was working at the Phillies' spring training camp when he was hospitalized with a brain tumor. Initially, it was stated surgery was successful and McGraw's long-term prognosis was that he would resume excellent health.

McGraw's identification with the "Ya Gotta Believe" theme was invoked while he was recuperating, even if it did not work that time. Instead, it turned out the tumor returned in inoperable fashion and McGraw died at 57 in early 2004. During the following 2004 season, Mets players wore a patch with the saying on their uniforms to honor McGraw.

Also beginning in 2004, the Philadelphia Baseball Writers Association instituted a "Tug McGraw Good Guy Award" presented to a player each season. A Tug McGraw Foundation was established in 2003 to enhance the quality of life of children and adults with brain tumors and in 2009 expanded programs to help those with post-traumatic stress disorder.

My journalistic time spent with Tug McGraw, especially at his home that long afternoon, was particularly enjoyable. At one point later, McGraw gave me a gift consisting of two collected volumes of the "Scroogie" comic strip. One of the books was autographed. Thinking back on the type of man who signed it, I treasure it to this day.

MINNIE MINOSO

Photo courtesy of BASEBALL HALL OF FAME

THE SETTING

The ballpark is where you most often found Minnie Minoso. The one-time star of the Chicago White Sox came to games regularly. He liked to mingle with the players and officials and watch his old team play.

In the early 2000s, when I visited the press box at the new Comiskey Park, and after it was renamed U.S. Cellular Field, I saw Minoso all the time and interviewed him periodically. Sometimes we just said hello. Other times we had lengthy conversations about his days in the majors.

Sometimes his words appeared in columns I wrote for baseball outlets. Other times we did interviews for books about the Chicago White Sox. Minoso was born in Cuba and even though he had been in the United States as a player since the 1940s, he still spoke English with a thick accent.

Yet when it came to Minoso and the White Sox, he was living, breathing history, a link to the good days of the franchise under Hall of Fame owner Bill Veeck, and a symbol of history himself since he was the first Black player to compete for the club in the early days immediately following Jackie Robinson breaking the color barrier.

Minoso did not wish to dwell on that topic, almost dismissing his own role in history at times, and other times appreciating it. But he was always a pleasure to talk to, someone who clearly still carried his own love for the game at all times.

When I was a youth and first watching baseball on television, Minoso was still a regular, though nearing the end of his career. It was not until adulthood that I realized what an important role he played in White Sox history. At a time when discrimination was still strong in the sport and insults hurled from the stands at Black and Latin players, both of which Minoso was, were commonplace, Minoso remained true to himself.

⟫⟫⟫⟫⟫⟫⟫⟫⟫⟫ *THE STORY*

The baseball player called "Minnie" was born Saturino Orestes Armas Minoso Arrieta on November 29, 1923 in Perico. Cuba. That is the date referred to now, but over the years it has fluctuated. The old Baseball Encyclopedia wrote that he was born in 1922. Minoso insisted he was born in 1925.

He grew up in poverty, but found salvation in baseball. He first played the game in his home country and then, in 1946, after World War II, he came to the United States to join the New York Cubans of the Negro National League. Minoso played parts of 1946, 1947, and 1948 with the Cubans and was a two-time All-Star.

More forward-thinking Major League Baseball clubs began searching the Negro Leagues teams for talent after Robinson became a star for the Brooklyn Dodgers and Minoso was signed by the Cleveland Indians. However, he did not make an impact until he excelled for the White Sox in 1951 as an All-Star outfielder.

That year, Minoso was the first Latin-American to play in a Major League All-Star game, but by then he had made his debut with the White Sox a historic one. Being the first Black to suit up for the South Side Chicago team established Minoso in team lore.

"The most important game of my life was May 1, 1951," Minoso said.

This was the first game Minoso played for the White Sox. It was against the New York Yankees in the original Comiskey Park. Vic Raschi was hurling for the Yankees that day and Minoso had never batted against him. Minoso decided to take his chances with aggressive swings.

"So, I went up to the plate my first time and I said I'm going to swing three times," Minoso recalled. "I hit a long one that went 439 feet into the White Sox bullpen and the umpire signaled home run."

Minoso smacked his blast in the first inning. Coincidentally, a rookie outfielder for the Yankees who would make a big splash in his career, hit his first home run that day in the sixth inning. That was Mickey Mantle. Minoso enjoyed telling the tale with the emphasis on the part about him getting his first homer before slugger Mantle did since Mantle hit many more in his own Hall of Fame career.

The Yankees, as they so often did during that era, won the game, 8-3. Minoso went two-for-four that day, but endeared himself to the 14,000-plus spectators – and all White Sox supporters – from the start.

"I made a good impression on the fans," Minoso said. "White Sox fans always liked me after that. I never heard any boos. Never. Since that opening day, nobody ever booed. I was in love with everyone."

It is likely fans could read Minoso's generosity of spirit coming through when he spoke to sportswriters. They always treated him kindly for his attitude in addition to his production.

Minoso did not ignore his special place in White Sox history as the first Black player, but he did not dwell on it or always draw attention to it, though he issued some thoughts when quizzed. The Dodgers were the first team to hire a Black player and the Cleveland

Indians did so with Larry Doby immediately afterwards in 1947. Some other teams such as the New York Giants made strong moves in rounding up Black talent. But some teams moved slowly, among the slowest being the New York Yankees, Detroit Tigers, and Boston Red Sox.

Coming to the United States to play baseball from Cuba, Minoso was aware of, but not well-versed in, the racism prevalent across American society in 1946. When he could, he chose to ignore it, but at times was verbally abused. Some suggest that it was no accident Minoso was hit by pitches 197 times during his career, the most in an American League season 10 times. He was even hospitalized from a severe concussion on a pitched ball. Was he a target or did he just crowd the plate and bring risk upon himself? MInoso did not shout about his plight.

He was grateful to get the chance to play in the majors when walls began crumbling.

"Mr. Jackie (Robinson) and Mr. Branch Rickey (the Dodgers' general manager) opened the door to us," Minoso said. "I don't ever look at race. I don't care for color, position, nationality, beauty, or ugliness. I knew about racism when I came from Cuba and that they say, 'You're not supposed to be there.' They have separate things and they don't let you eat there.

"I am the first Black player for the White Sox, but it had to be somebody. It is a good thing, but I am not a special person because of that. I paid my price, just like Jackie."

Others believe differently – that Minoso was a pretty special man in more than one way.

⟫⟫⟫⟫⟫⟫⟫⟫⟫⟫ CAREER

As many of the first Black players were getting their chance at the majors, Minoso was a little bit older than the average rookie player. He remained in the majors, primarily with the White Sox and Indians through 1964, but also made brief stops with the St. Louis Cardinals and the Washington Senators.

A nine-time All-Star, in addition to his All-Star selections with the Cubans, Minoso batted .299 and won three Gold Gloves. Possessed of great speed, Minoso twice led the American League in stolen bases and was one of the linchpins of the White Sox's so-called "Go-Go" offense of the 1950s stressing speed.

Although Minoso basically retired at 40 in 1964, later Sox owner Bill Veeck got the promotional idea to try and help Minoso make future appearances in later decades. He played in three games in 1976 and two in 1980 at age 56, making him a unique five-decade player. Somewhat overlooked among those who said this would be making a travesty of the game was that throughout his late forties Minoso kept playing ball regularly in Mexico and hitting pretty well at what was called the equivalent of AAA ball. He wasn't merely lying around on a chaise lounge.

There was even talk of Minoso putting the uniform back on for a game in the majors when he was 67, but Major League Baseball put the kibosh on that plan. However, in 1993, at age 69, Minoso unretired once more for the opportunity to take a few swings for the independent minor-league team in St. Paul, Minnesota. It was no coincidence that the chief operator of the club was Mike Veeck, Bill's promotionally minded son, who learned a trick or two from dad.

Then, in 2003, Minoso, at age 77, played in a game in a seventh decade, walking as a designated hitter for St. Paul.

Yes, it was a gimmick, but done in fun.

In 2004, the White Sox unveiled a statue of Minoso at the team's home park and Minoso shed tears on the occasion, saying, "I can't explain the way I feel in my heart."

In the early 2000s, a special committee was formed to try to bring Hall of Fame justice to the best Black players whose careers dated to before integration, or overlapped with it. There was a feeling among many that Minoso would be one of those honored, but it didn't happen. A group of 17 Black players were inducted in 2006.

Minoso was crushed he was overlooked then and by the Golden Era Committee. "Truly, I'm hurt," Minoso said. Of others who got in, Minoso said, "My records are better. That's what's breaking my heart."

At a 2011 Minnie Minoso Hall of Fame Forum in Chicago, many spoke of Minoso's impact on the game and the community and especially his role as a Latin American star.

"Minoso was the Jackie Robinson for all Latinos, the first star who opened doors for all Latin-American players," said Puerto Rican Hall of Famer Orlando Cepeda in a message sent to the Forum. "He was everybody's hero."

Minoso said he didn't want to be chosen for the Hall of Fame after he died, because he wanted to be alive to enjoy the connection. When he passed away in early 2015, most likely at 90 or 92 years of age, with that date of birth still facing discrepancy, Minoso had not been chosen and there was no indication he would be in the near future.

Then abruptly, when the Golden Era Committee met again near the end of 2021, there was newfound support for Minoso. He was elected to the Hall of Fame and inducted at the ceremonies during the summer of 2022. It seemed like a case of justice delayed but at least not completely denied.

Minoso was the leading hitter in the 1948 East-West All-Star Game.

JOE MORGAN

THE SETTING

Long after he played his last Major League game in 1984, Joe Morgan, the two-time National League Most Valuable Player, kept a locker inside the clubhouse of his old Cincinnati Reds team.

Whenever he could, Morgan would use the Great American Ball Park facilities to work out, stay in shape, take a shower, and hang out. The Hall of Fame second baseman never strayed far from the game he loved, but few guys who were not actively playing, coaching, or managing, kept a change of clothes in their old team's locker room.

Talk about having baseball in the blood. Elected to the Hall in 1990, Morgan, who rose to prominence on the organization's board of trustees, was about as well-known and popular as a long-time broadcaster after he parked his glove.

Morgan called games for the San Francisco Giants, plus NBC and ABC. At NBC, Morgan worked with Bob Costas and Bob Uecker, two stars of the booth. And then he had a longstanding partnership with Jon Miller especially, and Orel Hershiser, on ESPN's Sunday Night Baseball, one that got rave reviews. Morgan and Miller handled championship series playoff games and the World Series on radio, too.

Over time, Morgan also broadcast the College World Series, the Little League World Series, and Monday Night Baseball. If there was a baseball being tossed somewhere, sooner or later Morgan would show up.

One of the centerpiece players on the roster of the Big Red Machine Reds title teams of the mid-1970s in his second go-around in the game, Morgan actually broadcast former teammate Pete Rose's record base-hit when that Reds icon cracked Ty Cobb's all-time hits mark with his 4,192nd safety.

Periodically, when I was covering the Cincinnati Reds in the 2010s, I would see Morgan around the team. On one occasion we found a space to do a lengthy sit-down interview in the clubhouse.

⟫⟫⟫⟫⟫⟫⟫⟫⟫⟫ *THE STORY*

The 1975 World Series between Cincinnati and the Boston Red Sox has been hailed as perhaps the best Series of all time, full of drama, suspense, and moments of great achievement. By winning that championship round in seven games, the Reds put their initial stamp on being called a great team. By winning the title again in 1976, they confirmed their legendary stature.

Those Reds teams, managed by Sparky Anderson, set a high standard and featured a legion of great players, including Morgan, Rose, Johnny Bench, Tony Perez, Ken Griffey, Don Gullet, George Foster, Gary Nolan, Dave Concepcion, Jack Billingham, and Cesar Geronimo. At its core, it was much the same outfit in 1975 and 1976.

"I think that that team, I don't think there were any better teams in the history of the game," Morgan said. "We loved that challenge because we were, in my opinion, the only team that could beat you every different way. We had speed. We had great fielding. We had four Gold Gloves up the middle. We could run. We could steal bases. No team ever had that. One year we almost all hit .300."

Morgan extolled the baseball IQ of the group, too, saying the Reds played with smarts and savvy, making the right choices and right plays on the field and under pressure.

"We were not all Phi Beta Kappas off the field, but on the field we were," Morgan said.

Knowing that when talking all-time history and the groups the Reds were compared to included such outfits as the 1927 New York Yankees' Murderers Row, Morgan did not exempt that glittery team of Babe Ruth, Lou Gehrig, and others from his comparison.

Yes, those Yankees, with Ruth mashing 60 of them, could hit home runs with anyone, but could those Yankees outdo Morgan's Reds in other facets of the game?

"But defensively, they weren't like that," (equal to the Reds), Morgan said.

It is sometimes overlooked, however, that the Reds became noted as the Big Red Machine by winning back-to-back. In 1975, Cincinnati won its division by a 20-game margin, but the Reds won the famed World Series by a much thinner margin over the Red Sox. If the Reds lost to Boston in Game 7 after the remarkable Game 6 that held the country spellbound, would anyone have been talking about a Big Red Machine at all?

One of the greatest games in Red Sox history was the victory in Game 6 when catcher Carlton Fisk ripped an extra-inning home run and danced around the bases after seemingly willing his fly ball to land fair.

That set up the decisive Game 7 which could not quite match Game 6 for over-the-top theater, but benefited from the hoopla following Game 6 in attracting eyes to television sets.

Morgan, who had two hits, highlighted that game and that victory as the most special of his career. Not only because the Reds won the game and won the championship, but because he produced the game-winning hit.

Boston led 3-0 early and the Reds tied the game 3-3 in the seventh inning. Griffey was on second base when Morgan stepped into the batter's box. He stroked a single to score Griffey for the lead and the 4-3 margin stood up.

"I knew we were champions, but I couldn't believe it," Morgan said of the slow-to-sink-in glow of winning it all.

There was so much emotion, so much joy in the clubhouse after the game as the Reds celebrated their achievement. The scene remained a vivid picture in Morgan's mind long after.

"It was a madhouse in there, you know," he said. "But I can remember that we all talked to each other individually and congratulated each other and were just happy."

Morgan was convinced that the next year's bunch, the 1976 champs, constituted an even better team, but that the satisfaction gleaned from the first title provided more of a lasting feeling because it was the first Series win for the group. After going 102-60, the Reds defeated the Yankees, four games to zero.

"You know the old saying, 'You never forget your first girl?' Morgan said, "You know, even if I had won 10 more World Series, that first one would have still jumped out at me. That was the one."

 ## *CAREER*

Joe Morgan played his first big-league games at 19 in 1963 with the then-Houston Colt .45s, and remained with that franchise as the Astros through 1971 when he came to the Reds. In all, Morgan played 22 seasons, retiring in 1984.

Regarded as one of the most outstanding second basemen in baseball history, Morgan hit .271 with 268 home runs, 689 stolen bases, and 1,133 runs batted in. A 10-time All-Star and five-time Gold Glove winner, Morgan won the MVP award in both of those mid-1970s Reds title seasons and in both World Series.

In addition to being chosen for the National Baseball Hall of Fame in Cooperstown, New York, Morgan is a member of both the Houston and Cincinnati team halls of fame.

Morgan was a small man in an increasingly big man's game as athletes grew in size, standing just 5-foot-7 and weighing 160 pounds. For that reason, he was often referred to as "Little Joe."

As a broadcaster, he once humorously made the argument AGAINST his being considered the best second baseman ever when compared to Rogers Hornsby. Hornsby, who played between 1915 and 1937 compiled a .358 lifetime batting average, second best in history to Ty Cobb. Hornsby won seven batting crowns and hit higher than .400 three times.

In 1998, the Reds retired Morgan's No. 8 uniform jersey and he choked up during the ceremony. "It kind of got to me," Morgan said. "You know it's going to happen, but to see it happen is what makes it special."

Morgan recalled that when he was young and still learning, he teamed with another small-in-physical-stature middle infielder Nellie Fox, another Hall of Famer, who was then at the end of his career.

Fox told him, "'Joe, the guys who stay in the major leagues the longest are the guys who do the most to help their team win.' And that's the way I tried to play every day," Morgan added.

Joe Morgan died at 77 on October 11, 2020.

STAN MUSIAL

⟫⟫⟫⟫⟫⟫⟫⟫ *THE SETTING*

Ever-so-fleeting. For a brief period of time, out of courtesy, out of being the gentleman that he always was, Stan Musial hung out in the press box at Veterans Stadium in Philadelphia, just waiting.

"Stan The Man," the most revered of St. Louis Cardinals stars, and perhaps one of the more underrated of Hall of Famers in the history of baseball, was a polite guest-in-waiting, an observer like members of the press. All of us were mostly on hand due to a record watch, not for the results of any particular game in the home park of the Philadelphia Phillies.

Pete Rose, who had just turned 40 years old during that disjointed 1981 season, was closing in on the record for most hits by a National League batter. This was before interleague play when such records were still distinct and had not been blurred forever. The mark was 3,630 and it was owned by Musial, who played for the Cardinals between 1941 and 1963.

Rose, who spent most of his playing career with the Cincinnati Reds before going to the Phillies in free agency (a concept that did not exist in Musial's playing days) had ever-so-briefly overlapped in the sport with Musial. Rose was a rookie in 1963 and was in the field during Musial's final big-league game.

Alas, rather than a smooth transition from the old record-holder to the new record-holder, baseball was interrupted by a labor action that summer and the entire process of Rose surpassing Musial in base hits was delayed as a strike was sorted out.

Musial had long before seen Rose coming up behind him, much like a driver spotting approaching headlights in the rearview mirror. He said he would be happy to be present when Rose caught up. So, Musial traveled to Philadelphia for the passing of the torch and spent his waiting time speaking to members of the press in anticipation of Rose's single or double, maybe even a home run (though less likely given his batting tendencies).

It was just prior to a strike deadline ultimatum and Rose did not catch up to Musial before the unwanted roughly two-month-long intermission from the schedule.

》》》》》》》》》》》》 *THE STORY*

The story line was Musial and Rose, how they were different players from different eras, but when the labor movement intervened, the process essentially went on strike, too. No new record for Rose until the games resumed.

Instead, the gracious and available Musial was following developments like everyone else, while occasionally opining about Rose.

Musial was a much more significant power hitter than the singles and doubles specialist Rose. Musial mostly played the outfield, but also first base, while Rose played some outfield, but mostly the infield.

Musial revealed that after the World Series of 1980, when Rose was a member of the champion Phillies, he and Musial saw one another and that is when Musial said he would be glad to be present when Rose broke his hits record. In that way, Musial's presence was sealed months before this stretch when Rose crept up on the mark.

During this period Musial actually admitted he thought his league hits record would have lasted a bit longer than it was about to last. He had done the arithmetic, figuring that some unknown player would have to collect 200 hits for 15 years to reach 3,000 and Musial's total was well beyond that.

For a while, he didn't reckon on Rose, who could gather so many hits so often and keep on going at an even swifter pace. Then Musial realized Rose was enough of a hitting machine that he had totaled at least 200 hits in a season 10 times. That's when he began to think the time might come with Rose hovering on the edge of reaching and surpassing 3,630.

When Musial stepped away from the game, he was second on baseball's all-time hits list to Ty Cobb and his 4,191. There were only six others who had accumulated as many as 3,000 hits. Musial reached that level in 1958. Musial is still fourth all-time, although now there are 33 men who have reached the 3,000 milestone. The only one on the list and still adding to it in active play as of the 2023 season was Miguel Cabrera.

While chatting with sportswriters, Musial showed off a droll sense of humor. "The key to hitting for high average," he said, "is to relax, concentrate, and don't hit fly balls to centerfield."

Rose was one hit shy of Musial's record in June of 1981 when the strike began and had to wait until mid-August to pass him and claim the record.

When Rose did catch up to the record, then-president Ronald Reagan called him on the telephone at the ballpark to offer congratulations. Also, despite the lengthy, interrupted vigil, Musial was on hand. Rose said it meant a lot to him that Musial came. Rose's record-breaking hit was a single to left field on the ground through the infield.

As play was halted for acknowledgement, Musial walked onto the field, gave Rose a hearty handshake and the men exchanged a few words.

⟫⟫⟫⟫⟫⟫⟫⟫⟫⟫⟫⟫⟫⟫⟫⟫ CAREER

Stan Musial had one of the greatest careers in baseball history. Musial was selected for 24 All-Star teams, was a member of three World Series champions, won the Most Valuable Player Award three times and won the National League batting crown seven times.

Statistically, Musial batted .331 lifetime, accumulated those 3,630 hits, cracked 475 home runs, batted in 1,951 runs, and scored 1,949 runs. Not only were Musial's RBI and runs scored totals virtually identical, but his hits total was split exactly down the middle with half stroked safely at home and half stroked safely on the road. During his 22 years in the majors, all spent with the Cardinals, Musial exhibited an easily-recognized crouching left-handed batting stance and wore No. 6 on the back of his uniform.

The slugger had such a good eye at the plate that he struck out just 38 times in 722 plate appearances in 1949. Once, before a game, a teammate said that he felt like going four-for-four that day and Musial said, "Hell, I feel like that every day." Perhaps that determined outlook was one reason why Musial so often did that.

Musial was a collector and saver of souvenirs, Cardinals, and baseball memorabilia throughout his life. Although he saved quite a bit and many, many items were inherited by family members, there was still $1.2 million worth auctioned off after he passed away.

One item that stood out among the collectibles was a letter Musial had received from Cobb, who holds the record for most batting titles with 12. In 1951, Musial won one of his batting titles with a .355 average. Accusing Musial of being too nice a guy, Cobb wrote, "So now go out there and lead the league again and if you don't lead both Major Leagues this year, you should be shot in the behind with mustard seed."

Musial did go out and win the NL batting title once more, hitting .336, the following season. However, the lesser-known Ferris Fain batted .344 in the American League, preventing him from topping the entire majors. There was no known follow-up letter from Cobb discussing mustard seed delivery.

Musial, who was admired and beloved in St. Louis for his performance and his demeanor, was 92 when he died in 2013, a year after his wife Lillian.

PHIL NIEKRO

>>>>>>>>>>>>>>>>>>>> *THE SETTING*

While doing research for a book about the knuckleball, I met and spent time interviewing Phil Niekro at a minor-league ballpark in Lawrenceville, Georgia named Coolray Field and additionally had talks on the telephone.

We also shot some photographs. On the cover was Phil's right hand, gripping the ball as if he were about to deliver the tricky pitch he specialized in. Although he would not specifically claim the title (deferring to reliever Hoyt Wilhelm), Niekro is likely the most accomplished knuckleball thrower of all-time.

Niekro's often-used nickname during his playing career was "Knucksie." Coolray Field has a restaurant named after him and the menu included The Knucksie sandwich.

The native of Ohio who learned the knuckleball from his dad

Phillip in the backyard, and experienced much success with the Atlanta Braves and other teams, won 318 games in his long career, and pitched a no-hitter while relying on a pitch few others could control well enough to constitute a career.

Over a period of many years, Niekro, whose brother Joe also successfully employed the knuckler to win 221 games (the Niekros won more big-league games than any other brother combination) Niekro was always on friendly speed dial for other knuckleballers seeking advice to help their own careers along.

Aware of this, almost at the very beginning of our lengthy first conversation in 2014 in the Atlanta suburbs, I used the expression "Dr. Phil" as a way of noting the manner in which other active knuckleball pitchers relied on him, even though he was in retirement. I also made the mistake of applying a different phrase to Niekro, casually calling him "a master" of the knuckleball. Despite all his success and his place in the National Baseball Hall of Fame, he immediately intervened to clear up an impression.

Niekro said he knew a lot of people used such a term about him and the knuckler, "But I don't think you ever master the knuckleball."

It should be pointed out that Wilhelm, who also became a Hall of Famer, agreed with that sentiment. Neither of those men who employed the knuckler as their key weapon on the mound ever felt 100 percent in control of it. Those who could make a living off the knuckleball could make it work for them often enough to survive, but seemed too superstitious to claim mastery, as if an innate sorcery with the pitch might haunt them.

The pitch, when in the hands (fingers, knuckles) of the best, is a slow ball, sometimes moving from mound to plate at less than 70 mph and always slower than a fastball. It looks easy to hit, yet makes its swerves in the wind currents and goes where it wants. As far as a pitcher is concerned, it may go where he hopes it will.

"Everybody pretty much knew I was going to throw it," Niekro said. "I didn't care if they knew I was going to throw it. If I had confidence, I was going to throw it."

The knuckleball looked so easy to hit because it moved at such a first-gear pace. But hitters flailed and missed and Niekro spent 24 seasons in the majors, not retiring until he was 48. Pitchers who count on fastballs and curves can't take the strain on their arms as long.

It is often said the pitcher who relies on the knuckler puts so little strain on his throws his arm never wears out. One of the reasons why Niekro and I met at a minor-league park was because he still occasionally threw batting practice to the young professionals. He was 75 years old at the time, his arm apparently still in working order.

>>>>>>>>>>>>>>>>> ## THE STORY

Aspiring big-league pitchers do not grow up dreaming they will whiff Aaron Judge on a deadly fluttering knuckleball. They all seem to have the image of blowing the heat past hitters frozen with the bats on their shoulder and just shaking their heads trying to assimilate what that blistering last pitch did.

Scouts look for arm strength as much as anything, not 18-year-olds who toss knucklers. There are few practitioners, none in the majors at the moment, and pitching coaches did not throw the knuckler themselves, so it is not taught. If a knuckleball specialist runs into trouble, he is most likely talking to a coach who doesn't understand how the pitch works.

That is why well-respected knuckleball guys like Niekro got late-night telephone calls from desperate knuckleballers seeking private coaching sessions from a fellow pro. The men might have been strangers, but they shared the rare experience of making a go out of life by relying on a very unpredictable strength.

Woe is the young pitcher who realizes he won't graduate from AAA, or maybe not even make it that far, with the fastball and curve that was so good to him in high school and college. He looks ahead and sees his days are numbered unless he can try something new.

"They don't let you throw it in Little League or Pony League or American Legion," Niekro said of various levels of youth play. "Then you go to your high school coach and he says, 'I don't know anything about that. I can help you with this or that.'"

The problem might be with this or that, however.

"Then you go to college and you tell your college pitching coach, 'I want to be a knuckleball pitcher,'" Niekro said. "And he says, 'Can't help you. Sorry about that.'"

The big-league scouts still like the guy well enough to sign him, and no one is going to turn down the opportunity.

"You go to a minor-league camp someplace and you tell the minor league coordinator, 'I want to be a knuckleballer,' and they say, 'We got nobody here. We can't help. We didn't sign you to do that.' You're getting older and everybody is shying away from that. Guys have a hard time. They want you to throw a fastball."

When someone emerges to make a splash with the knuckler the way Tim Wakefield did with the Boston Red Sox in the 1990s and early 2000s and R.A. Dickey did with the New York Mets around 2010, there is sudden magnification of attention. Wakefield won 200 games. Dickey won 120 games and won a Cy Young Award as the best pitcher in the National League in 2012.

"R.A. Dickey was late in his career and when he won the Cy Young that opened the eyes of every pitcher, not in this country, but in other countries," Niekro said. "They thought, 'Hey, maybe I don't have to throw 92 mph.' He opened the eyes of a lot of people."

Dickey did not really jump-start a revolution. It was more that he may have represented the tail end of an era since there are zero knuckleballers in the majors now. However, Niekro said there was so much publicity about the knuckler during Dickey's 20-win season, every ball-playing kid became curious.

Niekro said kids on his grandson's Little League team were "trying to throw knuckle balls on the side."

Many have called the knuckler the pitch of last resort because some success stories have followed long apprenticeships and guys making the switch away from the fastball and curve that brought them to the dance. Niekro was one of the adherents, the true believers, who down deep always felt success with the knuckleball would only be possible if a thrower was mentally all in on the funky pitch, throwing it at least 85 percent of the time.

"You've got to commit to it," Niekro said. "The commitment, you've got to believe in it. The knuckleball is not a pitch you throw with two or three other pitches. I'm a knuckleball pitcher and everything feeds off that. Commit to it. Sacrifice to it."

⟫⟫⟫⟫⟫⟫⟫⟫⟫⟫⟫ CAREER

Phil Niekro was born on April 1, 1939 (he and I shared the same birthday). He broke into the majors in 1964 at 25 when the Braves were still in Milwaukee. In 1967, when he was 28, Niekro led the National League in earned run average with a 1.87 mark.

A five-time All-Star and five-time Gold Glove winner, Niekro's lifetime mark was 318-274 with a 3.35 ERA. He recorded 3,342 strikeouts. Niekro was a three-time, 20-game-winner. He threw as many as 342 innings in a season. On August 5, 1973, Niekro pitched a no-hitter against the San Diego Padres, winning the game, 9-0. He struck out four and walked three that day.

Niekro notched his 300th victory with an 8-0 shutout of the Toronto Blue Jays in October of 1985 when he was pitching for the New York Yankees. That made him the oldest pitcher to ever hurl a shutout.

Unbeknownst to his manager and coaching staff and teammates when going for the milestone win, Niekro decided to show he could have been a successful pitcher without throwing a knuckler. He recorded his first 26 outs using other pitches, then for the last batter only used exclusively knuckleballs.

After retiring as a player, Niekro became the manager of the all-women's Colorado Silver Belles professional baseball team, between 1994-1997 touring the country and playing against men's teams. The other coaches were also ex-Major League players, Joe Niekro, Joe Pignatano, Johnny Grubb, and Al Bumbry.

In 1997, while the group was still together, Niekro was chosen for the Baseball Hall of Fame and he invited the players to attend the induction ceremony.

Phil Niekro was 81 when he passed away in late December of 2020. I never did get to taste a Knucksie sandwich since the day Phil and I hung out there the restaurant was not open.

Then known as the Gwinnett Braves in the International League, the team's name was changed to the Gwinnett Stripers in 2018 because of the popularity of striped bass fishing in the area.

However, Braves or Stripers, the most recent menu still included the item labeled "Phil Niekro's favorite," the Knucksie, includes smoked pulled pork, caramelized onions, pickles, and coleslaw on skillet cornbread and is covered with barbecue sauce. Sounds like a multi-napkin meal.

BUCK O'NEIL

Photo courtesy of BASEBALL HALL OF FAME

⟫⟫⟫⟫⟫⟫⟫⟫⟫⟫⟫ *THE SETTING*

It was about 10 months before John Jordan "Buck" O'Neil Jr. died at 94 in the fall of 2006 when we met at the Negro Leagues Baseball Museum in Kansas City for an interview. I was glad for the chance to visit with the elegant and knowledgeable baseball man who had lived so long and knew so much about the game.

Although baseball statistics list O'Neil as just 5-foot-10, he carried his full height in a manner that left observers thinking he was taller. Standing erect, O'Neil seemed somewhat bigger even in his early nineties. White-haired and firm-voiced, O'Neil seemed to surrender little to age. When we shook hands, I was struck by both the size of his right hand and the very firm nature of the strength still residing in it.

O'Neil, who was born in Carrabelle, Florida in 1911, had long before enjoyed a prime as a player, at a time when Major League Baseball still shunned Blacks from competing and when the main way to make a living in the sport if someone had his dark skin color was to compete for Negro Leagues teams. Doing so, primarily as an All-Star first baseman for the Kansas City Monarchs from the late 1930s to the late 1940s wrapped around U.S. Navy service during World War II, O'Neil was enjoying a renaissance with new generations of baseball fans.

The one-time Monarchs manager, and then as a scout in the employ of the Chicago Cubs, O'Neil played a role in bringing such stars to the majors as Ernie Banks, Billy Williams, and George Altman. He then became the first African-American big-league coach with the Cubs.

Still, O'Neil had been out of the limelight for some time when he appeared in a stealing-the-show performance in Ken Burns' acclaimed documentary "Baseball." With his superior diction, distinctive voice, sterling memory and low-key demeanor, O'Neil introduced and reintroduced himself to baseball fans. He presented himself on film as an eloquent spokesman for the men of his youth, his contemporaries, who had been mistreated by the sport simply for having what was deemed the wrong skin color in a racist society.

While not being the type of person to demand publicity or credit, beyond his adopted home area of Kansas City, O'Neil's history and reputation had pretty much fallen by the wayside except amongst the most avid students of baseball, people possessed of excellent memories. Yet it was no accident that O'Neil and I set our rendezvous for the Negro Leagues shrine. He had been instrumental in its construction, its choice of location, and its development, and no one was happier when the doors opened in 1990 than he.

Inside these walls O'Neil was not only home, but somewhat of a landlord. After all, he was the honorary chairman of the board of the organization for nearly 25 years.

⟫⟫⟫⟫⟫⟫⟫⟫⟫⟫⟫ THE STORY

Once O'Neil stepped out of the shadows with his national exposure in the Burns documentary, he became sought-after for speeches and story-telling. He was good at that. What also struck so many when O'Neil spoke directly about the racism endured was the apparent lack of bitterness on what he may have lost out on and what his friends, teammates, and Black stars were deprived of experiencing in the majors.

O'Neil lived his life to the fullest by seizing opportunities where they came and making his own breaks. In Florida, he couldn't attend his local high school because of segregation. He worked hard in the celery fields under a hot sun and realized in his youth there had to be a better way to make a living, leading him to his baseball career.

While certainly there were hard times on the road barnstorming and traveling, with all Black teams discriminated against, there was baseball, camaraderie, and a life of excitement still taking place. O'Neil always talked of how the Black players may have been blackballed from white hotels, but they stayed in the finest Black-owned hotels. They may have been exiled from select entertainment venues, but were able to enjoy the finest Black entertainment, from Louis Armstrong and Cab Calloway to other stars.

When O'Neil was later asked if he wished he had been born later and avoided the discrimination and hassles, as well as the ban on Black players in the majors, he always offered a similar reply. "I was right on time," he said of his own life.

O'Neil was still on time, in his own way ensuring the future of his baby, which honored the past, but regularly participating in fundraising efforts to keep the museum a going and growing proposition. I had flown into the Kansas City airport and was driving to our meeting when I passed a billboard reading, "Stuck On Buck." It was advertising a combined birthday celebration for O'Neil and a fundraiser for the museum. Kansas City was definitely stuck on Buck.

Given the context of the museum's surroundings and the events that took place affecting and sidetracking O'Neil in baseball, it was inevitable there was discussion of race. While many have spoken about the shame accrued to Major League Baseball during its decades of ignoring Blacks, I, like so many others, expected O'Neil to leak a little bit of outrage, but it was apparently not in the man.

"Why would I be angry at baseball?" O'Neil said. "You have to be angry at society." That most assuredly did aim at the big picture, but it was still somewhat of a magnanimous outlook at the ills of the sport.

It may be that O'Neil, although a solid hitter, more of the .280s variety in his best seasons, was a better glove man than batsman. He was well aware that he surprised visitors with his firm grip and said, "I always had good hands and big hands." By the time he was fourteen he had hooked on with an adult team that traveled to games around Florida. "I had a natural talent."

O'Neil learned young that white society was not friendly to or partial to all-Black baseball teams and many hotels would not allow his squad to stay there. As a teen and young man, O'Neil wanted to enroll at Sarasota High School, but could not. He would have liked to attend the University of Florida, but wasn't welcome there. Instead, he spent some educational time at Edward Waters College in Jacksonville. O'Neil matriculated there for two years before striking out to pursue a baseball career.

Some touring Black teams played upon white stereotypes and did tricks with a ball much like the Harlem Globetrotters did with a basketball. Some clubs, notably the Zulu Cannibal Giants, were considered "clown" teams, meaning they performed elaborate acts, some of which were viewed as demeaning. The Zulu Giants dressed as African warriors, and although O'Neil stuck to "straight baseball" he did spend a month with that Louisville, Kentucky-based team in 1937 and said he had to apply warpaint and wear an African skirt.

Later that year, O'Neil was signed by the Memphis Red Sox of the Negro American League and the next season was swapped to Kansas City, remaining with the Monarchs the remainder of his playing days.

It was a remarkable moment, O'Neil recalled, when the Brooklyn Dodgers signed Jackie Robinson (who had been playing with the Monarchs) and then brought him to the majors in 1947. "That was the beginning of the civil rights movement," O'Neil said.

Baseball was called the National Pastime and compared to basketball, football, and hockey, which all had lesser followings than they did in the 1940s, baseball was viewed as the paramount team sport in the United States. The sport has also usually been seen as the best record-keeper linking past and present among the four. Even so, it has taken an enormous amount of work, research, and energy to uncover Negro Leagues box scores since most never saw daylight in major metropolitan, white-owned newspapers when the games were played.

While Robinson is well-remembered as a pioneer player – the pioneer player – and Frank Robinson is pretty well-remembered as the first Black manager, O'Neil being the first Black big-league coach is not a fact that always rolls off the tongue so readily.

"A lot of people don't remember it," O'Neil said of his break-through stint with the Cubs. "The baseball fan might remember it."

Illuminating the dark days is something O'Neil wanted to force. For a time, he was the leading spokesman for the Negro Leagues days gone by while reminding the world about the gifts of such players as Satchel Paige, Josh Gibson, Buck Leonard, and Judy Johnson. But he also knew he would not live forever and he wanted the so-called "black out days" to be remembered.

"That's why I wanted the museum here, so what happened would never be forgotten," O'Neil said. "To understand man's inhumanity to man, that's been a terrible thing. There was nothing fair about it at all. The tough part of it was I could go to Omaha and seventy percent of the fans were white, then when we left the park, we couldn't go to a restaurant or a hotel."

CAREER

Buck O'Neil was chosen to play in three Negro American League All-Star games, two in 1942 and one the next year. His lifetime average was .260.

One development that came under the heading of "We're going to make up for it the best we can," was a series of events honoring O'Neil in 1995 by the city of Sarasota. He was presented with a diploma from Sarasota High, where he couldn't attend. The Baltimore

Orioles training complex was named after him. Plus, there was a luncheon feting him and a reception with the title of "An Evening with Buck O'Neil."

Long after O'Neil retired, the National Baseball Hall of Fame began trying to retroactively honor players who excelled, but who never had the chance to play in the majors, or only made appearances over a few-year period.

The Hall first began selecting honorees in 1936, but did not hold its first induction ceremony until 1939. In 1971, Satchel Paige was the first Black player from the Negro Leagues chosen. Josh Gibson and Buck Leonard followed in 1972. Monte Irvin was selected in 1973, although like Paige he did have some productive Major League time. Cool Papa Bell was voted in with the class of 1974.

Several others followed, including Judy Johnson and Martin Dihigo, and then in 2006 a group of 17 men brushed aside by the majors in years gone by were accepted together. At this time, it was a shock for many baseball people that O'Neil was not chosen.

A few months after his death, O'Neil was awarded the Presidential Medal of Freedom for his contributions to American society. The Hall of Fame itself, which does not supervise the voting, created its own "Buck O'Neil Lifetime Achievement Award, gave the first award to O'Neil, and unveiled a statue of him near the front of its building. The Hall administrators assuredly demonstrated the belief they felt O'Neil belonged.

Four other individuals have periodically been presented with the O'Neil award. Then, in 2022, one of the Hall voting committees examining candidates from past eras, made up for the previous slight and voted O'Neil in as a regular member, as well.

Late in life and apparently, even in death, the baseball world could not get enough of Buck O'Neil.

For a man who was discriminated against in his baseball prime, O'Neil could never quite put his arms around the emotion that was applied to him by strangers. When those 17 Black baseball figures were chosen for the Hall of Fame in 2006 and O'Neil was left out, it was expected he might have something harsh to say. As he had many times before when discussing the racist world he had to cope with, O'Neil did not bite.

"I never learned to hate," O'Neil said once. "I hate cancer. My mother died of cancer. My wife died of cancer 10 years ago. I hate AIDS. A good friend died of AIDS three months ago. I just can't hate a human being."

JIM PALMER

⟫⟫⟫⟫⟫⟫⟫⟫⟫⟫⟫⟫ *THE SETTING*

For the most part, when one runs across Major League Baseball players, they are wearing a team uniform, though sportswriters do get to visit the clubhouse at times when players are dressing in their street clothes.

Still, Jim Palmer's clothing gig had little to do with either type of outer garb. For a time, he became an underwear pitch man, a somewhat unusual product endorsement deal in the late 1980s. Naturally enough, Palmer, who was regarded as movie star handsome, had to pose for magazine ads and the like in his skivvies.

For a while, it seemed, there were more photographs of bare-chested Palmer floating around than there were of him in his flannels (assuming baseball uniforms were still being made of flannel at that time). The writing on his clothing was more commonly stamped

"Jockey International" than Baltimore Orioles.

He was more regularly found in places where fine under garments were sold than in Memorial Stadium or other Major League ballparks. This was quite the gig for a middle-aged man who was 43 in 1989, some five years into retirement from a professional sport.

The right-handed Hall of Fame pitcher who spent his entire 19-year career with the Orioles, came to Alaska and signed autographs at a local department store named Lamont's in the spring of '89 when he would previously normally have been tied up at a baseball stadium.

At the time I was the sports editor of the Anchorage Daily News and noted that many women turned out for Palmer's appearance, some of them completely unaware that the man hawking underwear was even a baseball player. One young woman I knew who was a college athlete, showed up with a friend and he whispered she had never heard of Jim Palmer, but thought she was coming to see Arnold Palmer.

Half-right, but wrong sport. Wrong generation of athlete.

Palmer scribbled his name for the masses and I talked baseball – and underwear – with him.

⟫⟫⟫⟫⟫⟫⟫⟫⟫⟫ THE STORY

For sure, Jim Palmer had retained his youthful appearance. He looked as if he could take the mound that very day if someone like old manager Earl Weaver called his name.

At the time, his main baseball connection was doing broadcasts for ABC television, but he gave away the secret of his next upcoming scheduled pitching appearance. In contrast to the general belief he would never throw from a mound again, Palmer revealed he was going to suit up and play in an Orioles Old-Timers Day game between the 1969 Orioles and the 1979 Orioles. "Maybe I'll pitch for both teams," Palmer said.

The irony of that notion is that Nolan Ryan, a contemporary, who was still pitching for the Texas Rangers, was only a year younger and drawing his regular paycheck.

Palmer retired with 268 victories on his resume, his welcome apparently at long last worn out in Baltimore. He felt he could still pitch, he looked as if he could still pitch, but he would have had to shop himself around to other teams. Palmer said he did not want to move to a new city outside of Maryland because his two daughters were still in high school and he did not want to uproot them while he possibly jumped around trying to settle into a new place while chasing the milestone of 300 victories.

Jockey and Palmer first linked up in 1977, so by 1989 he had been a poster boy for quite some time. Originally, he was best known for his fastball and All-Star status, his results good enough that it was obvious he was on his way to the National Baseball Hall of Fame. Palmer was not anxious to become known as a hunk, the object of the female eye, outside of his family, but said other baseball stars paved the way. Pete Rose, Steve Carlton, and Steve Garvey were out there posing for pictures in their underwear.

"There was safety in numbers," Palmer said.

He signed a good few hundred autographs that day at Lamont's department store, but it was definitely a mixed-breed audience, some baseball fans mingling with modeling fans, women who admittedly had beefcake on their minds.

One woman was not playing hooky from work. She went about taking the day off legitimately, putting in for a day of annual leave just to come to the autograph session. Jokingly, she was asked if she had heard of baseball and said she had, but was not particularly a stats maven. "He's certainly well-known from the pictures," the woman said, dancing around her real motivation for showing up.

Palmer was a hard-nosed competitor who was known for his seriousness about winning. He was good at that, too, most of the time as a big winner for the Orioles. While eight times winning at least 20 games in a season, Palmer did not think of outside interests, making endorsement money posing in his underwear and certainly not thinking about being as well-known across the United States for modeling briefs as throwing accurate pitches.

"I never took a whole lot of time to ponder that," Palmer said.

He was more of a phenomenon showing bare skin than he might ever have imagined and there was no doubt there were women on hand who were fairly disappointed that he was wearing so many clothes in public. The company kind of made up for that real-life presentation by providing Palmer underwear posters that he could sign. Rather remarkably, some 20 women from a single business declared the day a virtual holiday and fled the confines of their office to make a Jim Palmer Day visit, getting their autographs and posing for photos with him.

They hovered around the hurler, laughed with Palmer, got his signature, and after hanging out for a while went off as a group to play Whirlyball. At the time, some newspapers were referring to Palmer as a sex symbol and calling him a male version of actress Bo Derek. Derek gained fame in the movie *10* which was rating her looks. In 1981, in a headline, the Atlanta Journal said of him, "Jim Palmer: America's male No. 10."

At the Anchorage store, one adult male baseball fan, whose 14-year-old son was in school and could not declare a holiday, made it to the front of the line to obtain an autograph on this late April day. Coincidentally, the man was from Palmer, Alaska, about 40 miles up the street and said the pitcher should come to the town that was not named after him to throw out the first pitch of the Little League season May 6.

Alas, Jim Palmer would not be sticking around Alaska long enough to perform the task. Palmer emphasized he would only be in Alaska "briefly." Really, the man selling briefs said that.

»»»»»»»»»»»» *CAREER*

Turning 78 in 2023, Palmer was born in 1945 in New York City, where he was adopted. After his adoptive father died of a heart attack, Palmer grew up in Beverly Hills, California and Scottsdale, Arizona and then attended Arizona State.

Originally, Palmer was known as Jim Wiesen, but when his mother married actor Max Palmer, Jim changed his name to Palmer and announced his desire to do so as a youngster at a Little League banquet as he was beginning to excel in baseball.

Palmer was 72 in 2018 when he learned the identity of his birth parents and discovered an entire trove of cousins and other relations through a genealogy search. But he always prized his relationships with the other families that cared for him.

"I lucked out," he said. "I won the lottery when it came to my adoptive parents and a step-father in Max Palmer."

It was in the Palmer household he learned to throw. He was just 19 when he broke into the majors in 1965 and retired in 1984, never having pitched for any other big-league team besides the Orioles on his way to a 268-152 record. He had an enviable 2.86 lifetime earned run average and won two league ERA titles.

Twice, between 1970 and 1973, and between 1975 and 1978, Palmer won 20 games per season four years in a row. He led the American League in wins three times and in innings pitched four times with a high of 319 innings thrown in 1977. Three times Palmer won the AL Cy Young Award and he was a six-time All-Star and earned four Gold Gloves. Palmer tossed a no-hitter in 1969 against the Oakland Athletics.

In 1991, several years after his retirement and inspired by the continuing older age success of Nolan Ryan and football player George Blanda, who remained in the National Football League until he was 48 years old, Palmer tried a comeback with the Orioles. It did not work out. He got the message from his body to stay retired when he injured a hamstring in spring training.

In 2012, the Orioles unveiled a sculpture statue of Palmer in the Garden of Greats behind centerfield at Camden Yards. At the time the only other statues were of Weaver and Frank Robinson, although more were added.

"The statue to me is symbolic …I was the greatest Oriole pitcher, but we had a lot of other great pitchers," Palmer said at the ceremony. "I had a chance to pitch with staffs that had three 20-game winners and four 20-game winners."

MAX PATKIN

THE SETTING

Max Patkin probably had the most storied career in baseball history of anyone who never played in the majors and he sported the best nickname, too, as "The Clown Prince of Baseball."

Although few who ever saw Patkin perform realized he actually did play the game in his younger days, what they witnessed was a show that played more dates off-Broadway than any theater performance, and was seen by more people than "My Fair Lady," "Cats," or "Chicago." Patkin's was a one-man comedy act woven into the fabric of baseball and he was so well-known that his rubbery face was his calling card and gift.

Well, maybe Max did not exceed every show in history combined, and there was no official count of the number of his performances. Still, he estimated he did 4,000 baseball shows in a 52-year career.

Patkin, who was born in 1920 in Philadelphia, began his baseball career as a serious player with the same dream of so many young men – he wanted to make it to the major leagues as a pitcher. He was pretty good, too, good enough at least to spend a few seasons in the minors in the early 1940s.

As a 21-year-old in 1941, Patkin, whose baseball measurements were given as 6-foot-2 and 165 pounds by Baseball Reference, went 10-8 on the mound for Wisconsin Rapids, a Class D affiliate of the Chicago White Sox. He pitched 178 innings and compiled an earned run average of 3.94.

That was a high point. A year later Patkin split time between Wisconsin Rapids and Green Bay and went 3-4, but suffered an arm injury. By then the United States was embroiled in World War II and Patkin joined the Navy.

His right arm recovered sufficiently that he could pitch in service ball and that brought him to a fateful moment in Hawaii hurling against New York Yankees star Joe DiMaggio playing for the Army. DiMaggio, who had mistreated many pitchers in similar fashion, belted a home run off Patkin.

Patkin knew who he was up against, but he went into a fake tantrum, displaying anger about giving up the long ball – and chased DiMaggio around the bases. The fans in attendance ate it up as a big joke and Patkin realized his showmanship might lead to something.

Fresh out of the Navy in 1946, Patkin thought he would give pitching one more try. This time in the Cleveland Indians' organization, he pitched for Wilkes-Barre in Class A, going 1-1. Reality struck and Patkin recognized he was not going to go far on the strength of his arm. At that time, the flamboyant Bill Veeck owned the Indians and he hired Patkin as a coach.

However, when Veeck sold the team in 1949, Patkin was a free agent anew of sorts. He began his itinerant, barnstorming career of baseball comedy, roaming the country as a clown for hire.

In the 1988 movie, *Bull Durham*, starring Kevin Costner and Susan Sarandon, focused on minor-league baseball, Patkin plays himself in a bar scene where the character Annie would rather dance with him than the younger, more studly Crash Davis. If there was any baseball fan in the United States who didn't know who Max Patkin was before that wildly popular film, they did afterwards, whether or not they realized Patkin was the real deal and not a fictional figure.

In the late 1990s, when I was researching a book called *Diamonds In The Rough* about the history of the Alaska Baseball League, I visited Veterans Stadium in Philadelphia to interview some players in the clubhouse.

I had a seat in the press box right next to Max Patkin, there just for fun, not work since he had retired his clowning act a few years earlier. I recognized him immediately and we chatted throughout the Phillies game.

≫≫≫≫≫≫≫≫ THE STORY

Appropriately, the title of "Clown Prince of Baseball" is a parody of the royalty reference of "crown prince." A few others of humorous bent made a living through baseball related comedy over the decades, including Al Schact, but Patkin hung onto the nickname longer than anyone else.

Patkin represented a simpler time in the sport before much of a big-league game's pre-game and between-inning entertainment was scripted and played out in front of Fan Cams or with music. Patkin did crazy facial impressions, spritzed water on himself like an out-of-control fountain, and dropped his pants in Vaudeville-like tricks. He journeyed all over the country to star as a gate attraction in the smaller minor-league parks where the fans were local and didn't have a big-league club to follow. He made friends everywhere.

As I learned from our conversation, yes, he even appeared at ballparks in Alaska for teams in the Alaska Baseball League. He said he had a terrific time making the journey and appearing before fans in the Far North. He really had been everywhere, man, as the Johnny Cash song goes.

There were two teams in Anchorage, the Glacier Pilots and the Bucs, who shared the same home park, Mulcahy Stadium, and Growden Memorial Park was the home field for the Alaska Goldpanners of Fairbanks. Patkin did shows in both venues in the 1980s, though he wasn't sure what year. When Patkin came onto the field in a baseball uniform he immediately provided a chuckle because instead of a number on his back he had a question mark.

Patkin estimated in conversation he traveled five million miles as a baseball clown and going from the Lower 48 states to Alaska and back certainly beefed up his total. Another estimate suggests he may have traveled seven million miles with his act, but there is really no official tally.

"The crowd treated me great," Patkin said. "It was the longest trip I ever took in my life. I enjoyed my trip there."

Patkin said he was paid $1,000 for his shows, which was of course more valuable in 1980s dollars. Unlike many of the towns in the Lower 48 where he had a long-established reputation and made repeated stops, Patkin said he was a fresh act for Alaskans.

"They didn't know who I was up there," he said. "I was new. I came in, rested, and went to the ballpark. I bragged about playing Alaska. No one knew they had ballclubs up there."

They still do, although they are not professional minor-league teams, but remain summer league amateur outfits where college stars can gain playing experience. No doubt, Patkin would be welcomed back if he was still a funny man professionally.

CAREER

Not only did Max Patkin have the most expressive of faces in order to enhance his jokes, he appeared to be double-jointed and capable of bending his body into a variety of shapes, a sort of human Gumby.

Patkin didn't just come out onto the field for one visit. Perhaps if he did basketball or football games he would have performed only at halftime. In baseball, he did his schtick all game long, while play was going on. By 1980, Major League Baseball had implemented new policies that made Patkin a less-than-welcome guest for big-league games because neither side could figure out how to adapt his act such as pseudo-coaching at first base and or gracefully accept him mimicking players.

On one of his advertising brochures, the material read, "Bring out the ladies and children," clearly emphasizing the family nature of his act. It also included a box reading "Now available for bookings."

Patkin was at the tail end of his career in 1995 at 75 years old but was slowly modernizing in terms of merchandising. He had an autobiography come out and sold autographed bats at his appearances and someone put him on some baseball cards.

As is often said of other athletes, including aging pitchers, the legs go first and that year Patkin said he was losing steam.

"My legs aren't what they used to be," Patkin said. "I had to slow down." For Max, that meant scheduling only 25 shows in '95. "I get tired. Get lonely. But I can't stop. I love to leave 'em laughing."

Spoken like a true showman. Yet Patkin did stop and he didn't cope well with the tameness of a solitary and stationary life in Paoli, Pennsylvania. He admitted to depression and said he missed being around people. He had out-lived his closest relatives, too.

Four years later, in 1999, the year after we met and the year before the Alaska baseball book came out, Patkin passed away at 79. Even in chance encounters, Max Patkin did leave 'em laughing.

TONY PEREZ

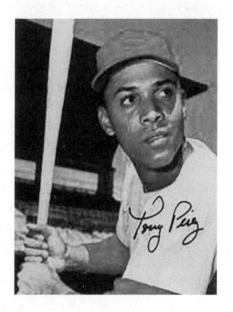

>>>>>>>>>>>>>>>>>>>>>> *THE SETTING*

Although Tony Perez had been long retired from active play before I began covering the Cincinnati Reds in 2010, he periodically was around the team for major events such as Reds team Hall of Fame occasions.

He also made a trip to Cooperstown, New York for the National Baseball Hall of Fame's induction weekend in 2012, a common enough visit since he was a member of that august body. While there, however, Perez joined his old friend and teammate Pete Rose in a sports memorabilia shop on Main Street for an autograph appearance.

The men, who have described themselves as close as brothers based on their time shared in Cincinnati helping the Big Red Machine win four National League pennants and two World Series championships, sat side-by-side at a table greeting fans and signing their names.

Rose, the player present who was not in the Hall of Fame because he was banned from baseball for life because he bet on the sport, actually drew a bigger crowd.

The quieter, friendly Perez, regarded as one of the most popular players in Reds team history, who was recognized with a Tony Perez Day in Cincinnati in 1986, was freed up a little bit more readily to talk. Besides me, the only sportswriter on hand, plenty of other baseball fans desired to chat with the native of Cuba, as well.

Rose, who is on the outside looking in, was gracious and effusive about Perez and his value when it was announced his close friend was voted into the Hall of Fame in 2000, the same year as Sparky Anderson, the Reds powerhouse's manager, was also chosen.

"I'm so happy for him," Rose said. "It's an honor well overdue. (He) was a fatherly type in the clubhouse, especially to the Spanish (Hispanic) players."

》》》》》》》》》》》》》 *THE STORY*

Cooperstown, New York, home of the National Baseball Hall of Fame calls itself a village. The population is around 1,750, but when the annual Hall induction ceremony and festivities are conducted each July, the community is inundated by visitors.

The attendance varies greatly depending on the popularity and prominence of inductees, but regardless, many thousands of visitors make the trek to the upstate New York community. Not only are all hotels filled to overflowing, the sidewalks are crammed with pedestrians. Streets are blocked off to prevent gridlock traffic and a system of shuttle buses is put in place to transport fans from satellite parking lots into the center of town where all the action takes place – except for the ceremony itself.

For a few days, Cooperstown is overwhelmed with love from tourists who struggle to get in the door of restaurants, by baseball believers who might bump into a Hall of Famer on the street. There are several ancillary events Hall of Famers may participate in, too, signing autographs and just meeting the public.

Some sessions are conducted in selected businesses like the one where Perez and Rose set up shop to scribble their names on everything from photographs to baseballs, bats, or team logo equipment.

In some ways the setting is a baseball nirvana, where baseball is the center of the world and nothing going on elsewhere on the planet draws attention for a short while. Hall of Famers themselves have some of their own events at the deluxe Otesaga Resort Hotel, the fanciest digs around, and some sequester themselves there. But many are on the move around town and mingle with fans, like Perez did.

Perez was born in 1942 in Cuba as Atanasio Perez Rigal and while he seemed to be a larger man in his playing days, his measurements were listed at 6-foot-2 and 175 pounds. That weight belied his power and Perez was renowned for his ability to drive in runs. He said when he was growing up coaches did not even have the word "mechanics" in their vocabulary.

"I never heard about mechanics when I played," Perez said. "Only later."

Perez broke into the majors in 1964 and that was a very uneasy time period for Cuban natives trying to make a living in baseball. Up until the Fidel Castro-sparked revolution that led the island nation into Communism, Cuba had long been a baseball haven with individuals crossing the water to the majors and Havana hosting a AAA minor-league team.

Things quickly became testier and in the early 1960s Castro began barring the free flow of baseball players to the United States. To keep playing, many individuals had to choose to stay in the U.S. and forsake their families. Perez was caught up in the painful forced separation from loved ones.

It was not until 1972 that Perez was given diplomatic permission to visit with family members he had not seen since 1963. Perez said he traveled with 17 suitcases of clothes, food, shoes, and medicine, necessities he thought might be needed for his parents, three sisters, and two brothers. They were located in his home city of Ciego de

Avila about 300 miles east of Havana, which he reached by train.

The reunion was emotional and remained vivid in Perez's thoughts for a long time.

"It was some kind of feeling," Perez said. "There's no way I can describe it. You would have had to be there to watch."

Perez was a notable member of the Big Red Machine that won two World Series in the mid-1970s. However, it is often overlooked just how close the Reds came to not winning the first one against the Boston Red Sox in 1975, a Series some consider the best ever played.

That was the showdown that lasted for seven games, and included Red Sox comebacks and Reds comebacks, besides the famous Carlton Fisk wave-it-fair home run when Boston captured Game 6, by a 7-6 score that left fans buzzing. Perez's brightest memory from a single game during his career was Game 7, when the Reds overcame the Red Sox for the championship.

"The last game of the World Series is my favorite game," Perez said. "We were ahead and they caught up. They won the night before in that great game. Then we were down 3-0 (in Game 7) and I got that home run."

That home run was a two-run shot in the sixth inning that began the Cincinnati comeback culminating in a 4-3 victory and the Series title.

Perez distinctly remembered his slow start in the Series, not getting even one hit for the first four games. Then he came alive with two home runs in Game 5 and two hits in Game 6.

"My home run in the seventh game made me proud," Perez said. "That brought us close. We won the game in the ninth inning. People say that was the beginning of the Big Red Machine. I agree with that."

≫≫≫≫≫≫≫≫ CAREER

Just 16 when a scout found him in Cuba's sugar cane country, Perez received neither a bonus to sign with the Reds nor any real renumeration. Oh, except for $2.50 to cover the cost of a visa that would get him into the United States.

"I just want to play ball," Perez said. "That is all I ever want to do."

Perez spent 23 years in the big leagues, ending in 1986. He made his reputation with the Reds, but was traded to the Montreal Expos for the 1977 season and played for Montreal, the Red Sox, and the Philadelphia Phillies before returning to Cincinnati for the final three years of his career. By then, in his early 40s, his pal Rose was the manager.

A seven-time All-Star, Perez ripped 379 home runs among his 2,732 hits and drove in 1,652 runs batted in. Seven times he knocked in at least 100 runs in a season with a high of 129 and overall knocked in at least 90 for 10 straight years. When he was a boy just being introduced to baseball, Perez said Minnie Minoso, the star with the Chicago White Sox and Cleveland Indians, was his hero.

Perez managed the Reds in 1993, but he was dismissed after one season. Many protested he was not given a fair chance to show what he could do in the job. He was Reds manager under the ownership of controversial boss Marge Schott. Perez also managed the Florida Marlins in 2001.

During his years in baseball, he earned the nickname "The Cuban Clouter." He was also bestowed with the nickname "Big Dog" by teammate Lee May and then modified to "Doggie" by Rose, Perez was only the big dog in the dugout for a short time. But he was put in the Hall of Fame forever. When he took his orientation tour of the museum, he said, "This is something, man. I tell you, baseball has been my life, so this is like home to me."

CHARLEY PRIDE

»»»»»»»»»» ## THE SETTING

It was a great name for either a singer or a baseball player and Charley Pride was both. Best-known as a rare Black star on the country and western charts, his true dream was to play Major League Baseball.

Quite good at the game, Pride did play ball for some of the last of the Negro Leagues teams as integration was taking hold across the National Pastime. If pressed for the truth within his heart, Pride would have likely admitted that he would have preferred seeing his life path take him down the road to the National Baseball Hall of Fame, though becoming a member of the Country Music Hall of Fame was a pretty darned good accomplishment.

As it is, Pride, who was born in Sledge, Mississippi in 1934, has a name that carries weight in the music industry, but except amongst historians, is not remembered for being a high-caliber baseball player. In that realm, he is pretty much the answer to a trivia question, albeit one of great Pride.

Pride was born into poverty, one of 11 siblings who were the children of sharecroppers. One of his brothers was a very sound catcher and Pride had a good arm that started him pitching. It was a little bit later, when he was 14 years old, that Pride taught himself how to play the guitar.

He learned that he not only had a fine throwing arm, but a voice that could turn heads. One of the eight boys in the family, older than Charley, was Mack Pride Jr. and Mack was a good enough hurler to make a mark in the Negro Leagues, too, playing for the Memphis

Red Sox and the Kansas City Monarchs. He was called "Mack the Knife" during his playing days. This brother also had a musical bent, but took it in another direction singing at weddings and funerals, and choosing a main career in religious broadcasting.

In August of 2012, Charley Pride and I turned up at the same lecture event at the Negro Leagues Museum as members of the audience. When I learned he was present, I hustled to introduce myself and after the program engaged in an interview about the famed singer's baseball background.

⟫⟫⟫⟫⟫⟫⟫⟫⟫⟫⟫ THE STORY

When he was a youngster, Charley Pride said his belief in his baseball abilities first gave him hope for a better life. He dreamed of a life outside the Deep South challenges that for his family manifested themselves as laborers living in poverty.

"Here's my way out of the cotton fields," Pride said of his encouraging outlook to possibly become a professional baseball player, even if at that time Blacks were still barred from being signed by Major League clubs. "That's the first thing that clicked in my head."

When the notion first struck Pride and took hold of his thinking to the point where he began telling others in his orbit that he was going to become a professional baseball player, their first reactions involved laughter. For two reasons, really, one being that the odds were stacked against any young player ever making the grade and secondly, at the time the only avenue open to him was the Negro Leagues.

However, Pride was still an early teenager when Jackie Robinson was signed by the Brooklyn Dodgers and broke the big-league color barrier in 1947, stoking hope in many Black ballplayers that the future could be brighter.

By 1952, opportunity was opening for many of the top Black players and the Negro Leagues were about to be edged out. Still, for a player like Pride, just 18 at the time, it could be a stepping-stone. That year he made his professional debut with the Memphis Red Sox.

Pride also suited up for the Louisville Clippers and the Birmingham Black Barons before playing in the New York Yankees' organization, all wrapped around a stint in the United States Army in the 1950s.

Hank Aaron played for the Indianapolis Clowns briefly before the Milwaukee Braves signed him. Pride said one of his most prideful pitching moments with the Memphis Red Sox was throwing four shutout innings against a lineup that included Aaron. Pride had the confidence he could make the big-time.

"I thought I was good enough, yeah," Pride said. "And I was good. I had three pitches, the hummer, the hook, and the change and I could get you out with all three."

Yet his was the story of so many pitchers of great promise who get sidetracked by one injury. In Pride's case he hurt his elbow in 1956 and that took the speed off his fastball and the swerve off his curve. Not willing to give up his baseball dream, Pride added a knuckleball to his throwing repertoire. He started over, playing in Class D in Fond du Lac, Wisconsin and in Class C in Boise, Idaho, as well as clubs in Montana.

Pride did not give up easily, even after his arm did and he could not rise higher. He represented Louisville in Black ball at the very tail end of the Negro Leagues and later went to tryouts with the California Angels and New York Mets. The major problem was that he never regained the speed on that hummer.

There were clues Pride was not really a hot prospect anymore, including when the Louisville club traded him and one other player for a new team bus. Make that another team bus since this was a used vehicle.

Even in the early days of the integration of big-league baseball, not all teams were equally welcoming and some teams added Black players, but unofficially capped the number of African-Americans they wanted on their team at the same time.

"I wanted to be the first (Black) Chicago Cub," Pride said.

The first Black Chicago Cubs turned out to be future Hall of Famer Ernie Banks and almost instantly thereafter Gene Baker, too.

"There were only 16 clubs in the major leagues," Pride said. "Some of them had only two colored players on any given team. That was their quota. In the minors, they had two. There were certain things that kept you boondoggled where you couldn't move up like the average person. You learn how to try to work around those things, just try to be the best you can be and still make it anyways.

Pride recognized he was receiving declining attention from big-league teams when he reached 25, a common enough practice for players at that time.

"They just marked you off," Pride said.

Friends who observed his struggles in the game, especially after the elbow problem, began urging him to take more advantage of his other natural talent, his voice.

"I said, 'No, I want to go to the major leagues and break all the records and set new ones by the time I'm 35 or 36, and then I'll go to singing,'" Pride said.

Instead, Pride's records broke records.

CAREER

By 1960, Pride's chances were fading in baseball and he set out for Montana where he played some semi-pro ball and showed off some bonus skills as a hitter. He spent five years in Helena and one season hit .372. He pitched and played second base. He also played in Great Falls.

Simultaneously, Pride was realistically inching toward a singing career and it became well-known that he had an extraordinary voice. He once put it on display between games of a double-header in Helena, a city where he became very popular on stages and on the field.

Between gigs in baseball, Pride held down gigs in local night clubs and then began playing some larger venues. He was on his way to the big-time in another discipline. His big break in the music world came after his last failed tryout with the Mets. Cutting through Nashville on his way back to Montana, Pride signed a recording deal with RCA.

Pride's recording years basically spanned 1966 to 1987 and he had 52 top-ten hits on the Billboard Hot Country Songs chart and 30-plus No. 1 hits. In 2000, Pride became the first African-American inducted into the Country Music Hall of Fame.

After he became famous, Pride, the would-be Major League player, became a part-owner of the Major League Texas Rangers. For some years, while he was still able, he sometimes took batting practice with the team.

In 1980, Pride meshed his two great interests by singing the National Anthem before Game 6 of the World Series between the Philadelphia Phillies and Kansas City Royals at Veterans Stadium in Philadelphia. He also sang the anthem before Game 5 in 2010 between the San Francisco Giants and the Rangers at the Ballpark at Arlington.

During that interview in Kansas City, it was suggested to Pride that life most definitely takes unexpected turns.

"It sure does," he said. "I'd like to be in Cooperstown, New York in the Baseball Hall of Fame. Now I'm in the Country Music Hall of Fame."

Charley Pride died at 86 years of age from complications of the COVID-19 virus in December of 2020.

ALBERT PUJOLS

THE SETTING

This truly was a locker room clubhouse talk, although it took place after all other sportswriters cleared out and Albert Pujols thought he was done dissecting the night's work on the field.

The site was the visitors' locker room at the Great American Ball Park, home of the Cincinnati Reds, when Pujols was still with the St. Louis Cardinals, before playing out his option to join the Los Angeles Angels and a decade before he rejoined the Cardinals for a finale ground tour of the majors in 2022.

As it so happened, Pujols, who walked away from the sport after becoming one of the few men to ever top 700 home runs in a career (an exclusive club containing Barry Bonds, Hank Aaron, and Babe Ruth), on this night in 2011 slammed a three-run blast that defeated the hosting Reds.

Pujols was so used to these defining moments in his lengthy soon-to-become Hall of Fame career that he was in no hurry to hang out with fidgety sportswriters trying to make deadline. His shower rained more water and lasted longer than some hurricanes. He was the story of the night for the average beat writer who would have liked to hear what allowed Pujols to drive the ball out of the park at rocket speed.

However, kings make commoners wait and often enough that is applied to journalists who ache for morsels from the mouths of royalty as they try to explain to readers of newspapers what makes the best players tick.

Eventually, Pujols emerged from the shower, pulled on his street clothes, and spoke briefly and succinctly to gathered sportswriters. I waited them all out, till the daily deadline guys split and Pujols was preparing to exit the locker room.

My approach was the appropriate one, because I had something besides that night's game I wished to talk to Pujols about, a broader topic. And my word choice hit the target and got his attention.

Some months before, I had visited the Dominican Republic, Pujols' native country on another baseball mission. By pure coincidence, I took the elevator to the hotel lobby after my first night in the building to await a ride. There was Pujols, the superstar baseball hero, back at home, checking out at the front desk and being surrounded by adoring hotel employees mobbing him for autographs and for selfies.

I recognized him instantly, but he was so popular with that crowd around him I didn't really have a chance to introduce myself or say a real hello before he exited the hotel. I did get close enough to issue a brief hi and toss off a one-liner, telling the perennial All-Star that I admired his game. What baseball fan didn't?

It came to my attention the reason Pujols was back in the Dominican was for a charity appearance. The day before, participating in a softball game, he had hit 11 home runs. Now that would have been something to see.

Months later, I caught up to him for real.

>>>>>>>>>>>>>>> THE STORY

Pujols had been perfunctory in his moment of glamor, explaining his connection to the game-winning home run. He had performed such an act so many times the words came automatically to him. "I guess I saw it pretty good," Pujols said of the bashed ball that was thrown to him by Reds pitcher Bronson Arroyo. "I hit it out of the park."

However, when everyone else had vanished I stepped up to the plate to address him and mentioned the scene in the hotel in Santo Domingo in the Dominican. Instantly, realizing what I was saying, Pujols' demeanor changed. He smiled broadly and said, "You have been to my country? Did you like it?"

I assured him that I had enjoyed my visit.

That 2011 season was a challenging one for Pujols. While being a native of the Dominican, he played two years of high school ball in Independence, Missouri, spent two seasons at Maple Woods Community College in Kansas City, and to that point had never taken a big-league at-bat for anyone besides the St. Louis Cardinals.

He was 31 and after one of the most accomplished decade's worth of a start to any hitter's career, he was being besieged about his future. Would he stay with St. Louis forever or would he test the free agent market to perhaps become the highest paid player ever? It was easy enough to imagine Pujols wanting to stay in Missouri, but wherever Pujols traveled, that's what everyone wanted to talk about, anyway.

Compounding the issue was that for the first time in his career, just when all eyes were on his performance status, Pujols was on his way to a sub-.300-hitting season for the first time and missed out on 100 runs batted in for the first time. An injury cost him 15 games. Did all this mean that Pujols, the 6-foot, 230-pound slugger, was in truth actually not invincible?

"Thank God it wasn't worse than it was," Pujols said of a broken bone in his wrist that sidelined him for three weeks. That was after the projection he would be out for four-to-six weeks. "It's a long season, man. It doesn't matter how you start, good or bad. It's not the first time I had a slow start."

At the time, in late July, the season was hurrying along, but the Cardinals still had about 60 games left. The end was too far away to contemplate. Baseball is a daily grind and the best players come to the park ready to play every day all summer.

Pujols said he tried to keep his focus narrow as the calendar pages flipped. Every little short streak could become distracting.

"The last thing you want to do is get caught up in the small things," Pujols said. "Believe me, these last two months will go quickly. We can't worry about last night. A lot of crazy things can happen. When you have two games left, you look at it."

When the games were over, St. Louis finished with a 90-72 record to place second in the Central Division. Then to the shock of many, Pujols departed the Cardinals for the Angels, signing a 10-year, $240-million contract.

⟫⟫⟫⟫⟫⟫⟫⟫⟫⟫⟫ CAREER

Almost as stunning to many baseball people, Pujols was never as good with the Angels as he had been with the Cardinals. Despite many terrific moments, his average steadily dropped. He incurred a variety of injuries and while he redeemed himself with his original team and the fan base with one final year – and one especially great run near the end of the season in 2022 – overall, Pujols was not missed in St. Louis while he played in California.

Still, as the owner of some of the most impressive statistics in history, Pujols will become a Hall of Famer sooner rather than later. Pujols won the National League rookie-of-the-year award in 2001, was a three-time winner of the NL Most Valuable Player Award, won two home-run crowns, an RBI title, a batting title, and two Gold Gloves

Pujols was an 11-time All-Star and won baseball's Roberto Clemente Award for his charitable acts. He was also on two World Series champions.

Due to late-in-career slumping, Pujols finished with a lifetime batting average under .300 at .296. But he is fourth all-time in home runs and his 2,218 runs batted in is second on the list behind Hank Aaron's 2,297. Pujols is also a member of the elite 3,000-hit club with 3,384 and he scored 1,914 runs. He played in an impressive 3,080 games. That ranks fifth behind Pete Rose.

For all his love for the Dominican Republic, along the way, Pujols became an American citizen.

Pujols hit his 500th and 600th career home runs while playing for the Angels. When he announced he would retire after the 2022 season, few thought he would make it to 700. Then Pujols, summoning the magic of the past, went on a late-summer run while fittingly back with the Cardinals. He got hotter and hotter, raising his average to .270 and closing in on No. 700.

It was late September, with the season waning, when the Cardinals faced the Dodgers in Los Angeles. Pujols smacked two home runs, one inning apart, to reach 700. He tipped his batting helmet to the cheering crowd, and then had to retreat briefly from the dugout to compose himself as his emotions overwhelmed him.

"What a special night," Pujols said later. His children were able to be with him to see the shots.

The Cardinals feted Pujols in the clubhouse afterwards, stuffing him into a laundry cart – which has become de rigueur for some teams – and poured beer on him.

It was a great curtain call to a 22-year career.

DERRICK ROBINSON

THE SETTING

The clubhouse after the Cincinnati Reds game of April 15, 2013 played against the Philadelphia Phillies at the Great American Ball Park in Cincinnati, is where Derrick Robinson lingered.

Although he could not know it at the moment, Derrick Robinson, a rookie outfielder from Gainesville, Florida, was in the midst of living out the most notable and memorable hour or so of his Major League career.

This was the 66th anniversary of the day when Jackie Robinson played his first big-league game after being a multi-sport star at UCLA and playing baseball briefly at an All-Star caliber for the Kansas City Monarchs of the Negro American League.

It was Jackie Robinson Day across the major leagues, a day when the sport pays homage to the Brooklyn Dodgers' Hall of Famer who broke the modern-day color barrier that previously kept Black Americans on the sidelines, unable to play professional baseball in the land of the free and the home of the brave.

In contrast to its shameful history, when African-Americans were not welcomed in the major leagues between the 1880s and 1947, when Robinson made his debut, baseball had adopted a genuine recognition symbol to honor the one-time Dodger. The number he wore on his uniform jersey was 42 and that number was permanently retired from all teams' active rosters.

One day a year – April 15, the date when Robinson played his first big-league game – the reverse procedure was introduced. On that game day, every player on every team in the majors wore No. 42. For that day, regardless of name, color of skin, or heritage, everyone was Jackie Robinson.

Derrick Robinson, who is also African-American, had been drafted in the fourth round by the Kansas City Royals out of high school and been touring the minor leagues for about seven years when opportunity shouted his name with the Reds.

The younger Robinson, no relation to Jackie Robinson, though his family was a long-time admirer of the historic figure, did not start the game. He entered in the eighth inning, pinch-hitting for Reds hurler Bronson Arroyo with the score 2-2.

##》》》》》》》》》》》》》》 THE STORY

Derrick Robinson was inserted into the game by manager Dusty Baker to lead off the home half of the eighth inning and he stroked an infield single off Phillies pitcher Jeremy Horst. The hit began the rally that won the game and saved the victory for Arroyo.

Shin-Soo Choo laid down a sacrifice bunt in front of home plate and Robinson was safe at second. Zack Cozart lifted a fly ball to right-center, but it was not clear if the ball would be caught, so Robinson had to hold up. The ball fell in, Cozart was credited with a double, but Robinson had to stop at third.

However, it didn't matter because after Joey Votto was intentionally walked, Brandon Phillips singled to right field, driving home both Robinson and Cozart. Robinson's go-ahead score was the winning run.

The Reds led, 4-2, and closer Aroldis Chapman entered in relief with his 100-mph fastball, striking out two of the last three hitters.

It was doubtful any of the other principals on this Jackie Robinson Day were more pleased or as satisfied with their roles than Derrick Robinson, who at his locker almost immediately began talking about finding a way to keep the No. 42 jersey he would no longer wear since his regular number was 15. Typically, teams gather up the 42 uniforms, launder them and put them into storage for another year.

This Robinson was proud of the other Robinson and being able to play in the game on the baseball holiday. "It means a lot," Derrick Robinson said. "He did a lot for African-Americans. I've heard about the good things he did. It's an honor to wear the jersey."

As a youngster, probably as early as Little League, Derrick Robinson said his father told him about the importance of Jackie Robinson to Blacks and to baseball. "My father was big on baseball and he let me know that African-Americans had opportunities because of this guy," Robinson said. "I've been asked if I'm related to Jackie Robinson. I take that as a compliment."

Once Derrick was anointed by Baker to pinch-hit, he said his mindset in a tie game was pretty basic. "I went up to get on base," he said. "I was going to bunt on the first pitch, but it ended up being a little swinging bunt. It worked out perfectly."

Phillips got the big hit, but Derrick Robinson got the big run on Jackie Robinson Day and Phillips said players took note of another Robinson making a critical play. "That's kind of funny," Phillips said. "We were talking about it in the dugout. It's a beautiful thing."

As players ran through post-game analysis, the clubhouse attendants circulated, collecting all those No. 42 jerseys. Quietly, as his was taken, Derrick Robinson said he would like to keep it if he could.

One by one, players dressed and left. So did the sportswriters. I looked up at one point and Derrick Robinson and I were the only ones left in the big room besides equipment workers cleaning up.

Then, a clubhouse staffer approached with a folded-over No. 42 and handed it to Robinson to keep. He beamed.

"I'm going to mail this back home to my parents in Florida," Derrick Robinson said of the memorabilia from his day as a Jackie Robinson Day hero. "I think I'm going to have it framed."

》》》》》》》》》》》 CAREER

That 2013 season turned out to be Derrick Robinson's best chance to make good in the majors – and the only season when he played at the top level of the sport.

That year, Robinson got into 102 games for the Reds, made 216 plate appearances and batted .255. No slugger, Robinson did not hit a single home run and he drove in eight runs while playing some days in the field at right, center, and left.

Robinson, who was signed by the Royals for $150,000, could have been a scholarship college football player at his hometown University of Florida, but made the tough call to choose baseball and the money right away over football and the educational opportunity nearby.

"There was just something about baseball," Robinson said. "Yeah, football was fun – a lot more action – but I loved swinging the bat in baseball."

Speedy on the basepaths, and a track sprint star, Robinson envisioned himself stealing a lot of bases while Florida envisioned him as a cornerback on two national championship teams coached by Urban Meyer. But once committed, Robinson said he never regretted selecting baseball as a career.

Still, while he may have thought he was home free at last in the majors, that 2013 season constituted Derrick Robinson's complete major-league career. He returned to the minors after 2013 and kept playing four more years, including in Puerto Rico, Mexico, and the Dominican Republic winters, without making another big-league roster.

But it was obvious Derrick Robinson made at least one very special big-league memory.

FRANK ROBINSON

THE SETTING

Frank Robinson was one of the featured speakers at the Negro Leagues Baseball Museum in Kansas City during a forum I attended in July of 2012.

The context of his talk and discussion was his mindset and experiences when he was named the first Black manager in Major League history for the 1975 season. There was much fanfare surrounding the Cleveland Indians' hire – as there should have been – and that was partly because many believe the milestone should have occurred long before.

This was all against the backdrop of Jackie Robinson becoming the first Black player given a job with the Brooklyn Dodgers in 1947 – something else which should have taken place long before – breaking the 20th-century color barrier in big-league baseball.

Frank Robinson, of course, had been a big-time star during his playing days, first with the Cincinnati Reds and then with the Baltimore Orioles, the key individual in a trade that has long been considered to be one of the dumbest in history for the Reds. But that was another kind of history.

During the mingling portion of the forum in K.C., which was attended by Jackie Robinson's daughter Sharon Robinson, Frank Robinson provoked chuckles when he told a small group that he was often asked if he was Sharon's brother or Jackie's son, or in some way related to the Brooklyn Hall of Famer. No, he just had the same last name.

Besides serving as his own barrier-breaker when he took over the Indians, Frank Robinson also managed the San Francisco Giants, Baltimore Orioles, and the franchise that began life as the Montreal Expos until becoming the Washington Nationals.

In addition to being the boss of the dugout for those clubs, Frank Robinson also worked in a variety of administrative positions for Major League Baseball. At the time of his Kansas City visit, Robinson was engaged in trying to involve more African-American youths in the sport early in life.

On October 15, 1972, only nine days before he died prematurely from heart and diabetes issues at 54, Jackie Robinson threw out the first pitch at a World Series game. During that appearance he spoke out trying to advance his latest cause – baseball's need to hire a Black manager.

Frank Robinson became that man and that symbol.

⟫⟫⟫⟫⟫⟫⟫⟫⟫⟫ THE STORY

Frank Robinson did – and did not – want to be baseball's first Black manager. At least not yet. He was not ready to retire from the field. But he said he felt an obligation to Black people to take the job from the Indians when it was offered, because if he said no then the reaction might have negative ripple effects.

It is sometimes forgotten that when Robinson joined the Indians he came as a player-manager. That role was already on the endangered species list in big-league ball. In the nearly 50 years since Robinson performed the double role, Rose has been the only other player-manager.

As happened with Rose, and many others through the years, gradually managing took precedent, working for the greater good, overshadowed individual play. In Robinson's case the timing was inconvenient for him to slow down and stop playing, if only from the standpoint of historical statistical reasons.

In 1974, Robinson was a full-time player, with the California Angels and at the end of the season with the Indians, and while he was aging at 38, he was not ready to retire his stick. In 1975, he played in just 49 games for Cleveland. In 1976, he appeared in just 36 games, ending his active career.

Over 21 seasons, Robinson played in 2,808 games, collected 2,943 hits for a .294 average, hit 586 home runs, and drove in 1,812 runs. If he played full-time those final two years, he almost surely would have reached the 3,000-hit milestone and 600-homer barrier and perhaps even reached 2,000 runs batted in.

To boot, taking on the high-profile position with all eyes on him as manager, and sacrifice the excellent chances of rising up the ladder on the all-time stats lists, Robinson wasn't really paid very much to combine the two jobs.

Robinson said he was paid $200,000 for the 1975 season from the Indians, but was due $180,000 as a player anyway. He was taken aback when the team offered that arrangement.

"You're only going to pay me $20,000 to manage the club?" Robinson said he asked team officials. "I wanted to be a manager one day. I didn't want to be a player-manager."

Robinson said the negotiations, as such, were take-it-or-leave-it, so he took the deal to attain his goal, but also while being very conscious of his position as someone who could make a difference for other Black players seeking to make the transition into managing.

"I wanted to further the cause for African-Americans and minorities in baseball," Robinson said.

Robinson had prepared for the opportunity, managing in Puerto Rico and handling teams in winter ball in off-season warm-weather climates for the experience. He felt he was ready for the offer that came from that standpoint, but inwardly was being tugged because he did not want to stop playing.

It was not as if Robinson felt he was the only qualified Black candidate for a managing job, but he did wonder how it would be received by both the baseball establishment and the Black community if he turned down the job.

"When will that door open again?" Robinson said.

By the time Robinson spoke of this period in his life nearly 40 years had passed. He was 77 years old, but still working in the game, if not in the dugout. Major League Baseball was establishing inner-city academies to provide opportunities for kids to start the game young and perhaps stick with it instead of drifting away to basketball and football as had been a trend.

"It used to be that you were able to get a bat or ball or stick or whatever and get right out on the street and play," Robinson said of changing times. "You can't do that anymore. That's the pity of it. But this is the next best thing, giving these kids a chance, a place to go. It doesn't cost them anything but their time and attention."

Frank Robinson was 11 years old, living in Oakland, California, where he did play baseball in the streets, when Jackie Robinson broke the color barrier.

"I knew then that if I had the skills and ability to play in the major leagues, I would have the opportunity," Frank Robinson said. "Before that, no chance."

⟫⟫⟫⟫⟫⟫⟫⟫⟫⟫⟫ CAREER

A 14-time All-Star, Frank Robinson broke into the majors in 1956 and played 21 seasons. He is the only player to be voted Most Valuable Player in both the National League and the American League, was the NL rookie-of-the-year, won a Gold Glove, and was AL manager-of-the-year in 1989. Robinson was inducted into the Baseball Hall of Fame in 1982.

Robinson was an instant hit with the Reds. Just 20 years old that season, the youthful Robinson still had some of that little boy in him that Hall of Famer Roy Campanella once said was essential to the baseball player. Some newspapers called him "Frankie," a friendly and youthful alteration of his name that would be harder to envision later when he was managing and taking everything more seriously.

When Robinson was living at the Manse Hotel during his rookie season, the owners presented him with an apple pie each time he slugged a home run. That season, Robinson equaled the then-rookie record of 38 homers, so he ended up with as many apple pies as Table Talk.

In 1970, Robinson became the rare player to hit two grand-slam homers in a single game.

For his play on the field, Robinson's jersey number was retired by the Reds and the Orioles. For his managing breakthrough, it was retired by the Indians, now the Cleveland Guardians. For all three franchises, he wore No. 20.

Despite his trepidation about accepting the player-manager job, when his first game came around as manager for Cleveland, Robinson described his debut by saying, "It's just tremendous." He did play that day, too, going 1-for-3 as the designated hitter.

Robinson was a man of extreme confidence and was an extremely aggressive player. He was shocked and insulted when the Reds traded him to Baltimore for three pitchers (the best of whom was Milt Pappas) during the off-season prior to 1966.

In 1970, Robinson got some revenge when his Orioles defeated his former Reds, 4-1, in the best-of-seven World Series.

Frank Robinson was 83 when he died in 2019.

SCOTT ROLEN

THE SETTING

Over a few-year period around 2010 and beyond, when Scott Rolen was a member of the Cincinnati Reds and I was writing about the team, I saw him in the clubhouse regularly.

He was a very business-like guy. It was easy to see how much effort he put into preparation, though he was still friendly enough and cooperative at his locker. This was Rolen at the end of a career that began with the Philadelphia Phillies, had many highlights with the St. Louis Cardinals, and could well have continued with the Reds after 2012 at age 37.

After playing for 17 seasons, however, Rolen retired quietly, when many baseball people believed he would return for another season. He was only a year removed from the All-Star team at that point and two seasons removed from his latest Gold Glove win.

Confusing matters, Rolen did not report to spring training 2013 with the Reds, but he did not announce his retirement from the game, either. It was a somewhat quirky departure from the sport, but eventually his name was advanced for consideration on the National Baseball Hall of Fame election ballot.

The all-around combination of Rolen's hitting statistics, hits, doubles, runs batted in, and home runs put him in the company of other Hall of Fame third basemen such as George Brett, Mike Schmidt, and Chipper Jones.

While Rolen compiled some impressive career statistics and was honored many times over for his fielding and with All-Star selections, his name did not initially meet with overwhelming support. He garnered slightly more than 10 percent of the vote when 75 percent is required for election.

However, as time passed and Rolen's credentials were more closely examined, he gained more and more support. Other names came and went on the ballot, as well, players either elected or dropped from consideration because of the 10-year limit. Rolen was in his sixth year of having his name on the Baseball Writers' Association of America ballot when he was voted into the Hall with the class of 2023.

The approval of Rolen for the Hall brought him back into the limelight and he was invited to participate in interviews reviewing his career. Since 2018, Rolen, who was as much a Hoosier as anyone who ever dribbled a basketball in that hoops-mad state, has been associated with the Indiana University baseball team. He was working closely with the school he almost attended before choosing professional baseball.

⟫⟫⟫⟫⟫⟫⟫⟫⟫⟫ *THE STORY*

Rolen's casual nature and his graciousness were on display in several ways after he took the phone call that confirmed him as an immortal. After hanging up the telephone, the first thing Rolen did in way of celebration at receiving the news he was going to be the newest member of the Baseball Hall of Fame was hug his parents.

He was sharing the emotion and issuing thank-yous to mom and dad for their help along the way. It was also pretty neat that Rolen somewhat returned to the roots of the game and one of its timeless images by also quickly stepping outdoors and playing catch with his son. Many imagine that picture and see the sport at its purest.

While thrilled with his selection, Rolen, who was 47, still didn't think it was worth getting all dressed up to meet the sporting press whom he once upon a time talked to in his jockey shorts. His rummaging through his closest for appropriate attire went only so far. He did wear a collared shirt and a sport coat, but did not break out a neck-tie.

"I haven't put on a suit in 11 years," Rolen said.

Although born in Evansville, Indiana, Rolen became a local sports legend in Jasper, where he was a star baseball, tennis, and basketball player and definitely explored continuing his basketball education at an NCAA Division I school. He had a brother and sister attending Indiana University, but he came closest to playing basketball for the University of Georgia on scholarship.

He originally hoped to be one of the few athletes who could juggle college basketball and minor-league baseball, but when the Phillies drafted him in the second round, he benched the basketball idea to concentrate on baseball. Some observers felt he might be the next Mike Schmidt for the Phillies, but Rolen backed away from such comparisons since Schmidt is regarded by some as the greatest of all-time at the third-base position.

That was thinking way above his pay grade, he thought, but so was having as much success as he did and being in the circumstance he was in at that moment, explaining his overwhelmed reaction to joining Schmidt in the Hall of Fame.

"That was never reasonable to me," Rolen said of being looked at favorably compared to Schmidt. "I never thought I'd be a Hall of Famer. I never thought I'd get drafted."

Someone asked Rolen if he had a baseball idol growing up and he said he did not really, spending more time and energy playing the game than watching it. But he said he did have a poster of Don Mattingly on his bedroom wall. Mattingly, who many feel deserves to be in the Hall of Fame, too, excelled with the New York Yankees and became a manager. The men know each other and Rolen said they do stay in touch.

"He was certainly a legend in our area," Rolen said.

As of 2023, Mattingly was a coach for the Toronto Blue Jays after lengthy stints managing the Los Angeles Dodgers and the Miami Marlins.

One of Rolen's proudest playing moments was being a member of the 2006 World Series champion St. Louis Cardinals. A few years later, in 2010, when Cincinnati was on the verge of clinching a National League playoff and Rolen was one of the small number of players on the team who had been there before, he counseled his mostly younger teammates on how to savor the moment.

"No, it's not just another day at the ballpark," Rolen said. "We have the opportunity for a big night. We'll wreck this place a little bit." In part by spraying champagne on everything and everyone in range. "I'm not sure the champagne is drinkable, anyway, no offense to whoever's label is on it."

CAREER

Scott Rolen played in 2,038 games, hit 316 home runs, drove in 1,287 runs, and batted .281. He won the 1997 National League rookie-of-the-year award, was a seven-time All-Star, and an eight-time Gold Glove winner.

Just 21 when he made his Major League debut in 1996, his true rookie season was the next year. His best single season was 2004 when he clouted 34 homers, drove in 124 runs, and batted .314 with a .409 on-base percentage.

Rolen always had an affinity for Indiana University and he made a large donation to the baseball team. Then, with a change of coaches, he became director of player development for the Hoosiers. Rolen is a role model for the players, offering advice and tips on the game and counseling those who seek professional careers. He also helps the program with recruiting.

One somewhat amusing and fascinating anecdote Rolen imparted to sportswriters after his selection to the Hall was how as a young major leaguer he approached Cal Ripken Jr. for advice. A Hall of Famer who played both shortstop and third base for the Orioles, Ripken is renowned for a work ethic that enabled him to play in a record 2,632 consecutive games as well as collect 3,181 hits.

Rolen said he knocked on the door of the Baltimore Orioles' clubhouse, introduced himself to Ripken and sought wisdom. It was exactly what a fledgling young player would expect to hear. The comments weren't about hitting well and fielding cleanly. They were more about just coming to work.

"You can have an impact on the outcome of the game by just being there and showing up and doing your job and playing," Rolen said Ripken told him.

It wasn't sexy stuff but gritty stuff. While Rolen said it's not as if Scott Rolen highlights play on a loop at his house to enlighten his children about his career, but when he was chosen for the Hall, they all performed a search on YouTube for some good plays to display.

Rolen said he watched himself make barehand plays at third. "I'm reliving them," he said. "I'm like, 'Oh yeah, it looked like that hurt.'"

PETE ROSE

》》》》》》》》》》》》》》》》》》》》》》》》》》》》》》》》》》》》 ### *THE SETTING*

My first contacts with Pete Rose occurred during the 1980 baseball season when he was a key member of the Philadelphia Phillies team that won the franchise's first World Series. I was involved in some of the coverage for the Philadelphia Inquirer.

Over many years, I saw Rose during some of his public appearances signing autographs in Cooperstown, New York during Hall of Fame week festivities, and in Las Vegas where he routinely signed his name for fans.

We also did a lengthy interview about the 1980 season when I was working on a retrospective book about the championship 40 years later and we spoke on the telephone about the issue of whether the prominent star who had been banned from the game for life for gambling should be reinstated and thus be eligible to have his name appear on the Hall of Fame ballot.

This became a particularly intriguing situation as Rose aged into his 80s – raising the question of whether voters would ever be able to pass judgment on his career through Hall of Fame procedures while he was still alive. And also, given how Major League Baseball, along with other professional sports in recent years, had become more entangled in the world of sports betting.

Pete Rose was banned from baseball during the summer of 1989, nearly 35 years ago. The man whose time on the field made him a no-brainer candidate for the Hall of Fame, has been on the outside looking in ever since. Not only is Rose not allowed on the roster of those enshrined by the sport in Cooperstown but forbidden from any active job in baseball.

Especially since MLB has become increasingly involved in sports gambling, with odds on various combination bets even appearing on the screen during televised games, and betting parlors being constructed inside ballparks, it seems logical that Rose should be freed from the chains of his punishment. He should be pardoned or paroled, whatever the appropriate term is, and reinstated in the sport.

Rose was long ago sentenced to death row, but others have been pardoned from death row even when scheduled to be executed for murder. Rose has lived in a prison without bars, almost as if he was unable to cross an invisible barrier that would have set off an electric charge, for all these years. It can be argued that his punishment has been sufficient. His sentence should certainly be reviewed against the backdrop of baseball's new, cozy relationship with betting.

There has never been the slightest doubt that Pete Rose the player, the all-time hits leader in baseball history, amassed the type of statistical record that earned him a place in Cooperstown. It was the rash of bad judgments that landed him in this morass.

But with the turn towards legalized sports betting in so many ways, in so many places, it is Major League Baseball that comes off looking hypocritical in failing to grant Rose the freedom from his sentence. Rose, at his age, is not about to manage again. What is at stake is his legacy of being considered a Hall of Famer. Or at the least freeing him up to see his name on the ballot for voters.

≫≫≫≫≫≫≫ THE STORY

Pete Rose was still an icon in the eyes of fans in 1981, the season after the Philadelphia Phillies won the World Series, but a season during which baseball underwent a wrenching labor dispute leading to a strike.

That summer Rose, whose long-term outlook was to surpass Detroit Tigers great Ty Cobb's record of 4,191 hits, was chasing Stan Musial to become the leading harvester of base hits in National

League history. There was no inter-league play yet, so the league marks were distinct.

The season had been abruptly disrupted when Rose was just shy of passing the St. Louis Cardinals' great. They were tied at 3,630. Everyone went home, stopped playing after June 10, and then the season resumed August 10. Baseball revved up again with an All-Star game in Cleveland.

Since an air traffic controllers strike loomed and he had missed out on enough games already from the baseball strike, Rose did not chance flying to Philadelphia for the first game back. Instead, he drove nine-and-a-half hours to make sure he was in the lineup.

By happenstance, the Phillies were playing the Cardinals. St. Louis actually won the game, 7-3, but Rose's quest out-shined the rest of the night at Veterans Stadium. Rose went just 1-for-5, but the hit, a single in the seventh inning, gave him the new NL record.

The Phillies were definitely ready for the moment. The game was halted and a celebration commenced with 3,631 balloons unleashed on the skies, fireworks were set off and Stan Musial himself congratulated Rose. Rose told Musial he wasn't going to make him stick around another day.

After the game, Rose said he was keenly aware of the approaching moment. "I had goose bumps for six or seven innings," he said. "I'll probably have pneumonia tomorrow."

Things became more entertaining when President Ronald Reagan called in to offer congratulations and the phone lines from the White House to the ballpark seemed to get crossed up.

When the phone rang the first time and Rose picked up, he said, "Tell the president to wait a minute." Rose apparently then got cut off twice more and when Reagan finally came through, he said, "I think I had to wait longer than you did to break the record." Rose joked back, "We were going to give you five more minutes and that was it."

Eventually, Rose did break Ty Cobb's record and no one is close to catching Rose. His life started to go haywire when he was banned from baseball. He made his living selling autographs and he was often interviewed. Periodically, he sent applications to the then-commissioner of baseball for reinstatement, but he was not able to move any of them.

There was an ebb and flow to Rose's public emotions. Sometimes he said he was over the fact he was still banned. Other times he let on how much he missed being left out. It was a purgatory of sorts.

"After 30 years, I'd be the happiest guy in the world (to be elected)," Rose said in 2020.

That was during the COVID-19 shutdown of much of the world and he said he was "going stir crazy" in Las Vegas with no one coming to the tourist town. He wasn't going to bug Commissioner Rob Manfred about his case while the boss was trying to figure out a season.

"No, no, they're too busy for me," Rose said.

Even after COVID passed its peak of disrupting American life and the sports world, it seemed as if MLB was going to stay too busy for Rose. There was no movement on his case and no indication he was going to receive the pardon that would allow him to be placed on the Hall of Fame ballot.

>>>>>>>>>>>>>>> CAREER

As a player, Rose appeared in a record 3,562 games over 24 seasons, setting records for plate appearances, official at-bats and of course hits, enabling him to embellish his autograph with the words "Hit King." He batted .303, won a Most Valuable Player Award, and was a 17-time All-Star.

Rose, whose nickname was "Charlie Hustle," bestowed on him early in his career when he even ran out walks, won three batting titles and even won two Gold Gloves, which was surprising because he so often switched fielding positions on the diamond. He was the National League rookie-of-the-year in 1963 and was a member of three World Series champion teams, being a key cog in the Big Red Machine clubs that twice won titles in the 1970s, in addition to that Phillies squad.

Although Rose remains banned, he is a beloved figure in his hometown of Cincinnati and is appreciated by the Reds, the team for which he toiled most of his career. There is a Pete Rose Way next to the Great American Ball Park in downtown Cincinnati. Rose is honored in the Cincinnati Reds Hall of Fame. The team has retired his No. 14 jersey. In 2010, the team recognized his breaking of Cobb's record on the 25th anniversary of the event.

Rose was present, but did not speak to fans. He said he was glad he didn't because he probably would have been crying. "You only get to see me cry once," he said at the time and the once was when he set the mark in Riverfront Stadium.

However, during a roast of Rose at Hollywood Casino in nearby Lawrenceburg, Indiana attended by about 500 people, including former teammates Tony Perez, Tom Browning, Cesar Geronimo, and George Foster, Rose spoke and he did shed tears.

"I disrespected the game of baseball," he admitted. He also apologized to those players and teammates who were not present. Admitting he was "a hard-headed guy," Rose said he was a better person than he had been. "I'm a different guy. I love the fans. I love the game of baseball and I love Cincinnati baseball."

NOLAN RYAN

⟫⟫⟫⟫⟫⟫⟫ *THE SETTING*

If Nolan Ryan had been from Boston instead of Texas, people would have been calling him "wicked fast" from the time he was twelve years old. To illustrate the speed of his fastball, though, he was nicknamed "The Ryan Express." That made him verbal kin to Walter Johnson and his fastball, a man nicknamed "Big Train."

The fastball defined Ryan on the mound, his pitches a blur to the mere mortals who stepped into the batter's box and exited with eyes bulging, muttering unintelligible words and shaking their heads.

Other pitchers won as many or more games than Ryan's 324 – not many, though. But no others pitched as long as his 27 seasons and no others struck out as many opponents. Ryan's strikeout mark of 5,714 will never be touched. The proof of how insanely good Ryan could be when his right arm had the good fortune aligned with the planets, is that he also has seven no-hitters on his resume. The next-best mark is four.

It should also be noted that Ryan had bouts of wildness and also walked 2,795 hitters, more than anyone else in history, too. One game in 1974, while hurling 13 innings against the Boston Red Sox, Ryan struck out 19 batters, walked 10, and threw 235 pitches.

One night that season in a game versus the Detroit Tigers, Ryan's fastball was clocked at 100.9 mph. A couple of weeks later, in the ninth inning, he was clocked at 100.8 against the Chicago White Sox.

Anyone who came to the ballpark on a day when Ryan was scheduled to pitch had to at least harbor the thought of seeing a no-hitter in the back of his mind. He could hope, for sure. Ryan, who led his league in strikeouts 11 times, with a high of 383 in a single season, was having a bad day if fewer than 10 enemy batsmen struck out in a game.

Some baseball people don't remember that Ryan was just 19 when he broke into the majors in 1966. They might remember that he was a member of the 1969 Miracle Mets championship team at 22, though – and this is eye-opening to say – he was basically a spare arm with a 6-3 record that year.

Still, he gained early fame by being part of that joy ride. For one thing, people took note of his tiny hometown of Alvin. Some joked it was the only community in the country named after a chipmunk, Alvin and his friends being household words at the time. Fellow Mets pitcher Jerry Koosman said Alvin was so small it didn't even have a last name. While Alvin did have just 5,600 people in the early 1960s, it has more than 27,000 now.

Ryan's Mets years represented his learning days in the big leagues, the years when he was harnessing his power. It was not until he moved to the California Angels in 1972 when he won 19 games and led the American League in strikeouts for the first time with 329 that Nolan Ryan became Nolan Ryan.

Post-Angels, he was either a Houston Astro or a Texas Ranger, his final pitching efforts with the Rangers at age 46. One year with the Astros he posted a 1.69 earned run average to lead the National League.

Ryan was a member of the Astros when I had the chance to interview him in the Houston clubhouse in 1980. The Astros out-lasted the Los Angeles Dodgers to capture a division title and set up a National League Championship Series versus the Philadelphia Phillies when I was at the Philadelphia Inquirer.

Another time, Ryan provided the foreword for a book I was doing about his old teammate and fellow pitcher J.R. Richard from that era.

One was a glad occasion and the other was a somewhat sad occasion. When Ryan was in the locker room, it was a glad occasion. When Ryan was talking about Richard it was a sadder occasion because J.R. had suffered a career-ending stroke when the men were playing together.

⟫⟫⟫⟫⟫⟫⟫⟫ THE STORY

For all his individual success, and the Hall of Fame nature of Ryan's career, there were only a few times when he had the opportunity to compete in the post-season. He won a game in the NLCS for the Mets and he appeared in relief in the World Series when they beat the favored Baltimore Orioles for the title. He made one playoff appearance for the Angels 10 years later, too. So, when the Astros qualified for the post-season in 1980, Ryan knew these opportunities did not come along like clockwork.

A party atmosphere prevailed in the Astros' clubhouse. Houston was born as an expansion team for the National League at the same time as the Mets in 1962, originally named the Colt .45s before switching their names to the Astros. Until this moment, though, they had not won anything.

As the 1980 regular-season wound down, the Phillies had clinched the NL East and were waiting on an opponent. The Astros took a three-game lead on the Dodgers into the last weekend of play, but Los Angeles swept all three scheduled games to reach a tie for first place and require a one-game playoff.

That meant there was a 163rd regular-season game, a must-win for both teams. After nearly fading into oblivion, the Astros pulled out a 7-1 win to advance. Knuckleballer Joe Niekro pitched a complete game and won his 20th game of the season simultaneously.

Ryan was just a spectator on that day, but a happy one. He had signed a $1 million free agent contract to get back near his Texas home of Alvin and to buttress the starting Houston rotation.

Ryan went just 11-10 in his first season with Houston but was another big arm to count on. He did not play in this deciding game, but afterwards compared the feeling to the successes of the Mets and Angels he experienced.

"I enjoyed all of them," Ryan said as he felt his hair wetted by celebratory champagne. He glanced around the locker room at other players wearing champagne as much as drinking it, a similar scene to what he lived with New York and California. "I don't see any difference. They're different individuals, different uniforms, but I'm just as wet."

One Houston player who could not revel in the merriment was pitcher J.R. Richard. Like Ryan, Richard, who stood 6-foot-8 and weighed 220 pounds, was a flamethrower. Between 1976 and 1979, Richard three times won 18 games and once won 20 games. He had emerged as a 300-strikeout man himself.

Earlier that summer, carrying a 10-4 record and a 1.90 earned run average, Richard had been the starter for the National League in the All-Star game. Only before the end of July, Richard, just 30 at the time, was throwing a workout when he felt ill. In a stunning development, he had suffered a stroke from a blood clot. Hospitalized, but hopeful about his future, Richard sought to return to top form and play again but never could make a comeback.

"J.R. Richard was the mainstay of the starting rotation at the time," Ryan said of when he joined the Astros. "...and he was at the top of his game. At the time we were both probably among the hardest throwing pitchers in the major leagues, and for the Astros, having us both in the rotation meant that opposing hitters were going to have to face two guys who threw their fastballs about 100 mph.

That's a tough task for any team to take on.

"It is fair to say that J.R. was one of the best pitchers in baseball when he was felled by a stroke."

It is the type of maybe that no one can ever suggest since it involves a rewriting of history, but along with many others, Ryan wondered if J.R. Richard had been healthy, in his usual form for the rest of the regular-season, there may not have been a need for the Dodger playoff game. Or after that if the Astros might well have defeated the Phillies and that Houston, not Philadelphia, would have won the World Series in 1980.

Ryan pitching in Atlanta June of 1983. The Astros won 4-3. Teammate Jose Cruz is in the background.

⟫⟫⟫⟫⟫⟫⟫⟫⟫⟫⟫⟫ CAREER

Nolan Ryan's lifetime record was 324-292 with a 3.19 earned run average – and all those strikeouts. He appeared in 807 games and threw 5,386 innings, the fifth-most in Major League history. An eight-time All-Star, Ryan had his jersey number retired by the Angels, Astros, and Rangers, and he is a member of all three of those teams' Halls of Fame. He was inducted into the Baseball Hall of Fame in 1999.

Not only did Ryan hurl a record seven no-hitters, the first one in 1973, the last one in 1991, he threw an astounding 12 one-hitters and 18 two-hitters. Ryan recorded 15 seasons with at least 200 strikeouts.

Among his activities after retiring from the field, Ryan headed the main ownership of a AAA club, then became president and Chief Executive Officer of the Rangers. He followed that up with a five-year stint as a special assistant in the Astros' front office.

Ryan's sons Reid and Reese, both pitched collegiately at Texas Christian University and also played summer ball with the Alaska Baseball League's Anchorage Bucs. Ryan sometimes quietly dropped in to watch them throw in Alaska. Reid Ryan later operated the Round Rock minor-league team and served as president of the Astros.

One thing Nolan Ryan did not do like a good ranch cowboy was ride quietly off into the sunset when his pitching career ended. He went out with an ouch. Ryan's right arm went dead on him abruptly, in the first inning of a game against the Seattle Mariners in September of 1993. He tore the ulnar collateral ligament in his elbow.

Ryan was escorted from the mound at the Kingdome by medical personnel and inside the clubhouse he admitted immediately that the injury was devastatingly final.

"There's no way I'll ever throw again," Ryan said. "It's just a hell of a way to end a career."

RYNE SANDBERG

THE SETTING

I admit I chuckled when Ryne Sandberg told me his family members were such big baseball fans that he was named after 1950s relief pitcher Ryne Duren. It had never occurred to me there could be a connection.

You have to be a big-time baseball fan to know Ryne Duren's story, or at least of a certain age. He was well-known when he played, but not well-known in baseball history for his actual day-in and day-out performances.

Ryne Duren was born in 1929 in Wisconsin and he had a bazooka of a right arm, capable of throwing a fastball as fast as anyone else in the game. He also wore glasses with extremely thick lenses and while he was sometimes wild, he used the combination to his advantage, too. Duren was not above flinging an inaccurate heater to scare batters wide-eyed. When he was with the New York Yankees, his manager Casey Stengel, was also not above perpetuating the image of the half-blind, supersonic thrower as being out of control while saying if hitters dug in and got hit by Duren they might end up in "the past tense."

Duren never won more than six games in a season in a 10-year career, but he did lead the American League in saves once with 19 and was chosen for four All-Star teams. Duren had the tools for greater success, but it came out that he was a serious alcoholic, an affliction that hampered him. Ultimately, Duren overcame his addiction, wrote a book called *I Can See Clearly Now* and worked with other alcoholics.

That was the backdrop to Ryne Sandberg's first name. It is most probable his parents just liked the sound of it rather than delved too deeply into Duren's story. Besides, Sandberg was born in Spokane, Washington, far from any big-league outposts. However, those parents had already named his older brother Del after former Phillies outfielder Del Ennis, so you can never tell what they really knew.

Ryne Sandberg was a terrific high school athlete, an All-American quarterback who was recruited by NCAA Division I colleges. He signed a letter of intent to play for Washington State in nearby Pullman, but being drafted by the Phillies tugged him in the direction of baseball.

It proved to be a wise choice, with Sandberg becoming one of the greatest second basemen of all time, recognized for his hitting and fielding excellence. Only not so much for the Phillies, his original suitor, for whom he played just one season. After he made his debut in Philadelphia in 1981, the Phillies traded Sandberg and shortstop Larry Bowa to the Cubs for Ivan DeJesus.

Sandberg had not yet established much of a reputation, playing in only 13 games (he got his first big-league hit at Wrigley Field), but Dallas Green, who oversaw the Phillies' player development and then led the team to the 1980 World Series title as manager, knew how talented Sandberg was. Green had become the Cubs' general manager and made the swap that essentially fleeced Philadelphia.

The Phillies had Manny Trillo and Julio Franco to cover second. Bowa was aging, but when making the trade, Green casually mentioned to Phils management, "Oh, why don't you throw in Sandberg, too" and they fell for it.

Change of scenery, change of future for Sandberg. He said, "Dallas Green remembered me."

Sandberg's main exposure in the infield up until then had been at third base. When the team reported to spring training, Green and manager Lee Elia told him he would be playing second and Bowa, an experienced veteran, worked hard with him on technique. Sandberg credited Bowa's preparation and help with instilling a pregame routine for him that he stuck with for his whole career.

>>>>>>>>>>>>>>> *THE STORY*

Sandberg was a surprisingly strong hitter for a middle infielder, who as a group in the past had been counted on more for fielding than battering the ball. He was able to do both well, smack the ball around, or pick it up and throw out speedy runners.

There was one game, however, over the course of his 16 seasons in the majors that stood out to fans and to Sandberg himself as a special one when what he did at the plate made all the difference. In fact, in Cubs lore it came to be known simply as "The Ryne Sandberg Game," as if it was the name of a stage play or something.

The occasion was a game against the St. Louis Cardinals at Wrigley Field on June 23, 1984. The season was a break-out for Sandberg, indicating he had arrived as a next-level player, and for the Cubs as a team, who won a division title and played in the National League Championship Series.

It was not a game that shaped up early as anything special to remember for Cubs supporters. By the end of four innings, the Cardinals were leading 7-1. Later, the game was tied, went into extra innings, and Chicago prevailed, 12-11, in the 11th inning. That was after things had been tied again in the 10th inning, with each club producing a two-run rally.

Over the course of this nearly four-hours-long adventure, Sandberg cracked five hits, scored twice, and drove in seven runs. He homered in the ninth inning and the 10th inning. Both of the home runs came off of Hall of Fame reliever Bruce Sutter.

"I've heard that phrase, 'The Ryne Sandberg Game' about a million times," Sandberg said in an interview. "It absolutely is a memorable game. Ever since 1984, when I'm approached by fans, they've all mentioned it."

The fans asked if he remembered that game and he would routinely reply, "Absolutely!"

Sandberg was 24 years old and just about everything stood out to him about that season. The Cubs were big winners for the first time in a while. Sandberg won the National League Most Valuable Player

Award. He batted .314, hit 19 triples, 19 home runs, drove in 84 runs, scored 114 runs, and banged out 200 hits. He was also named to his first All-Star team and picked up his second Gold Glove.

"That was a game that changed me as a player, for one, and also gave our team a huge boost," Sandberg said. For the first time, manager Jim Frey told Sandberg to consider going after select pitches to hit for power.

Sandberg said he already had three singles by the time he came to the plate in the ninth inning to face Sutter, whom he respected as possibly the best reliever in the sport at the time.

"Bruce Sutter was a notorious ground-ball pitcher," Sandberg said. "At best you might hit a hard grounder off of him. But I looked at a pitch down and in. I got underneath it, hit it for a home run in the ninth, and then I hit another one off of him in the tenth. The place (Wrigley Field) was going bananas."

While the attendance at Wrigley was 38,000, Cubs Nation was apparently paying attention to the game in full force, one way or another, and every Cubs fan Sandberg runs across as the years go by feels compelled to discuss that contest.

"It seems like everybody was at that game," Sandberg said. "I guess they were, one way or another, in person, watching on TV, or listening on the radio."

»»»»»»»»»»» *CAREER*

Except for that brief call-up with the Phillies, Sandberg spent the rest of his Major League days playing in a Cubs uniform. He hit .285 lifetime, with 282 home runs and 1,061 runs batted in. A 10-time All-Star, Sandberg won nine Gold Glove awards and seven Silver Sluggers. He was inducted into the Baseball Hall of Fame in 2005.

A few years later, Sandberg began a managing career with the Cubs' minor-league affiliate in Peoria. He then handled the Tennessee Smokies and finally, the Iowa Cubs, the team's AAA club, winning the 2010 Pacific Coast League manager-of-the-year award. When Sandberg was passed over for the Cubs' field boss job, however, he made a move to the Phillies and ran their AAA team, the

Lehigh Valley IronPigs.

Instead of managing the Cubs, Sandberg ended up as manager of the Phillies starting in mid-season of 2013, but two years later, also in mid-season, he resigned with the Phillies in last place. Sandberg rejoined the Cubs in 2016, acting as a goodwill ambassador for the team.

When Sandberg was inducted into the Hall of Fame, in his speech, he talked of having respect for the game. Known for normally being a quiet figure in the clubhouse, he also made a joke about that image. "This will come as a shock," he said, "I know, but I am almost speechless."

RON SANTO

THE SETTING

Wrigley Field was pretty much Ron Santo's second home address, the ballpark where he played out 90 percent of his career representing the Chicago Cubs and in later years served the team as a popular broadcaster.

Often enough during the days I lived in Chicago and attended Cubs games, the former long-time third-baseman for the franchise was present and available, easy to chat with, to interview, just to pass hello regards with.

Other times, when I was researching Cubs history for books about the team, I interviewed Santo on the phone. There was no greater booster or believer in the Cubs than Santo and his friend Ernie Banks, who shared an infield together and shared a dream that the Cubs would one day win a World Series championship that they could witness.

Santo and a few others excelled when the team as a whole could not. There was a core group of players who were regulars in All-Star play, but there were not enough of them to win the Cubs a pennant during the 1960s or 1970s. They led the league in passion, but not in victories. They led the league in heartaches, but not titles won.

Some of the greatest of all Cubs overlapped on the roster for years and shared special times together, stoked the passions of Cubs die-hard fans, but could not give them the reward they all so desperately sought.

Santo, always a strong believer in what his team could accomplish, was one of the symbols of this near-greatness, but also a symbol of the futility of coming close, and failing.

Beyond that, his story was one of overcoming odds, though not everyone knew it, at least not for many years, and one in private that was filled with sadness as his health declined. Banks, Santo, Billy Williams, Ferguson Jenkins, and some of the others, were tight-knit comrades in arms. If Ernie Banks had not been nicknamed "Mr. Cub" before Santo arrived on the scene, surely he would have been granted the nickname.

He meant so much to the Cubs and the Cubs meant so much to him that the two were almost entwined in an everlasting public hug.

>>>>>>>>>>>>>>>>>>>> *THE STORY*

Ron Santo was a closet diabetic when treatment for the life-threatening disease was not as sophisticated. And with not enough public knowledge about it, he legitimately feared Major League Baseball teams would not take a chance on him if his afflictions were known.

So, for years after being diagnosed with juvenile diabetes at 18, he kept his illness secret. He took his medicine, privately, injecting himself with needles, but not telling either his employer or his fans that he needed it to ensure he could suit up and play a professional sport.

Growing up in Seattle, Santo, who was born in 1940, was so good at the game that scouts from all 16 teams in the bigs knew about him and wanted to talk to him about wearing their uniform. There was no Major League ball in the Pacific Northwest at the time to soak in, though there was minor-league baseball and the majors were on television.

It was TV that first attracted Santo to the Cubs, even though that team was not a big winner, didn't offer the largest signing bonus and wasn't a team his neighbors rooted for or supported. Through "The Game of the Week," Santo saw and heard Banks, as well as watched him play, and he saw Wrigley Field.

Both the man and the ballpark attracted Santo through the small screen.

"I don't know why, but there was just something I loved about that ballpark," Santo said. And that was through the miracle of black-and-white television, not even in color since there was not much color TV around in 1959. "And Ernie Banks was special to me, just the way he conducted himself."

Santo gradually, but steadily learned his value from representatives of the teams that dropped in for visits. His parents had divorced when he was young and his mother re-married, but the family was not wealthy. When the Cleveland Indians offered Santo $50,000 to sign, members of the family stifled their surprise, as planned. Santo later said, "I couldn't even swallow."

That amount of money in 1959 was huge. The Santos listened to everyone as scouts came to the door and came through the living room. The Cubs were among those willing to ante up, just not as much as the Indians. Their offer to Santo was for $20,000. There really was no comparison between the Cubs' deal and the top deals, but a voice kept whispering to Santo, telling him he should become a Cub. And that's what he did.

By 1960, at age 20, Santo was already in Chicago, easing his way into full-time work. He showed enough to finish fourth in rookie-of-the-year voting while playing in just 95 games. From 1961 through 1973, Santo was the Cubs' starting third baseman. He played one more season in the majors, with the cross-town White Sox, and retired at 34.

Santo made a splash from almost the first moment the Cubs brought him up to the big club. Santo hooked up with the team on the road in Pittsburgh during the days when the Pirates still played in Forbes Field. He said he had never even been inside a big-league ballpark and he was a bit starstruck viewing Roberto Clemente, Dick Groat, and Bill Mazeroski going through their batting practice paces. It turned out they were good guys to watch that season since the Pirates won the World Series a few months later.

Lou Boudreau was managing the Cubs and with a double-header scheduled that day thought it would be a good time to break Santo into the lineup. Santo was told he was going to start and got himself ready to play – so he thought. But he was quite edgy.

Banks, living up to Santo's preconceived good-guy notion, watched Santo's inability to hit the ball out of the cage in batting practice and took it upon himself to soothe him.

"Are you nervous, kid?" Santo recalled Banks asking him. When he confessed that he was, Banks told him to look at the Pirates pitchers that day as just two more AAA minor-league guys. Since the starters were Bob Friend and Vernon Law, both big winners, Santo had difficulty playing that game in his head.

Yet Santo got two hits and drove in three runs in the opening, 7-6 win, and he had another hit and two more runs batted in during the 7-5 night-cap triumph. He was going to be sticking around the Cubs.

The first time Santo actually set foot on the grass at Wrigley Field and absorbed its greenness in color, he felt a special thrill, too. "I knew exactly I was in the right place," Santo said, adding he felt as if "I was walking on air."

Santo did not let the world know he was a diabetic until 1971, but after that he worked tirelessly to raise money for research to combat the disease. Santo and his family have long been associated with the Juvenile Diabetes Research Foundation and the Ron Santo Walk to Cure Diabetes in Chicago has raised more than $65 million.

>>>>>>>>>>>>>>>>>>>> *CAREER*

Santo battled .277 lifetime, with 342 home runs and 1,331 runs batted in and he stroked 2,254 hits. A nine-time All-Star, Santo won five Gold Gloves. When he retired, he felt he had the credentials to be elected to the National Baseball Hall of Fame.

As year after year passed without Santo's selection he was regularly interviewed about his chances and about being passed over. He was disappointed and was candid about being overlooked. Simultaneously, Santo had a fresh career going as a Cubs broadcaster, a role he filled from 1990 to 2010 and fans loved that he was unabashedly one of them, always on their side. He was not an objective newscaster, but an I-love-'em-too commentator.

The tinge of sadness surrounding Santo, one he battled to combat, but which others felt, was that he was physically fading even as he fought to keep up with the Cubs. The diabetes ate at him literally, causing the bottom parts of both legs to be amputated. He had heart problems.

Not only was daily life becoming a full-time struggle for Santo, his son Jeff, a film-maker, made a poignant documentary about his dad called "This Old Cub." The film demonstrated to the outside world what kind of obstacles Santo overcame just to show up in the radio booth.

Periodically, there would be a swell of attention as the Hall of Fame's committees gathered to vote, with hope running high that this would be Santo's year. Then came the let-down. Santo, who was also suffering from cancer, died in 2010 at age 70. The loss of a major member of the Cubs family was dramatized even more so when exactly what Santo feared would happen, actually did – he was elected to the Hall of Fame the year after he died. It was a cruel denouement.

Widow Vicki and three adult Santo children, two males, one female, represented their father at his Hall of Fame induction in Cooperstown, New York and spoke eloquently about their old man even as they mourned him and shed some tears for him. Calling their active presence somewhat "strange," Jeff Santo said it all really with the simple sentence, "We wish our father was here."

Busloads of fans traveled from Chicago to Cooperstown to honor Santo at the ceremony and as they walked the streets of the small, upstate New York community, Santo family members were stopped repeatedly by well-wishers who recounted stories they heard Santo utter on his broadcasts.

Old Cub teammate Billy Williams said those Cubs stars from the Santo era were friends as well as baseball partners. "Everybody wanted him to be here," Williams said. "He is looking down on us."

MIKE SCHMIDT

⟫⟫⟫⟫⟫⟫⟫⟫⟫⟫⟫⟫⟫⟫ *THE SETTING*

I first met Mike Schmidt in the Philadelphia Phillies' clubhouse during the season of 1974 when I was traveling the country doing freelance baseball stories. He was in the early stages of making a name for himself in the game, though just a lone season removed from the horrendous experience of batting .196 in 132 games, one of the worst essentially full seasons recorded by a Hall of Famer.

By the time I interviewed Schmidt, however, he was on his way to becoming the Mike Schmidt, an all-around star slugger and superb fielder which eventually caused some baseball experts to call him the best third baseman of all-time.

Later, as a member of the Philadelphia Inquirer sports department, I had many occasions to visit the Phillies' clubhouse when the team was fighting its way towards the 1980 National League pennant and the first World Series championship recorded by a franchise that began play in 1883 as the Quakers.

The Schmidt that I interviewed in 1974 was 24 years old and on his way to leading the NL in home runs with 36 for the first of eight times in his career. In an 18-year big-league career that ended in 1989, Schmidt grew into a player who was chosen for the All-Star team 12 times.

In 1980, when the Phillies needed him the most, Schmidt, who was periodically as friendly as anyone in the locker room and other times prickly enough to refuse to talk after games, was the Most Valuable Player in the National League. That was one of three times he won the award.

When the Phillies bested the Kansas City Royals in the World Series, Schmidt was also voted the MVP of the Series and amidst the chaos I put together the Mike Schmidt MVP story for my newspaper.

⫸⫸⫸⫸⫸⫸⫸⫸⫸⫸⫸ *THE STORY*

The 6-foot-2, 195-pound Schmidt, who had the agility to play the infield and the power to sock home runs, was from Dayton, Ohio. He attended Ohio University and the Phillies saw his potential and made him a second-round draft pick.

He made a 13-game cameo for the Phillies in 1972 and then played third as a regular in 1973, trusted with the keys to the position, but shaky at the plate the entire season. From there, Schmidt's gears meshed and he became an all-time great. One thing I joked about when writing about Schmidt that first time was that a year earlier, the most prominent display of the name Schmidt's was the beer that sponsored the team. By summer of '74 that was no longer true. When fans thought of Schmidt, they thought of Mike, and they were cheering.

It was going on the home stretch of the season and Schmidt was powdering home runs, driving in runs frequently, and had been chosen for his first All-Star appearance. It was cheeky to suggest he was as refreshing as a cold glass of the beer, but he was beginning a run that would make most forget about the suds.

So much had changed so quickly, the issue was how did he do it?

"I'm more patient," Schmidt said of his improved hitting style at the plate. "I'm not swinging at bad pitches. I wait for my pitch more. Because of that I'm not striking out as much. I'm hitting the ball, putting it in play. It's all part of the growing process in the majors. I learned a lot last year. That was just the first step."

It was a common process for a young player to go through and Schmidt was fortunate enough to be allowed to cope with those growing pains in the majors rather than in the minors. Maturity had kicked in and Schmidt's state of mind was calmer in his second season.

"I'm relaxing," Schmidt said. "I'm relaxed at home plate 100 percent of the time. I have much more confidence in the field, too. Last year, I didn't know until I came to the ballpark whether or not I would be playing. Then, when I did play, I'd be pressing to get a couple of hits so I could play again."

In 1973, the Phillies finished 71-91, in last place in their division. In 1974, they were nine games better at 80-82, and Schmidt said there was a feeling the young club was on the move.

"The main difference is that it's more fun to go the ballpark," he said. "It's not like work. Everybody is happy with each other. You can play looser and more relaxed."

Schmidt concluded by saying his goal was to someday win a World Series ring. In the years between that conversation and 1980, the Phillies became an all-around first-rate team, making the playoffs and finally going all the way and capturing a World Series.

There was pandemonium in the Phillies' clubhouse when they clinched the title – as to be expected – and Schmidt was in demand for his thoughts on the moment and on his performance in the six-game Series. Schmidt, who had belted a home run in the victory that gave the Phillies the division crown, smacked two home runs and batted in seven runs while collecting eight hits against Kansas City.

For all the wild celebrating going on around him, Schmidt was comparatively placid, pleased enough to grasp a champagne bottle in his hand and his thick hair drenched with the bubbly, but not so demonstrative at his locker to jump up and down and hug everyone who walked past.

Biggest hit of his life, Schmidt conceded of the bases-loaded single that drove in two teammates with all the runs his club needed in a 4-1 victory in the deciding game.

"I can't think of one bigger than that," Schmidt said. While admitting it was "a great thrill" to be named Series MVP, he wasn't sure he deserved the honor. "It could have gone to any number of guys on our team. My performance didn't stand out. I just did something every game."

Of course, doing something in every game mattered.

It was slow to sink in that the Phillies had actually accomplished their goal. At one point Schmidt said, "I'm still sort of in a coma."

When manager Dallas Green raised the championship trophy in the air and shouted to him, "Look at this! Look at this, Schmitty!" Schmidt's smiled wildly.

The Phillies brought some baggage to the season and to the Series, accused of being uncommunicative, a team that couldn't win the big ones, and roiled internally.

"I don't think anyone would dislike me personally if they spent enough time with me," Schmidt said. "The real image of the Phillies? Let me see. You can write a book on the subject. People are looking at the world champions."

>>>>>>>>>>>>>>>>>> **CAREER**

Philadelphia sports fans can be rough on even the best players on their favorite teams if they do not perform perfectly, and Schmidt was one of the Phillies greats who also was heckled at times.

Winning the Series helped win those demanding fans over, though, he thought. "The warmth that was felt from the fans during the World Series washed away every boo that had ever come out of those stands."

During his career, Schmidt appeared in 2,404 games, hit 548 home runs, collected 1,595 runs batted in, and won 10 Gold Gloves, all of which helped him with three regular-season MVP awards.

Actually, more relaxed at the plate or not, Schmidt did continue to strike out frequently throughout his career, four times leading the National League in that category. But he also always drove in bushels of runs, nine times topping 100 in a season. Three times he topped 40 in homers, with a high of 48 in 1980.

Schmidt was inducted into the Baseball Hall of Fame in 1995 and he made a speech that was widely appreciated. In part, he said, "I really do stand before you a man that's totally humbled by the magnitude of this entire experience. It's unbelievable."

Some years later, the Phillies honored some of the greats of the team by erecting statues and Mike Schmidt was one of the first ones installed.

RED SCHOENDIENST

>>>>>>>>>>>>>>>> THE SETTING

Despite a couple of short intermissions representing other ball-clubs, Red Schoendienst seemed to be a St. Louis Cardinal for as long as the colorful birds perched on a bat on team jerseys.

He began playing for the Redbirds in 1945 at age 22 and competed in the field for the Cards for much of his playing career. Schoendienst also managed the team three different times, coached for St. Louis at other times, helped out in the front office, and pretty much spent much of his adult life wearing that famously designed Cardinals uniform.

Although Schoendienst was still playing when I was a kid, he did retire in 1963. Even if he was a National Leaguer, I somehow became aware of the second-baseman despite growing up in an American League city and was a fan from afar.

This was especially emphasized, not only because he had the type of ability that would eventually land him in the Baseball Hall of Fame, but because I became conscious of a key element in his back story.

During the off-season following the 1958 campaign and the start of the 1959 campaign, Schoendienst was diagnosed with and hospitalized from tuberculosis. At the time, after he had surgery to remove a lung, Schoendienst was told he would never play Major League ball again. For centuries, tuberculosis was regarded as a scrounge of mankind and, until sophisticated treatments were applied, was often considered a death sentence.

When Schoendienst did bounce back and resume his baseball career, I admired his courage and that always stuck with me. Many years later, when I was specializing in outdoors coverage for the Chicago Tribune, I ended up spending some time talking to Schoendienst more under the umbrella of hunting than baseball.

We were at the County Line Hunting Club in Whittington, Illinois and Rend Lake Resort in November of 2005 as part of the Illinois Conservation Foundation's Celebrity Quail Hunt. Although there are two ballclubs, the Chicago White Sox and the Chicago Cubs, located in Illinois, this Southern Illinois location was closer to St. Louis, so most baseball figures invited to participate were affiliated with the Cardinals. It made more sense geographically. Chicago wasn't completely ignored, though.

There was considerable partying at the bar the night before the mid-November hunting date, so for some it was a struggle to arise early the next morning.

Among those keeping company with Schoendienst were former St. Louis pitcher Danny Cox, former Cardinals third baseman Mike Shannon, former St. Louis football player Jackie Smith, former Chicago Bear Tim Norman, and former NFL defender Tim Kearney, who played for a few teams, including the Cardinals, before they moved to Arizona.

>>>>>>>>>>>>>>>> *THE STORY*

Schoendienst, who turned 82 that year, admitted that he might have spent a little bit too long hanging out at the bar with the guys telling stories the evening prior to the hunt, confessing to a bit of a hangover. But he was still pleased to be involved because money raised by the event was donated to programs supporting beginning youth hunters and anglers.

"It's a good, charitable thing," Schoendienst said, and said he enjoys being with those who participate. "And they're all outdoor people."

During his off-seasons, when he was playing mainly for the Cardinals, and also the New York Giants and Milwaukee Braves a short time each, Schoendienst was a bird hunter. He did not shoot Cardinals – that might have been viewed as sacrilegious – but he did hunt ducks and geese. That meant he knew his way around a shotgun about as well as he knew his way around a Louisville Slugger.

Schoendienst, clad in hunter orange as the uniform of the day, was grouped with a half-dozen shooters, though there were around 130 hunters and guides out on the land. In deference to his age and

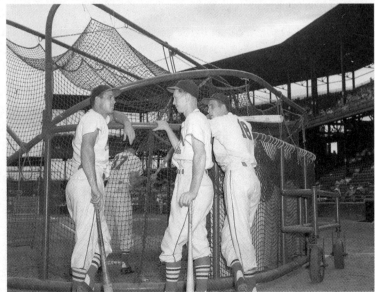

Schoendienst (center) at Sportsman's Park with fellow teammates.

Photo courtesy of Missouri State Archives

seniority in the bunch, Schoendienst was allowed to use a small Jeep to travel on trails through the woods instead of remaining on foot for long hikes. He whispered that the real reason he had the vehicle was probably because of the hangover, not his number of birthdays.

He said he ordinarily preferred to walk, but had to admit to elder frailties, as well. So, he drove and tried to coax birds close enough to shoot. He brought down his first quail after he jokingly sought to convince it to land in the Jeep via voice command.

"Come here, bird," Schoendienst called out. The strategy did not work as well as envisioned. "I tried to get him in the front seat."

Not quite. Instead, the quail landed in a nearby field. A pointing dog flushed the bird and it darted skyward. Schoendienst aimed and fired and the bird plummeted to earth. His throwing arm may have weakened, but his shooting eye was as sharp as ever.

Schoendienst, and the others in his group, accounted for a count of 27 quail and four pheasants, a satisfying harvest for them.

After an accurate Schoendienst shot, resulting in a quail tumbling into a field about 50 yards away, he drove his Jeep-on-loan to the spot as other hunters and dogs focused attention on a different bird that had been scented.

Schoendienst motored over to the dead bird and when he climbed out of the vehicle teasingly posed as a dog on point. He retrieved the bird without a dog's assistance and as he held it up – one in the hand – he glanced at his poised hunting partners scanning the field, he laughed, and said, "Better than two in the bush."

≫≫≫≫≫≫≫≫≫≫ CAREER

Born in Germantown, Illinois in 1923, Alfred Fred "Red" Schoendienst was 19 when he began playing minor-league ball in the St. Louis chain. He made the majors just as World War II was ending and became best friends with Stan Musial, the greatest Cardinal of them all, remaining in the lineup for St. Louis until 1956.

St. Louis fans were outraged when Schoendienst, a 10-time All-Star with a lifetime .289 batting average, was swapped to the Giants in a massive trade. Schoendienst, Jackie Brandt, and Bill Littlefield, plus later adds Bob Stephenson and Gordon Jones, were transferred to New York for Alvin Dark, Whitey Lockman, Ray Katt, Don Liddle, and cash.

Schoendienst spent almost exactly one year with the Giants, who traded him to the Braves for Ray Crone, Danny O'Connell, and Bobby Thomson. The Braves were shoring up their lineup for their run to the National League pennant. He hit .310 in 93 games for Milwaukee, who did win the league flag, and the World Series in seven games. Schoendienst felt sickly for some time and even in late September near the conclusion of the regular season underwent an X-ray that came up negative. He played in the Series, but still feeling ill had additional tests and became a bed-ridden victim of tuberculosis.

The infection was in Schoendienst's right lung and his baseball future was clouded. But with good recuperative powers and an optimistic attitude, he was back with the Braves for five games in 1959 and 68 games in 1960 at age 37.

Interviewed extensively about his battle with tuberculosis, Schoendienst became weary of discussing the topic and at times indicated it didn't seem like that big of a deal. Sports Illustrated put his smiling, freckled face on the cover in June of 1960, but he thought all the description of his TB was too dramatic.

"I had something to overcome and I overcame it," Schoendienst said. "I'm just like anybody else that's got rid of it, and we may as well forget it."

Subsequently, he returned to the Cardinals for the last years of his playing career, continued in Cardinal colors as manager, and coached for what seemed like forever.

Between 1965 and 1976 he managed nearly 2,000 games and then filled in for stints in 1980 and 1990 for shorter stretches. As player, manager, and coach Schoendienst shared in five World Series championships. Somehow, Schoendienst escaped St. Louis for two years to coach with the Oakland A's, but during the latter stages of his life he was basically a special assistant to the general manager for the

Cardinals, often hitting balls in batting practice.

"I just like baseball," Schoendienst explained in 1987, more than
40 years after he played in his first
Cardinals game. "I like to be around
it. I like to be on the field more than
anything else."

Schoendienst was credited with
spending some time in a Major
League uniform for about 70 straight
years. He was elected to the Hall
of Fame in 1989. When he died in
2018 at 95, the end of his life was announced during a Cardinals game
and his picture was shown on a ballpark giant screen. Players and fans
gave him a standing ovation.

FRANK THOMAS

>>>>>>>>>>>>>>>>> **THE SETTING**

Not only did Frank Thomas and I overlap in the Chicago White Sox clubhouse many times, talking near his locker, but we later worked together on a book about home-run hitting. Thomas, who was football-sized in build, hit 521 home runs during his Major League career.

That 521, amongst the all-time leaders in the sport, was a popular number. Boston Red Sox slugger Ted Williams also retired with 521 home runs and by coincidence, so did San Francisco Giants slugger Willie McCovey. This represents a rare cluster of all-time greats with the exact same statistic on one of the sport's most prestigious life lists. Both Williams and McCovey were voted into the National Baseball Hall of Fame.

During his 19 seasons in the majors, Thomas was an extraordinary player who won two American League Most Valuable Player Award honors and acquired the nickname "The Big Hurt." That appellation was added to his given name based on two things: 1) He could put a big hurt on opposing teams with his bat; 2) He was a big man. Thomas stood 6-foot-5 and weighed 240 pounds. He did play college football at Auburn University in Alabama and some believed the native of Columbus, Georgia could have been a National Football League player if he had not committed to baseball.

Although some controversy followed Thomas during his mostly sterling seasons with the White Sox, often related to contract disputes, for the most part Thomas displayed a mild, smiling personality around the locker room and was open and friendly with sportswriters.

One aspect of Thomas' commentary during his 1990-2008 years in the majors was his out-spoken, forthright statements decrying the use of performance-enhancing drugs by some players who used them to improve their numbers.

During this so-called steroid era, Thomas was one of the only big sluggers who said baseball should test players for drug use and volunteered to be tested. He disparaged those who cheated and when the United States government and the court system intervened in cases, Thomas also volunteered testimony under oath.

He was probably the embodiment of the "clean" player whose statistical stature suffered next to others who did take drugs, with the result his performances may not have been as much admired as they would have been. The cheaters took drugs to improve their own status, but on the flip side players like Thomas were harmed because their statistics were lower than they might have been if they had cheated.

Given his starry performance for many years, Thomas should have understood it was a no-brainer that he would be elected to the Hall of Fame, but I was struck by how he wished to avoid talking about the topic. He said he didn't want to jinx his chances, that there was no such circumstance as a sure thing, and that he wasn't in the Hall of Fame until it was real. He not only said that to me, I witnessed him dance around the question with well-wishers in public. The fans told him how it would be great when he was elected, but Thomas demurred, not ever wishing to dwell on the subject – until it finally was real.

Frank Thomas was inducted into the Hall in Cooperstown, New York in 2014.

THE STORY

Thomas was elected to the Hall of Fame in his first year on the ballot and much was made by sportswriters at the time that he was never tainted by even a whiff of scandal, unlike so many other big hitters who got caught up in taking drugs, or were rumored to take drugs.

Besides ducking the matter of whether or not he would be se-lected for the Hall of Fame – there was no reason to worry, Frank – mostly Thomas and I met away from the ballpark in Chicago to discuss home runs.

His home runs. Other stars' home runs. The greatest home runs in the game. His thinking, comments, and swinging, you could say, were all part of a book called *Going Yard: The Everything Home Run Book.*

For a ballplayer who hit as many home runs as he did during his career, Thomas never led his league in homers during an individual season. He did bash at least 40 in a season five times and more than 30 four other times, so he was hardly a stranger to the long ball.

One reason Thomas never hit even more home runs in a sea-son is because he was not a reckless swinger. He was a smart one, who took pitches for balls that soared above his head or bounced in the dirt, rather than just going for the fences. That is why Thomas walked 1,667 times during his career, four times leading the AL in bases on balls and 10 times walking at least 100 times in one season. He took the old adage, "a walk is as good as a hit" to heart. That's also why his on-base percentage was a terrific .419. Not only did Thomas lead the league in that category four times, but one year, in 1994, he compiled an other-worldly .487. He also had a startling .729 slugging percentage that season.

Thomas' overall thinking about the home run was straight-for-ward. He emphasized that each one was "special" and that each time a four-bagger was catalogued it represented the confluence of cer-tain conditions. The pitcher had to throw the ball in the right place and that above all, a batter has "got to be focused."

Fans might routinely watch a close game and say out loud that it would be nice if their team's most prominent batter could hit a home run right then. Thomas said he never brought such thoughts to the batter's box with him.

"I never really went to the plate thinking about hitting a home run," Thomas said. "I was always taught that the home run happens." Throughout his entire career, Thomas said, his "goal was just to hit the ball hard." Where it landed could be measured later.

Thomas correctly pointed out that for many years a player who hit 30 homers was among the league leaders. Then during his playing era, 30 homers was surpassed many, many times. Hitting 40 was a good standard, but for a stretch of time players who never seemed to approach such seasons again, topped 50 in a year and others revisited Babe Ruth territory by slamming 60 or more.

"I consistently hit 40," Thomas said. "That's a testament to hard work."

He said he never got caught up in the frenzy of chasing homers and remembered the lessons he was taught by his coaches when he was younger, and the principles stressed by White Sox hitting coach Walt Hriniak. Thomas basically said that he never lost sight of who he was.

One thing Thomas reflected on with me was the Deadball Era of Major League baseball, the period from 1876 when the National League started up, and the early 1920s, when the lively ball was introduced and Babe Ruth's moon shots energized the public.

"Boy, the Deadball Era had to be tough," Thomas said. "They had to be big, strong guys to hit home runs then. It's amazing how big some of the ballparks were. No wonder nobody hit many home runs. You would need a bazooka to hit one out."

When he was young and growing up in Columbus, Georgia, just 105 miles from Atlanta, Thomas habitually watched the Atlanta Braves as his hometown team – and cheered for Hank Aaron as he progressed towards passing Ruth's lifetime record of 714 home runs.

Never mind the games, but the sports news on TV always seemed to be showing Aaron ripping a ball out of the park and trotting around the bases. Thomas watched Aaron's famous 715th home run, too.

"It was exciting to see Aaron's big home run breaking Babe Ruth's record," Thomas said. "Aaron didn't hit tape-measure home runs a lot, but he hit them consistently."

>>>>>>>>>>>>>>>>> *CAREER*

Thomas' lifetime average was .301 in 2,322 games, primarily at first base when he played the field, but later as a full-time designated hitter. Most of Thomas' finest years were with the White Sox, but near the end of his big-league days he also had a fine season for the Oakland A's and one for the Toronto Blue Jays.

Selected for All-Star teams five times, Thomas won the 1997 AL batting title with a .347 average. Twice, he was named league MVP. The White Sox retired Thomas' No. 35 jersey after he formally stepped away from the game on a one-day contract with the club. A statue of Thomas was erected in the home ballpark, now known as Guaranteed Rate Field.

Besides investing in a wide variety of business interests, Thomas has been a regular studio analyst for baseball, seen on television in Chicago and nationally.

When Thomas was voted into the Hall of Fame it was coincidental timing that it was a big Atlanta Braves year featuring the inductions of that team's 300-game winners Tom Glavine and Greg Maddux and manager Bobby Cox. Thomas said that was great with him and he would also benefit from the Georgia-flavored turnout in Cooperstown.

"I'm a Georgia kid and the whole state of Georgia is going to be there," he said.

For a guy whose baseball dreams just about all came true, in 2021, Thomas had the distinction of being a major part of a financial group that bought the Field of Dreams in Iowa. That was the location of the ballpark in the 1989 movie *Field of Dreams* based on the magic realism movie made from W.P. Kinsella's novel about "Shoeless" Joe Jackson and his ghostly contemporaries coming from heaven to play ball again.

JIM THOME

>>>>>>>>>>>>>>>>>>>> **THE SETTING**

When it comes to sluggers and slugging, Jim Thome is in the top echelon of home-run hitters to ever play the game. During his playing days, as he greeted sportswriters with charm and warmth in front of his locker in the clubhouse, he was viewed by the people who cover the game as the nicest guy in the sport.

Thome and I had a particular overlapping area of interest – besides baseball – because when I saw him, we often discussed the outdoors. I was the outdoors-adventure writer for the Chicago Tribune and Thome was a passionate outdoorsman who had set aside some property for family use to take advantage of hunting and fishing opportunities.

When Thome played for the Chicago White Sox he was already well-established from his days with the Cleveland Indians, but he was cultivating new fans by the day with his play and demeanor.

A big man by most standards of definition at 6-foot-4 and 250 pounds, Thome looked strong, like the kind of guy who could bash a baseball 600 feet into the ozone. Indeed, he actually seemed even bigger than those dimensions, carrying the size of a pro football lineman if someone had pointed him in another direction.

A native of Peoria, Illinois, Thome pursued his baseball dreams in bigger cities, but he was well-remembered in that midwestern community. One day, several years ago, when I was on a long-distance drive, I glanced at the gas gauge in my car and realized it needed a pit stop. The next exit advertised gasoline for sale. I happened to be passing through Peoria.

When I got off the highway, eyes peeled for a service station, the first thing I saw was another sign of a different type. I had pulled onto a street named "Jim Thome Highway." Approved by the Illinois legislature, the name represented a change from a simple numbered road. The locals just felt it was a cool way to honor a native son.

Thome was primarily a first baseman and designated hitter over his 22 seasons in big-league ball, but some forget he was actually a third baseman in his earlier days with Cleveland. The Indians represented his longest-term allegiance, and he did some good work for the Philadelphia Phillies, too, but in about four seasons with Chicago, Thome stamped himself as a team and fan favorite. He boosted his overall image by smashing frequent home runs, three times topping 30 in a single season and one of those years going over 40, for the White Sox.

Thome's father Chuck introduced him to baseball by playing catch in the yard in Central Illinois and was a great influence in developing Thome's love of hunting, fishing for bass and bluegill, and baseball, three shared devotions.

"My dad and I practiced a lot," Thome said, "and I was successful playing just about right away. I wanted to play baseball from day one after I started doing it. I was just a huge, huge baseball fan."

However, not a White Sox fan. Father and son spent hours together watching televised baseball, but rooted for the Chicago Cubs, the other area team, since WGN, that superstation, made it so easy to cultivate a fondness for the National League club. Later, Thome took his father along to the Baseball Hall of Fame when he presented officials there with one of his milestone game balls.

Not well-remembered by Thome's Major League fans, was that after high school, where he starred in baseball and basketball, he enrolled at Illinois Central College, a community college in East Peoria. He also played sports there and later the home park for the school's baseball and softball teams was named Thome Fields.

⟫⟫⟫⟫⟫⟫⟫⟫⟫⟫ THE STORY

Even if it was not suiting up for the Cubs, when Thome joined the

White Sox in 2006 at age 35, he called it a homecoming. Peoria is not the suburbs of Chicago, but it is only 165 miles away.

The White Sox were the defending World Series champions and for years had relied on another future Hall of Famer, Frank Thomas, as a powerful designated hitter. But Thomas had been injured and the White Sox wanted a newcomer on the roster. Thome was having his own injury woes, periodically struggling with hamstring issues, so there was a question-mark surrounding his acquisition. Then Thome went out and slammed 42 home runs with 109 runs batted in and a .416 on-base percentage and he was the new hero in town.

Still, the hamstrings were worrisome and in 2007, the next season, Thome was forced onto the disabled list for a time. Often, in an older player, having little physical things go awry is a herald of bad news to come, perhaps of a career-ending day.

For that reason, when Thome returned to the lineup for Chicago in time for a game against the Oakland Athletics in May of his second season with the White Sox, he gleaned great satisfaction from an "I'm-back" performance. His number one goal was to show the baseball world he was healthy again, but he did that and more.

Thome returned to the lineup with a bang. He went three-for-three at the plate, hit a home run and drove in five runs in a 10-4 Sox victory.

"When you come off the disabled list like that you want to be healthy, first of all, and ready to go," Thome said. He was. "You want to try to contribute in any way you can. You don't know what's going to happen. The game came at a great time. There is always a little uncertainty about what's going to happen when you come back. You definitely want to get back in a rhythm."

Later that season, on September 16, Thome hit his 500th career home run, a blast that won the game, too. The White Sox came from seven runs down to defeat the Angels. Sox manager Ozzie Guillen said he called the shot, too, telling outfielder Jermaine Dye sitting next to him in the dugout that Thome was going to win the game with the clout.

"It's amazing," Thome said. "It really is. Like a movie script. I would never have imagined doing it in that situation."

The White Sox actually dug up home plate at was then called U.S. Cellular Field and presented it to Thome as a souvenir of the occasion. Soon after, Thome signed 150 photographs of his 500th homer and gave them to team employees.

The fans had already been rewarded, first by witnessing the key blow, and also because a White Sox giveaway to ticket buyers that day was a Jim Thome bobblehead doll.

Rather than simply shipping the home-run ball to the Baseball Hall of Fame, Thome and his father took an off-season road trip to deliver it in person.

》》》》》》》》》》》 CAREER

Jim Thome retired after the 2012 season at age 41 with 612 home runs, one of a tiny number of players ever to top the 600 mark. He drove in 1,699 runs and batted .276 with a lifetime on-base percentage of .402. His single season high for homers was 52 for Cleveland in 2002, but he led the National League with 47 for the Phillies a year later. A five-time All-Star, he was also named the winner of the Roberto Clemente Award for his excellence on the field combined with charitable work.

Thome, who was once called "The world's nicest man," by pitcher Joe Nathan, donates to several causes, especially those benefiting children, and some on an emergency basis such as when a tornado hit a town not far from Peoria. He also set up trust funds to cover the college costs of 10 nieces and nephews.

It is humorous to note that coming out of high school Thome was considered underweight and not large enough to become a professional athlete. He improved his credentials and packed on muscle weight at Illinois Central.

Although he was the 333rd draft pick coming out of school, Thome was still only 20 when he broke into the majors. He ascended to stardom with the Indians and the franchise erected a statue outside Progressive Field to honor him after he retired.

Thome has worked as a special assistant to the general manager for the White Sox and also did broadcast studio work. He has said he might want to become a manager at some point.

Thome was voted into the Baseball Hall of Fame and inducted in 2018. After being informed of his selection and on his orientation visit to Cooperstown, New York, Thome had tears in his eyes on tour.

"How do you ever dream of this happening?" Thome said when he strolled through the plaque gallery in the Hall on his visit, "walking through and having all of those great players stare at you?"

BILL VEECK

>>>>>>>>>>>>>>> **THE SETTING**

There was never a more fan-friendly owner of a Major League Baseball team than Bill Veeck. He was a hero to the supporters of the teams he owned in Cleveland, where in 1948 the Indians/Guardians won their most recent World Series title. He rejuvenated the Chicago White Sox for a time. And he delighted and surprised fans at the ballpark with promotions and stunts that had them talking for years.

It is no surprise that Veeck's devotion to the sport and his theatrics in promoting it resulted in his being inducted into the National Baseball Hall of Fame in 1991. When it is said Veeck grew up in baseball, it was not a metaphor. His father, William Veeck Sr., a one-time sportswriter, became president of the Chicago Cubs. One of the younger Veeck's tasks in 1937 was installing ivy in the outfield walls at Wrigley Field, one of the game's still-enduring and most iconic looks for a park.

As he aged and itched to run his own franchise, Veeck became a showman to entice butts into the seats at Milwaukee (when it was a minor-league town), Cleveland, and elsewhere. He helped pave the way in the integration of baseball when he signed Larry Doby for Cleveland as the second Black player, just three months after Jackie Robinson broke in with the Brooklyn Dodgers. He also gave legendary pitcher Satchel Paige his chance in the majors – twice – even though he was already in his forties.

Although he stepped into a similar role just three months after Robinson did in a more openly racist society, Doby never quite got the attention the Dodger player did, although Doby also became a

Hall of Famer. And, Veeck later made him the second Black big-league manager.

"When I signed Larry Doby, the first Negro player in the American League," Veeck said, "we received 20,000 letters, most of them in violent and sometimes obscene protest. Over a period of time, I answered all [of the letters]. In each answer, I included a paragraph congratulating them on being wise enough to have chosen parents so obvious to their liking."

Famously, when he was operating the sad-sack St. Browns, who were in a losing attendance war with the St. Louis Cardinals, Veeck sent a 3-foot-7 midget, Eddie Gaedel, up to the plate to hit.

When parents brought a little one to a Browns game, they might receive a certificate reading "St. Louis Browns, Baby Brownies, Future Player's Contract." This was in the early 1950s and part of the message at the bottom of the certificate said the individual was "a member in good standing of the sub-junior affiliates" of the Browns and "will be expected to report for spring training March First 1970."

Presumably, junior would be all-grown-up by then and capable of hitting .300. By 1970, of course, the Browns were long gone, moved to Baltimore and transformed into the Orioles and Veeck's stake in the Browns was also long gone. If the Browns were still in place, it would have been fascinating to see how many "Baby Brownies" showed up for a tryout those many years later.

Veeck was known as "sport-shirt" Bill because he never wore a tie. He viewed his fellow owners as hidebound and as stuffed shirts and they hated him, sometimes making it difficult for him to operate in the manner he wished. Unlike most of them, Veeck was not independently wealthy, and even today is said to be the last big-league owner who bought a team without having the bank account of a corporate giant.

Instead of heading to his savings account to buy a ballclub, Veeck put together coalitions of several well-off individuals. Periodically, the changing economics of the sport caught up to him and that led to him selling off his teams and putting him back on the sidelines.

During one of Veeck's interludes from baseball, for two years he held the position of chief executive of Suffolk Downs Racetrack in East Boston, Massachusetts, which at the time in the early 1970s was a place the locals came to place bets on thoroughbred horses.

As usual, one of Veeck's missions was to lure fans into the arena (though once there they were supposed to lose money gambling). Veeck ran the track for a bit and then wrote a book about his experience called *Thirty Tons A Day*.

I had to be one of the few sportswriters in Veeck's long sports promotional career, who had the mission to interview Veeck about a sport other than baseball. I was still in college and writing for a publication called Boston Sports Record Weekly.

For the most part over his years in baseball, Veeck had made many thousands of individuals laugh. I made him laugh during a telephone interview with my first question.

⟫⟫⟫⟫⟫⟫⟫⟫⟫⟫ *THE STORY*

I asked Bill Veeck what the title of his book meant.

"You could say it's the end result of 1,500 horses a day," he said. The euphemism was vivid and certainly gave people an idea of the scope of the racetrack's size.

Veeck, who made his permanent home in Easton, Maryland, admitted he didn't know much about horse racing when he accepted the assignment of bringing more excitement to Suffolk Downs. His mental outlook, as he explained in the book and in conversation, was essentially this when he was approached by the owners: "If it isn't promotable, why would they want me?"

At the time, shortly before Triple Crown winner Secretariat helped to rejuvenate thoroughbred racing across the country through his brilliance in the Kentucky Derby, Preakness, and Belmont Stakes – setting records that still stand – horse racing was in an era of decline. Behind the scenes, Veeck said, he also found that he was pitted against "the most corrupt politicians in the world" and poor luck in timing when bad weather ruined carefully-thought-out promotions.

Veeck did not depart the horse racing industry undefeated. He made it sound more as if the horse racing industry defeated him. The usually staid Suffolk track staged Ben-Hur-style chariot races and set off fireworks and the season-long handle topped $1 million, a mark not reached again for more than 25 years. But the parent real estate company was struggling and that led to Veeck's exit.

"Two years later, fortune having taken one look at my weathered features and shaken its hoary locks, I retreated smiling gamely," he said.

Veeck always was game. He was generally irrepressible in the face of great odds and his heart was always fixated on the baseball world. When we spoke, he was about to renew a previously syndicated baseball column and had plans to travel the country making speeches.

Do those and "just be a bum," he said. "One thing I'm not, is bored. I haven't discovered boredom yet." Veeck did author or co-author some auto-biographical books, including the notable *Veeck As In Wreck*. At this time, however, he said he was working on a novel tentatively called *Scrap Iron*, which he had scribbled off and on for years and expected to rewrite still more. No such book under that title was ever published.

Veeck, while in ownership, regularly spoke up for innovation in baseball to make the game livelier from any public podium he commandeered. When we spoke, the American League was about to introduce the designated hitter rule and unsurprisingly, Veeck said he thought it would be good medicine. He said he first talked up such an idea 20 years earlier.

"I think it'll make the fans more interested," Veeck said. "One-to-nothing and 2-0 games are fine and they're artistic successes, but I personally would rather watch a 9-7 game. The DPH (as he called it rather than DH as the rule popularly became referred to) is specialization and it's more attuned to the times."

Before the Boston Patriots morphed into the New England Patriots, when they were suffering financial difficulties and failures on the field, Veeck's promotional acumen caught the attention of a local sportswriter who suggested the football team turn over its operations to him. The same writer said Veeck was too sane to accept the job.

"Yes, I am," Veeck said. "I've got enough troubles of my own." He was laughing when he said that if Billy Sullivan, the Patriots' founder and front man, telephoned, he would have told him, "Billy, you've got to be off your rocker." It would have been fun, though. And you know something, almost all of the things I ever did were fun. We weren't always successful, but we had fun."

By 1973, Veeck had owned the Cleveland Indians, the St. Louis Browns, and Chicago White Sox, but had been out of big-league baseball ownership since 1961. He stepped away from the White Sox when he was suffering from health problems. Veeck had coped with numerous health issues since he served in the United States Marines during World War II.

During combat, a recoiling artillery piece rolled over and crushed part of Veeck's right leg. Amputation of his foot and the lower leg was required. When he returned home, he relied on a wooden leg, but in keeping with his spirit and outlook, Veeck carved an ashtray into the wooden leg for convenience since he was such a chain smoker. The leg seemed to be a source of never-ending aggravation and Veeck had 36 operations on it over the course of his life.

After the old Washington Senators abandoned the nation's capital by becoming the Minnesota Twins, Veeck, who lived close by in Maryland, sought to purchase the rights to the expansion franchise baseball granted the city. He was shut out of that deal, however.

When we talked, Veeck was a bit disingenuous when he downplayed his current feelings about his life-long passion for baseball.

"I miss it about four days a year," Veeck said. "On opening day, opening day of the World Series, and a couple of days during spring training when the sun is out and it hasn't been discovered that the new phenom can't hit a curveball.

"As far as getting back in baseball goes, the only place I would consider is Washington and only partially because of its closeness. I think it was a mistake to move from there."

Veeck was correct in that baseball has never been able to stay away from Washington D.C. for long. But he was lying when he said Washington was the only place he would consider for a return to the game.

In 1975, with the threat of the White Sox moving to Seattle looming, Veeck put together a new ownership group and became the owner of the Chicago American League team for a second time.

>>>>>>>>>>>>>>>>>>>>>>>> **CAREER**

Taking over the White Sox just in time for the nation's Bicentennial in 1976, Veeck re-introduced himself to the fans on opening day of that season with a "Spirit of '76" parade. Employing his wooden leg to advantage, Veeck played the one-legged fifer in the march.

Although Veeck's second time around generated some excitement, it was the lack of finances that made it impossible to compete at the beginnings of free agency, although he did believe the players should be able to dictate their futures.

During this run, broadcaster Harry Caray was working for the White Sox and Veeck forced him into leading renditions of "Take Me Out to The Ball Game" with fans during the seventh-inning stretch. This became a Caray signature, made more famous after he jumped to the cross-town Cubs.

When he was the owner, Veeck always wandered Comiskey Park, mingling with the crowd, taking the temperature of the fans who bought the tickets. He was no ivy-tower guy. Later, after he stepped away from ownership, he attended games in the Wrigley Field bleachers sitting there shirtless in the sun working on his tan, and having some brews with the other regulars.

The man who listed his number in the phone book and always answered his own telephone, completely in keeping within character as just another "everyman" ticket-buyer, Veeck died at age 71 in 1986 after suffering from cancer. His was a unique baseball voice stilled.

BILL VIRDON

>>>>>>>>>>>>>>>> **THE SETTING**

Sometimes people forget that Bill Virdon had a lengthy and rewarding career on the field and as a manager even when he wasn't running the New York Yankees under George Steinbrenner. That's because the spotlight was so bright in New York everyone had to wear shades and the soundtrack was so loud that everyone needed ear plugs, whether they wanted to or not.

Although being the field boss of the Yankees was only a small portion of Virdon's lengthy baseball career, it cast a long shadow. Normally a calming presence, Virdon is lucky he did not develop nail-biting, facial tics, and other signs of anxiety while working for New York in what was only 1974 and 1975, but probably seemed like decades. Besides the constant churn from above, Virdon actually got a death threat at one point because he played Elliott Maddox in the field instead of Bobby Murcer.

Sometimes also overshadowed were the excellent parts of Virdon's playing career, as the rookie-of-the-year with the St. Louis Cardinals and as a member of the Pittsburgh Pirates' 1960 World Series champions.

Virdon, who made his home in Springfield, Missouri for many years, was always a cooperative figure when reached for interviews by telephone. But we spent the most amount of time talking during the 1978 baseball season when he was managing the Houston Astros.

For Virdon, both as a player and a manager, there was life before the New York Yankees and life after the New York Yankees.

Virdon, who was renowned for his superb fielding, played in the majors from 1955 until 1968. Before running the Yankees, Virdon managed his old Pirates for two years and later he ran the Astros from 1975 to 1982. His last managing job was overseeing the Montreal Expos in 1983 and 1984.

In Houston, in 1978, proving he was still in solid athletic shape for a 47-year-old, Virdon was smacking around ground balls with a metal bat to his fielders as part of pre-game workouts. He sometimes threw batting practice, too, but not at that moment because the elbow on his right throwing arm was irritated.

One way that Virdon was often recognized from afar, as a player and as a manager, since he didn't really change with modernization, was his wearing of glasses on the field. Not contact lenses, but solid-rim glasses.

By the time we met up, his Yankees' experience was deep in the rearview mirror and fading quickly. Instead, he was focused on the future with a young Houston team.

⟫⟫⟫⟫⟫⟫⟫⟫ THE STORY

Virdon looked as much like an active player as he did the leader of the operation out on the field at the Astrodome. He had his glove folded and stuffed into his back pocket, ready to fill in for other potential tasks.

"I throw some batting practice, but I've got a bad elbow right now," Virdon said. "I even hit a few." He smiled as he made that comment, as if no one would believe an old guy like himself could handle that assignment. He did tend to wait to enter the batting cage until one of his coaches, not one of his young flamethrowers, was hurling. "I pick my spots."

Virdon had a certain amount of talent, was signed out of a try-out camp in Branson, Missouri by the Yankees. Famed scout Tom Greenwade, who among other players, discovered Mickey Mantle, spotted Virdon and signed him to an $1,800 bonus deal.

Gradually working his way up through the low minors to the high minors, ironically, as a centerfielder, Virdon was always destined to be stuck behind Mantle on the long-term depth chart. That fate got Virdon traded to the Cardinals' organization, where he excelled and turned in his special debut season in 1955.

Virdon always knew he wanted to stay in the sport after he could no longer play and started his own baseball academy in 1956 when he was still a youthful player. He managed for a few years in the minors and then his old team, the Pirates, hired him as a coach.

As one of the regulars with the beloved Pirates team of 1960 that featured Roberto Clemente, Bill Mazeroski, Don Hoak, Dick Stuart, Dick Groat, Bob Friend, Vernon Law, and Roy Face under manager Danny Murtaugh, Virdon always had a warm welcome in Pittsburgh. Virdon said there was no doubt his biggest thrill in baseball came when that team defeated the Yankees in Game 7 of the World Series on Mazeroski's legendary home run.

Virdon's reunion with the Pirates began as a coach in 1968 and he interviewed for the manager's job when Larry Shepard left in 1969, but Pittsburgh rehired Murtaugh. Murtaugh stepped away from the stressful job because of health reasons and the second time around Virdon was hired.

In an oddity, in 1968 when several Pirates were called up for military service because of the Vietnam War, Virdon was re-activated to play and appeared in six games at age 37 after a big-league absence of three years.

Virdon led the 1972 Pirates to the National League East division title, though they lost in the playoffs to the Cincinnati Reds. The next year was a difficult one in Pittsburgh. Clemente was killed in a plane crash in the off-season and famously, pitcher Steve Blass lost all of his control. The team was under .500 when Virdon was fired and Murtaugh returned yet again.

That led Virdon to New York and then to a fresh start in Houston. The Astros had young talent and optimism, but hovered around .500.

"I never figured we'd win, but I thought we could stay close and make it interesting," Virdon said of his first Houston teams, which placed third in their division. "We're not getting consistent pitching or defensive play or clutch hits. We're a young team and we make more mistakes on the fundamentals. But there's no simple solution."

It did not help matters that star outfielder Cesar Cedeno had injured his knee and been sidelined.

Virdon contrasted this 1970s group of players with the players he played with and against in the minors when they came to the majors. In his generation, players spent longer in the minors and were older when they broke in, he said.

"Now they have less experience and they're more curious," Virdon said. That was a subtle way of saying the young players questioned authority more than the old-timers did. "They demand more answers. There's got to be more explanations. They're more educated. They have a right to ask questions."

Virdon sounded like someone who knew his team was too low on horse power to make a big, sudden move in the standings, but felt things could change for the better.

"I think we've got a good pitching staff and some championship ball players," he said. "You can always use more, though."

Those puzzle pieces did fit together for Houston in 1980. The Astros finished 93-70 to capture the National League West. Houston and the Los Angeles Dodgers tied for first at the end of the regular-season, but the Astros won a playoff, 7-1, then lost to the Philadelphia Phillies for the NL pennant. The Phillies won the World Series.

》》》》》》》》》》》》》》 CAREER

Virdon was 24 when he broke into the majors with the Cardinals and stirred things up by batting .281 with 17 home runs and 68 runs batted in. He had a slow start in 1956 and the Cardinals swapped him to the Pirates for Bobby del Greco and Dick Littlefield, a trade that paid major dividends for Pittsburgh.

Virdon spent the rest of his playing career with the Pirates.

Always steady, committed, and hard-working, but never flashy, Virdon was not a great fit with the Yankees of the 1970s. He was perhaps better suited to bring a team to maturity with wisdom and care like the Astros.

"He's very patient," said Bob Lillis, one of Virdon's coaches with Houston and who was one of the original Houston Colt .45s before the team changed its name. "He provides a comfortable atmosphere. He sets the tone and it's especially important with young players. He's a calm person when making decisions."

Virdon was 90 years old when he died in 2021 and in early 2023 a book about his years in the game was published called *Bill Virdon: A Life in Baseball.*

HOYT WILHELM

THE SETTING

The first relief pitcher enshrined in the National Baseball Hall of Fame, Hoyt Wilhelm astonished fans repeatedly for years. Not only did he pitch in the majors until he was nearly 50 years old after getting a very late start in the big leagues, he practically performed magic by relying on one singular weapon to baffle hitters.

Wilhelm was the king of the knuckleball throwers, a one-trick pony, in essence, who relied on the knuckler for 90 percent of his arsenal. A pitch that even the best of knuckleballers say rules them and not the other way around, the ball floats to the plate appearing for a moment as easy to smack with a bat as a beach ball and then swerving out of reach into unhittable territory like a fast-moving bird.

Wherever Wilhelm pitched, for whatever team he excelled, remarkable feats followed. Along the way on his long journey, Wilhelm hurled for the New York Giants before playing with San Francisco, the Baltimore Orioles, and the Chicago White Sox, as well as for short stints with other teams such as the Atlanta Braves and the Los Angeles Dodgers.

Rarely did Wilhelm have the benefit of a manager or pitching coach who even understood the knuckleball's mysterious workings, so he never had any administrative help to pull him out of slumps or positively redirect his motion.

The history of knuckleball use since the early part of the 20th century, is a checkered one. There are only a tiny number of knuckleball artists who made good by relying on the pitch full-time. Those who have done so make up a small, private club.

Sometimes years pass without multiple knuckleball pitchers excelling simultaneously in the majors. Over a few eras there was some overlap and those who specialized in the knuckler world were known to help one another when it came to advice for the lack of anywhere else to turn.

In recent years, since about the mid-2015 time period, there have been zero pitchers in the majors who have been using the knuckler regularly or well. It may be the pitch has died out. Presently, especially with the passing of 318-game-winner Phil Niekro, who even said Wilhelm was the best of all knuckler throwers, there is no one regularly counted on to teach it.

Wilhelm, who grew up in North Carolina and whose age was shrouded in mystery (off by a year) because no one bothered to ask or correct it, was a rookie at 29. He often ran into knuckleball prejudice from some managers, coaches, and teams, but he resolutely stuck with his money pitch, aware that he did not own big-league stuff otherwise. He wasn't going to make it with his fastball and curve, but knew the knuckler could carry him a long way.

I got the chance to interview Wilhelm during a visit to spring training in Florida in 1977. Although knuckleball pitchers and the baseball experts who watch them acknowledge a sore arm is never going to force such a thrower into retirement, everyone who defies time in the game does ultimately remove himself from the playing field.

Pitchers rarely survive at the top of the game for 21 seasons the way Wilhelm did. The adage for most athletes comes into play – the legs go first. And if not the legs, then certainly the throwing arm.

On a sunny, warm spring day, five years had passed since Wilhelm had thrown his last Major League pitch for the Dodgers, his last in the majors, and he had eased into the role of being a minor-league manager and coach in the New York Yankees' organization.

⫸⫸⫸⫸⫸⫸⫸ THE STORY

Hoyt Wilhelm was a man of faith in the knuckleball as a weapon of choice. However, he was a pitcher whose faith was so deeply rooted he had doubts about late converts. He had taught himself how to throw a knuckler after being inspired by a newspaper story featuring 1930s big-league star Dutch Leonard.

His success that followed convinced him a pitcher had to learn the knuckler when he was young, in childhood or in his teens perhaps, rather than in his 20s or later. There are some pitchers who turn to the knuckler as a way to stay in baseball when their other tools fail them. They come under the heading of desperation knuckleballers.

Most of the other successful knuckleballers at least had some rudimentary training and background with the pitch when they were young, even if they were discouraged from using it or had other skills that carried them in high school, American Legion ball, and the minors. Phil Niekro and his brother Joe were taught the pitch in their Ohio backyard as kids by a father, Phil Sr., who had experimented with it and used it.

There may have been some who felt that once Wilhelm got ahold of young arms in the minors, he would turn out a parade of future knuckleballers, but he understood that was neither his role in the employ of a big-league outfit that had scouted the young arms and liked their abilities, nor a pattern that was likely to succeed.

"I don't try to teach it," Wilhelm said on a grassy field. "You've got to be born with it."

Born with it was a Wilhelm shorthand synonym for growing up with the knuckler.

At that time in baseball, which was heavier in the use of the knuckler by some prominent throwers, the sport still was not densely populated with knuckleball proselytizers.

"There was no real knuckler heyday," Wilhelm said. "There've never been too many guys who could throw it. Today are there only a few I can think if – Phil and Joe Niekro, Wilbur Wood, and Charlie Hough."

Although neither Wilhelm nor I was conscious of it at that moment, it is possible by listing that group of hurlers he was actually really describing a knuckler heyday.

It is possible that never in baseball history has a young pitcher been scouted and signed because he threw an exceptional knuckler. In the modern game, teams are looking for abnormally strong arms with the capacity to throw nearly 100 mph, not arms that loop the ball to the plate at 67 mph. The same was essentially true some 45 years ago, even if a high mph speed was more like 92.

"The scouts are looking for a young pitcher who can throw hard," Wilhelm said. "Nobody asks me to teach it (the knuckleball). It would be stupid to do it."

If the knuckler was easy to throw – and Wilhelm, Niekro and the other practitioners eschewed the use of the word "master" because they confess the knuckler is the boss – then everyone would try it.

"They just can't control it," Wilhelm said of how few pitchers were using the knuckler and who used it well.

Rather than becoming a salesman for the knuckleball, by this time, with his days on the mound behind him, Wilhelm refused to get nostalgic. The knuckler put so little stress on the arm that the best knuckleballers pitched well into their forties, but even then he said, the rarity of those pitchers and their advanced ages might spell the death of knuckleball use.

"I guess Hough is the only young knuckleball pitcher around," Wilhelm said of one of the brethren who ended up pitching in the majors until he was 46, some 17 years later than Wilhelm was speaking.

"But I really wouldn't be sad if the pitch died out. It served its purpose for me. It was the reason I was able to stay on so long. I didn't have to worry about blowing the ball past people."

CAREER

After a long apprenticeship in the minors and a career interrupted by World War II, Hoyt Wilhelm reached the majors in 1952 with the Giants. That season he stunned the baseball world by going 15-3 and led the National League in three categories. He recorded the circuit's best earned run average at 2.43, had a winning percentage of .833, and appeared in the most games as a pitcher at 71. In 1959 with the Orioles, Wilhelm won the American League earned run average title with a 2.19 mark.

Overall, Wilhelm won 143 games, 124 of those in relief, which is the record. He became the first reliever to 200 saves and concluded with 228 saves in an era when relief pitchers pitched several innings at a time, not coming into games simply to throw to one batter or to throw just one inning.

Wilhelm was the first pitcher to appear in 1,000 games, breaking the previous record set by Cy Young with 906. Ultimately, Wilhelm pitched in 1,070 games, a record since broken.

Off and on over the years, Wilhelm was employed as a starting pitcher by a given manager, and late in the 1958 season he pitched a no-hitter against the Yankees.

Over and over again, wherever Wilhelm played, the catchers on those teams had nightmares trying to tame the knuckler. His clubs routinely led their leagues in passed balls. This continuing problem led the creative Paul Richards with the Orioles to invent an oversized catcher's mitt. While this counteracted the problem somewhat, eventually Major League Baseball outlawed the glove.

Wilhelm was an eight-time All-Star and won a World Series with the 1954 Giants. He was 80 years old when he died in 2002 in Florida. It was not until then a one-year discrepancy in his age was discovered. Wilhelm, so often had his "old age" remarked upon in sports pages, yet it turned out he was actually another year older.

BILLY WILLIAMS

⫸⫸⫸⫸⫸⫸⫸⫸⫸⫸⫸ *THE SETTING*

Billy Williams made himself into one of the all-time Chicago Cubs greats coming out of Mobile, Alabama. Nicknamed "Sweet Swinging Billy Williams" because of his beautiful way of twirling a bat, Williams is one of the most popular Cubs players in history. In his prime, he shared the spotlight with Ernie Banks, Ron Santo, and Ferguson Jenkins as a quartet of fan-friendly all-stars who sought to bring a National League pennant to Chicago.

Frequently around Wrigley Field to watch the Cubs play, even after retiring as a player and front office administrator, Williams was available to talk baseball– and sometimes engaged to telephone interviews.

His was a Hall of Fame career that was outstanding, but not flashy, as was his down-to-earth personality. He settled in the Chicago suburbs after he finished playing, within easy access of the ballpark.

Occasionally, Williams and I said hello on the fly. Other times he sat for interviews. Other times still, we spoke on the telephone as he reminisced about the team's past.

Respected and appreciated for his accomplishments and his demeanor, Williams was honored by the unveiling of a forever statue of his likeness outside of Wrigley at the corner of Addison and Sheffield in 2010. Not only did Williams like the looks of the finished product, he was grateful to be so recognized.

Appropriately, using baseball terminology, when he got a glimpse of the final product after previously only seeing the statue in its stages of development, Williams said, "It's a grand slam."

Williams liked the way he looked in bronze, but he also had a great sense of moment about the symbolism of the statue and its enduring value.

"It's a bronze statue that stands there and typifies what you did for this organization," Williams said. "Most of all, I think my family will get a chance to enjoy it. Different generations will have a chance to come to the ballpark, can come, and say, 'This is what my father looked like when he played the game of baseball.'"

Or grandfather. Or great-grandfather. And all other fans.

⟫⟫⟫⟫⟫⟫⟫⟫⟫⟫ THE STORY

Technically, Billy Williams grew up in Whistler, Alabama, just outside of Mobile, in the 1940s. He said he and his brothers were outside all the time. He particularly enjoyed riding a bicycle.

If they were not playing baseball together, (or sometimes even softball) they were going fishing, although he offered the mixed metaphor about their neighborhood's real passion for the diamond game saying, "We were swimming in baseball."

The 6-foot-1, 175-pound Williams was from the same area as Hank Aaron and he remembers the great outfielder being a pitcher on some youth teams. Williams excelled early and by the time he was 16 years old said he was playing with grown men. That put the pressure on him to improve and to keep up with the more experienced teammates.

When he was really coming of age, Williams was scouted by Buck O'Neil, the famed manager of the Kansas City Monarchs who had joined the Cubs after the break-up of the Negro Leagues. O'Neil thought he had the makings of a good player and the men were close. In a famous story, when Williams became homesick and said he was very lonely while playing in the minors, he jumped his team and returned home. O'Neil was dispatched to bring him back and soothe his worries.

The Cubs brought Williams to the majors for short stints in 1959 and 1960, but his true debut year was 1961 and his 25 home runs, 86 runs batted in, and .278 average won him National League rookie-of-the-year recognition.

Williams was a six-time All-Star and despite his quiet nature spoke loudly with his bat. There was one memorable day in 1968 when in a double-header sweep of the then-Milwaukee Braves, Williams drove in nine runs with a home run, double, three singles, and a sacrifice fly.

Still, that was not the favorite day of Williams' career. At one point, Williams played in his 896th consecutive game, an NL record, breaking the mark set by Stan Musial, and the organization threw a Billy Williams Day party.

"Before the ceremonies started," Williams said, "the Cubs organization gave me a lot of stuff." He ticked off a list of goodies, including a new car, a fishing boat, a watch, a pool table, and a washer-dryer set.

Williams said that often when a team honored a player (such appreciation days with gifts have disappeared from the scene since players make so much money now), they often had a poor performance day because of nerves. In his case, Williams scored the winning run in the first game of a doubleheader and then topped it.

Williams called this the syndrome of "trying too hard" to justify the situation. "Yet, in the second game, I hit a single, double, and triple. I needed a home run to hit for the cycle. My last time at the plate I tried so hard to hit a home run, and you know when you try so hard, you don't do it. I wound up striking out, but fans gave me a standing ovation."

Oh, the Cubs did win both games that time, too, besting the St. Louis Cardinals 3-1 and 12-1. The Cubs were in a rare pennant race at the time and the wins were valuable.

"We held on to first place," Williams said. "So that was a joyous day. Doing what I did on the baseball field and staying in first place, so it was great."

Williams, who was selected for the Baseball Hall of Fame in Cooperstown, New York in 1987, said it was very meaningful to him as a Black player to be present at the Hall's ceremony when 17 former Negro Leagues players were inducted.

Not only were those players victimized by discrimination that held them back from participating in the majors, their road, literally, was more demanding in situations when they did play as barnstormers and the like.

"I think the thing we don't realize is the hotels weren't five-star hotels and the buses weren't air-conditioned," Williams said. "They had to travel 1,200 miles and get off a bus and play a game of baseball. They did it because they loved the game and they wanted to perform."

»»»»»»»»»» CAREER

Williams spent 18 seasons in the majors between 1959 and 1976, all but the last two with the Cubs. He played for the Oakland Athletics at the end of his career.

The Sweet Swinger belted 426 home runs, drove in 1,475 runs, and had a lifetime average of .290. In 1972, when he hit .333, he led the league in average. He once had a 5-for-5 game and another time swatted four doubles in one game.

Williams, whose No. 26 uniform number is retired by the Cubs, also coached for the team for about two decades.

Not viewed as a high-profile prospect, the Cubs got a steal of a deal when signing Williams. There was no signing bonus, he said, only a cigar for his father and a bus ticket to Ponca City, Oklahoma to begin his minor-league journey.

Yet three decades later, Williams was able to reflect on what it felt like to become a Hall of Famer. He said it truly sunk in that he was among the greats of the game during the 1987 ceremony when he looked around and saw himself seated with Ted Williams, Bob Feller, and Mickey Mantle.

"That's when you really feel that you are now a member of the Hall of Fame," Williams said.

TED WILLIAMS

Photo courtesy of BASEBALL HALL OF FAME

⟩⟩⟩⟩⟩⟩⟩⟩⟩⟩⟩⟩ *THE SETTING*

From an early age when I was growing up in the Boston area, I was a Red Sox fan. That meant going to bed listening to Red Sox games on the radio – at the time Curt Gowdy, who would go on to much greater fame, was the chief Sox broadcaster. It also meant watching them on television as often as possible.

Red Sox fandom was a generational thing. I had a grandmother on my father's side who devotedly listened to the Red Sox on the radio whenever they were on. I had a grandfather on my mother's side who followed them avidly, more through television. Jacob Kristal was a factory leather worker who had a standing annual bet with a co-worker, the cynic in the twosome. Each spring they made the same bet. My grandfather bet the Red Sox would have a winning season. His co-worker bet they would have a losing season.

For much of my youth, in the 1960s, the Red Sox let my grandfather down. However, when the Red Sox thrilled the fan base in 1967 with their "Impossible Dream" American League pennant, my grandfather got a payoff, too. It was not exactly as if he had won a bundle on the lottery, but he gathered in a little bit of cash and also had (at last) bragging rights.

My father, Joseph Freedman, was not a serious fan, but he followed the Red Sox's progress. During my early years of awareness of baseball and the Red Sox, I naturally developed an appreciation for Ted Williams. Even when the team was losing, Ted was hitting. Instinctively, if not statistically yet, I knew he was something special. As a result, he became my favorite player – and remains so to this day.

One day in 1960, my father and grandfather colluded and cooperated in a plan to take me to my first live Red Sox game at Fenway Park. Gracious to the point of being ludicrous, since I had absolutely no conception of the layout of the famous old ballpark opened in 1912, when we approached the ticket office, they asked me where I wanted to sit.

I had no clue of common sense to suggest box seats behind the plate, which I would most likely choose now, if given a wide-open choice. Instead, my mind raced to the Ted Williams Factor, a fixture pretty much since 1939 with the interruption of service in the military during a couple of wars in left field. I remember loudly proclaiming, "Left field!"

Obligingly, and I don't know who paid, but my relatives anted up for three tickets to sit in the left-field stands. I was counting on proximity to Williams, not only nearness, but being able to watch him field his position up close. Clearly, if I had known a little bit more I would have once again leaned towards those seats behind the plate and being up close to watch Williams hit, which was his thing. I may have been the only fan in history who voluntarily urged the purchase of seats to watch Williams field. From certain things I have read over the decades, it didn't even seem likely Williams would have paid to watch himself field.

This all became moot when the game started and that particular day the Red Sox chose to rest Williams. He was not in the lineup at all and his place was taken in left field by journeyman Gene Ste-

phens. I had nothing against Stephens – even had him in baseball cards – but I had come to watch Ted Williams hit, not Gene Stephens fail to hit.

That was the year Ted Williams decided to retire from baseball. If we went back for another game that season, I don't remember it, not nearly as vividly as I recall the excitement and letdown of my first Fenway Park outing.

However, that was not the absolute end of the story. Some 18 years later, in 1978, when I was a sportswriter working for the Florida-Times Union, the larg-

er of two Jacksonville newspapers, I visited several spring training camps for feature stories. A friend from Tampa, a non-sports journalist, was accompanying me on the day I headed to Winter Haven, the then-spring home of the Red Sox.

We had parked the car and were cutting across a grassy plot of land leading to the ballpark when I looked up and was forced to blink, then double-blink. Walking our way, by his lonesome, clearly headed to where he parked his own car, was Ted Williams. No friends surrounding him. No entourage. I had not prepared for an interview, but seized the moment.

Approaching Williams, we stopped him, asked if we could talk and for the next 15 minutes or so, mind running at 100 mph, dreamed up questions to discuss baseball. Once in a while, to help me as conversation threatened to flag, my friend popped a question. It seemed Ted Williams was congenitally unable to walk away from any discussion about hitting a baseball. Periodically, a straggler passerby recognized the tall man in the middle of our small huddle and came by and interrupted, though respectfully, and tentatively, seeking an autograph. Ted kept on talking to me and my friend right through his scribbling.

Time ran out on us and Ted headed for his car. Although my mission, aka topic, had changed, I did bother to enter the ballpark, but instead of discussing the Sox's outlook on the year I talked to players about Ted Williams. I had invested my time wisely by chatting with an immortal.

⟫⟫⟫⟫⟫⟫⟫⟫⟫⟫⟫⟫⟫ *THE STORY*

At that time, Ted Williams, born in 1918, was 60 years old. We were speaking in bright sunshine and he was seemingly well-tanned already, early in the year.

Based on what I had long heard about spring training and envisioned as a New Englander living with snow into March, never mind from December on, a casual encounter with Ted Williams represented the casualness of that time of year in big-league baseball.

Spring training was as much fantasy as anything else if you lived up north and your team prepared for the real season down south. The scores of the games they played didn't matter at all. Grapefruit League standings were nothing. Whose pitching was sharp might matter. Which unheralded rookie might make the final roster, that was news. This was the first time in my life I had ever turned spring magic into spring reality and the mood and atmosphere was exactly as I had thought it would be – no pressure, ballplayers littering the green landscape, easy-going in mind and conversation.

Nowadays, spring training in Florida and Arizona is big business, with the cities hosting teams building fancy new ballparks and the talk as much about how much their presence contributed to the economy. The players are much more serious. But at this time, a bump-into-Ted-Williams impromptu interview was much more likely to happen, and in many ways was a perfect metaphor for the tenor of those times.

Somebody in the area called Williams a recluse and a fisherman, both of which might have had truth in the descriptions, but he was also the Red Sox' organizational hitting instructor, that semi-official title perhaps pushing him in the direction of feeling obligated to talk with me. Or maybe he was just in a good mood.

If anything, Williams, not hardly in a baseball uniform, was dressed in a wardrobe more appropriate for golf. He had on baggy pants, brown-on-brown shoes that reminded me a little bit of girls' saddle shoes, and a green button sweater. Williams also wore dark glasses, but it didn't disguise him from me, not even at a distance, though it might have worked on others.

This was 1978, before the age of video games and an electronics age to come that some societal monitors view as stealing away the impulse to play outdoors among youth. Still, Williams already thought those who shied away from being devoted to the so-demanding task of hitting a baseball with a bat, were sloughing off.

"Young hitters don't have the dedication we had," Williams said of his days of growing up in San Diego where perpetual sunshine made it possible to practice baseball virtually year-round. "But I understand it. We didn't have as much to contend with. It's hard to devote as much time. It's not their fault. There are so many distractions, so much vacation time, great sporting events on TV. I'd be doing the same thing."

Williams, who had almost never suggested he might pursue an off-field future in baseball when he was playing, surprised many when he accepted the Washington Senators' managing job in 1969. The Senators, who had been bad for decades, weren't that bad that year, winning 86 games.

Williams presided over the Senators for two more seasons and was the field leader in 1972 when the club moved and became the Texas Rangers. The Rangers lost 100 games that year and that was it for Williams as a manager.

Whether or not anyone else wanted to try him as a manager was irrelevant. When I asked if he would give that experience another shot, he did not hesitate. "No," he said forcefully.

I double-checked if no really meant no, or maybe not. It was for sure.

"You can bet on it," he said. "When you're winning, it's great, but when you're losing, it's terrible."

Williams had co-authored a book called *The Science of Hitting*, so the man considered perhaps the greatest hitter of all-time could also say he wrote the book on the theme. His job with the Red Sox was trying to teach young Red Sox players some of what he knew, to watch their at-bats with eagle eyes and alter their stances or approaches to hitting while standing in the batter's box. Maybe a little bit of Ted could rub off, management thought.

For all of that, Williams was of the belief that hitting a pitched ball was the most difficult task in sports and that slumps were inevitable. But he had a strategy for limiting them.

"The more you know about what you're doing when things are going right, the easier it is to get out of it when they're not," Williams said. "When you know, boom, you can just get out of it."

Maybe if you are Ted Williams, but not so many other hitters could just wish away slumps.

As the autograph crowd expanded, Williams figured it was time to split. He tapped me lightly on the shoulder and said, "I've got to go."

⟫⟫⟫⟫⟫⟫⟫⟫⟫⟫ CAREER

"The Splendid Splinter," who was also called "The Kid" early in his 19 seasons, all with the Red Sox, or "Teddy Ballgame," had his Major League career twice interrupted by his role as a pilot during World War II and the Korean War. His wing man was future astronaut and U.S. Senator John Glenn. It was somehow appropriate that Williams' speaking voice sounded so much like actor John Wayne's given the way they both swash-buckled through life in their own ways.

He batted .344 overall and won six American League batting title. Williams hit .406 in 1941 and that made him the last player to bat

.400 in a season.

Williams hit 521 home runs and knocked in 1,839 runs. He was twice named Most Valuable Player and was a 19-time All-Star. Williams' career .482 on-base percentage is the best in baseball history. He was elected to the Baseball Hall of Fame in 1966. Williams is also a member of the International Game Fish Hall of Fame. He fished like he hit, with concentration and precision.

A student of hitting throughout his career, Williams said his ambition was to have people say, "There goes Ted Williams, the greatest hitter who ever lived." While an immodest proposal, it basically came true. It was also somewhat borrowed by the Robert Redford character in the movie *The Natural*.

Williams was a legend in life, in his sport, and wrote a fitting coda to his departure from baseball when he smacked a home run in his final at-bat. The man who sometimes feuded with sportswriters, and even Boston fans, refused to tip his hat as he rounded the bases for the last time, despite the begging of the Fenway Park crowd.

At that time author John Updike, writing in the New Yorker, stated, "Gods do not answer letters." It was humorous some years later when Ted Williams appeared on a postage stamp, when someone said gods could be used to mail letters.

Williams was 83 years old when he died in 2002, very much viewed as a god of baseball by the multitudes.

DAVE WINFIELD

>>>>>>>>>>>>>>>>>>>>>> *THE SETTING*

It is unfortunate that some older baseball fans, especially those who follow the New York Yankees, have never cleared the smoke floating around their heads about Dave Winfield. They fell victim to the irrationality of team owner George Steinbrenner's frequent rants of frustration when he decided the free agent he hired – and thought was the greatest invention since the airplane – was not all he was supposed to be.

The reality was that Winfield, the one-time multi-sport star who went on to be enshrined in the Baseball Hall of Fame, was as good as advertised overall, but Steinbrenner refused to see it. While much of Steinbrenner's unfortunate behavior was just George being George, Winfield pretty much took the high road, not rolling in the mud with the owner, as some others on the receiving end of needle-sharp criticism did.

During this era, the Yankees operated as if money was no object and once Steinbrenner set his focus on an available player, he went after him with checkbook wide open. In December of 1980, after Winfield had become an established big-leaguer with the San Diego Padres, he entered free agency. At that time the Yankees made him an offer he couldn't refuse. He signed a 10-year, $23-million contract that made him the highest paid player in baseball history – at that moment.

Rather foolishly, Steinbrenner did not read the fine print in the contract and thought he was paying $16 million. However, there was a cost-of-living clause that provided Winfield with more money and somehow Steinbrenner felt he had been hoodwinked.

This resulted in the distraction of Steinbrenner issuing verbal assaults on Winfield and friction that could not have benefited clubhouse harmony. Winfield played well through it all and the Yankees did their share of winning.

At one point, as the New York tabloids kept running to Winfield for retaliatory comments to answer Steinbrenner, aka "The Boss," the player said, "I have no problem with Bruce Springsteen." Winfield made the listeners snicker since iconic singer and Steinbrenner shared the nickname.

The Yankees' locker room in the post-season playoffs was one place I encountered Winfield. Another time he was the master of ceremonies of a special program at the Negro Leagues Baseball Museum, which I attended.

Unlikely as it was, Winfield and I shared an Alaska connection. When he was in college at the University of Minnesota, Winfield spent two summers playing in the Alaska Baseball League for the Alaska Goldpanners of Fairbanks. This was not something routinely touted on his resume, but he had been a star in Fairbanks, as he was everywhere he competed.

Once, at a major national sports memorabilia and card show, I spotted Winfield weaving his way through the sellers' booths. Thinking quickly, and hoping to get his attention, even if he had a determined moving-on look on his face, I yelled across a distance of about 10 feet: "Dave Winfield! Fairbanks Goldpanners!"

It was obvious Winfield was rarely addressed in such a manner and his head spun around abruptly, almost as sharply as the character in that famous scene in the movie *The Exorcist*. Not quite a 360, but a pretty big swing. He was smiling as he did it. I introduced myself as someone who wrote about the Alaska Baseball League during my journalism career.

>>>>>>>>>>>>>>>>>>>> *THE STORY*

Dave Winfield was a spectacular athlete. Born in 1951 in St. Paul, Minnesota, Winfield grew to be 6-foot-6 and 220 pounds, dimensions that aided him in all the sports he tried. And he tried – and stood out – at several of them.

Although Winfield was drafted in the 40th round of the amateur draft by the Baltimore Orioles coming out of high school, he enrolled at the University of Minnesota. He spent two summers playing baseball in Fairbanks, but he was on a Big Ten championship basketball team for the Gophers, as well as a baseball player.

This time when he came out of school, professional teams salivated over his prospects. The Padres made Winfield a No. 1 draft pick. The Atlanta Hawks of the NBA thought he could play pro basketball. So did the Utah Jazz of the competing American Basketball Association. And even if Winfield had not sniffed the gridiron in college, his hometown Minnesota Vikings drafted him to offer a shot at playing pro football.

Winfield spent the summers of 1971 and 1972 in Fairbanks, some few thousand miles away from his Minnesota home and seeking to gain high-level experience to improve. He was as much a pitcher as a fielder at the time.

The annual goal for the best Alaska league teams was to travel to

Wichita, Kansas for the National Baseball Congress championships for amateur clubs. It galled Winfield when the Goldpanners lost the title to their local rival the Anchorage Glacier Pilots. Winfield was so frustrated by that result, he said, "I hate this game." His other year, though, the Goldpanners won it all.

Winfield was good for at least one legendary hit at Growden Memorial Park, the home of the Goldpanners. He bashed a home run that not only traveled out of play, but over the left-field fence marked at 325 feet, and landed across the street on the roof of the local curling club. Long-time Goldpanner fans still talk about it. It should be noted that some skeptics said the ball really did not land atop the building, but hit it on one bounce.

About a dozen years later, Winfield brought his wife on an off-season vacation to Fairbanks and when he showed her the ballpark, she looked beyond left field and said, "Is that the building you used to hit the balls off the roof?" Yes, dear, absolutely dear, all the time.

Fifty years have passed, so it is unlikely any additional light will be shined on reality.

Winfield was enraptured by Alaska's mountain and river scenery, but was nervous hearing exaggerated grizzly bear tales, a special of his Fairbanks manager Jim Dietz. Dietz, who coached Tony Gwynn at San Diego State, and was succeeded as the head man at the school by him, was a master storyteller and prankster.

However, Alaska bear stories are often grounded in reality. On a getaway trip to a remote woodsy cabin, hosted by a team fan, Dietz, Winfield and other players had a bear approach as they were playing the card game of hearts.

Suddenly, their host leapt to his feet, grabbed a handgun, and began blasting away at the bear seeking to break into the food cache. Dietz claimed Winfield was so frightened that for the rest of the trip he wouldn't go out to use the outhouse and he skipped a fishing excursion to stay close to the building.

As big a man as Winfield is, grizzly bears are bigger – and they have bigger claws – so Winfield had every right to be wary.

By the time he wrapped up his stay at the University of Minnesota, Winfield had no doubt about which sport he ranked No. 1. In 1981, the split season, due to a players' strike, Winfield and I crossed paths in the clubhouse of the Yankees when they were romping over the Oakland Athletics, 13-3, on their way to a World Series matchup with the Los Angeles Dodgers.

Winfield had two hits, drove in two runs, scored two runs, and stole a home run with his glove. Before the Yankees took command and led just 1-0 in the second innings, Oakland's Tony Armas stroked a deep fly to left that threatened to go into orbit.

"It carried and carried," Winfield said. "It's tough to fight the wall and the sun. As I caught the ball, I hit the wall at the same time."

But Winfield held on and stifled an A's rally. Oakland manager Billy Martin, who lived his own soap opera with George Steinbrenner when he managed the Yankees, called Winfield's catch "just a sensational play."

CAREER

Even if Winfield went 9-2 as a pitcher for the Goldpanners one summer and could throw 90 mph, he ended up in the majors as an outfielder and a hitter for 22 years ending in 1995 at the age of 43. Winfield was inducted into the Baseball Hall of Fame in 2001.

Winfield batted .283 lifetime with 465 home runs and 1,833 runs batted in. He collected 3,110 hits, making him a member of the sport's exclusive 3,000 hits club. A 12-time All-Star, Winfield won seven Gold Gloves, was on the Yankees team that won the World Series in 1982, and was honored with the Roberto Clemente Award for his community service.

Winfield had his own David M. Winfield Foundation for charity, jump-starting it with a payroll set-aside when he signed his initial rich contract with the Yankees. Subsequently, he donated time and money to other causes, including the Paralysis Project of America and Little League. He made a trip to Ghana to promote baseball and then extended his stay to work with former President Jimmy Carter on the distribution of medical supplies.

Besides working in different capacities for the Padres, he did some broadcast work.

In 2022, a true old-timer in baseball was chosen for the Hall of Fame and no relatives could be found to act to represent him at the induction ceremony that summer. The player known as Bud Fowler, born in 1858, died in 1913, was originally known as John W. Jackson.

Ironically, early in life, Fowler/Jackson lived in Cooperstown and that was his main home despite moving around steadily from team to team to play ball. As a Black man no one wished to sign him for a Major League club, but he played everywhere that would have him, sometimes as the only Black on an otherwise white team.

Winfield took on the task of acting as the player's presenter. "Much of his record has been lost to time," Winfield said of the man who claimed to play some pro ball in 22 states and Canada. Fowler integrated several teams and tried to form his own teams and leagues in the late 1800s.

"My skin is against me," he said. "The race prejudice is so strong that my Black skin barred me."

Winfield became Fowler-Jackson's champion for a day and made a field trip to nearby Frankfurt, New York to visit the pioneer ballplayer's grave.

WILBUR WOOD

THE SETTING

When I was a youngster and first began collecting baseball cards, I always had my eye on members of the Boston Red Sox. In the 1960s, one of the guys trying to break in was pitcher Wilbur Wood. Wood was just a rookie fighting for a spot on the roster, but what appealed to me was that he was a local guy.

Wood was from the Boston suburb of Belmont so that empha-sized reasons to root for him. Unfortunately, despite a vaunted high school career, Wood never quite caught on with the Red Sox. The Sox traded him to the Pittsburgh Pirates and he never really caught on there, either.

This went on until the late 1960s when the southpaw landed with the Chicago White Sox and then everybody learned who he was. Wood had adapted to his near-misses by going all-in on the knuckleball and it had transformed his career from someone almost being forced out of the game into an All-Star.

While it was different than anticipated when he was a young player counting on a fastball and curveball like almost everyone else, Wood went on to have a splendid career because he became one of the small number of hurlers who weaponized the knuckleball.

Although he benefited from time spent as a teammate with Hoyt Wilhelm and his expertise, Wood already knew how to throw the pitch. Wilhelm steered him in the direction of counting on it for all situations.

They were teammates with the White Sox for a time, and compadres in the knuckleball fraternity. Proving that the knuckleball could be harnessed sufficiently to produce classic results Wood illustrated better than most of those who specialized with the pitch that such a hurler could get by on much less rest than a regular pitcher.

Wood said that while Wilhelm was helpful, it seems to always be assumed and misunderstood what their relationship was, with sportswriters believing Wood learned the rudiments of the knuckler from the Hall of Famer.

"My father helped me more than anyone else," Wood said of his junior high days when he was introduced to the knuckleball. He admits for sure, though, "I would never have had the career I did if I hadn't had the knuckleball."

Especially in light of the way Major League Baseball has drifted with starters' work loads being reduced typically by 80 or more innings a season, their number of starts cut back and the increase in the number of relief pitchers carried on rosters, Wood has some of the most astonishing statistics of the last half-century or so attached to his name.

In 1972, Wood threw 376 2/3 innings, the most by any pitcher since the 1910s. In 1973, Wood's record was 24-20. No pitchers ever win and lose 20 games in the same season anymore. Once, after lobbying his manager for a considerable length of time, Wood got the nod to start both games of a double-header on the same day.

For a time, Wood was as sturdy a relief pitcher as existed, appearing in 88 games one season. He only became a starter, and a four-time 20-game winner, after the White Sox had a regular sidelined by injury.

Over the years, Wood and I have conducted numerous interviews about the knuckleball, his success, his eye-opening statistics, and the unlucky way his career ended. Unlike many long-term pitchers, a sore arm did not do in Wood. A fluke line drive taken off his knee, ruined the end of his career.

Most recently we again visited the topic of the 376 2/3-inning season. Wood agreed it is unlikely that number of innings will ever be topped by a big-league pitcher again.

"Unless they make changes in the way the game is played," Wood said. "Not unless the game changes a lot."

⟫⟫⟫⟫⟫⟫⟫⟫⟫⟫⟫⟫ *THE STORY*

The knuckleball is so difficult to control, not even pitchers who know how to throw it always trust it. It was Wilhelm's thesis, and the firm advice he passed on to Wood, it was impossible to succeed twirling the knuckleball if it was part of a mixed bag of pitches.

The man who accepted the risk of balancing his career on the back of the knuckler was the one who could save himself, was the belief.

"If you're going to throw the knuckleball," Wood learned, "you've got to throw it and throw it and throw. It's not a pitch you use once in a while."

After a half-dozen years of bouncing between the Red Sox and the minors and the Pirates and the minors, Wood almost abandoned baseball. In a discussion with his wife, he decided to give his baseball efforts one more year and wed himself to the knuckleball to revive his career. Otherwise, he said, he was going to go back to Massachusetts and look for a new way to make a living.

In 1967, six years after his first appearance with Boston, Wood went 4-2 with a 2.45 earned run average and pitched in 51 games.

Things got better from there. In '68, he appeared in those 88 games with a 1.87 ERA and he led the American League in games finished with 46.

Beginning in 1971 as a starter, Wood won at least 20 games for four straight years, 22, 24, 24, and 20. He was a three-time All-Star. Over those four seasons, Wood never threw less than 320 1/3 innings. He was having a grand time. He hadn't had much fun with the Red Sox, failing to stick long with the big club, but there were a couple of memories, the type that stick with every big-leaguer from the start of a career.

Wood made his Major League debut on June 30, 1961, when he pitched four innings and gave up two runs in a 10-2 loss to the Cleveland Indians. Wood had some no-decisions and lost a game here or three, but never won one between 1961 and 1964.

But he had stepped on a mound in big-league games in a professional uniform, so that counted for something. "It was a great thrill," Wood said. "It was absolutely something special. It was a good feeling every time you put a big-league uniform on. Obviously, I wasn't very successful."

That came later.

When Wood recalled his favorite performances of his Major League career, his mind drifted to late May of 1973 when he was with the White Sox. The evening of May 26 began with a home game for the Sox against the Cleveland Indians.

Wood was not scheduled to pitch and Stan Bahnsen was the starter in a contest that became a strange one. The game lasted 21 innings and more than six hours. In an illustration of how different the times were for pitchers, Bahnsen hurled the first 13 innings. Then he was relieved by Terry Forster for three innings.

The game remained tied at 2-2. It should be noted, as well, that Cleveland starter Gaylord Perry, the Hall of Famer, also went 13 innings before the Indians called for relief help. As the game went on and on, the umpires suspended play after 17 innings with the score still knotted at 2-2.

By then, Wood had been summoned from the bullpen and was one inning into his stint. The two teams were not scheduled to play on May 27, but were to face one another again on May 28 in another night game.

Before that, however, the Sox and Indians picked up from their intermission in the game of the 26th. Wood ended up pitching five innings of extraordinary ball in all, allowing just two hits and one unearned run. However, that run did come in the top of the 21st inning and could have cost Chicago the game. Instead, the White Sox rallied in the home half of the inning with four runs. Slugger Dick Allen blasted a three-run homer to end the game and give Wood the victory.

That was only part of the story. Wood was the scheduled starter for the game of the 28th and he took the mound, per usual. On top of his relief win, Wood went the distance, pitching nine innings of four-hit, shutout ball to give the White Sox a 4-0 win on the same calendar day as the completion of the previously unfinished game.

The first game was halted because it dragged on beyond the Chicago curfew. The second game lasted just under two hours.

"When Chuck Tanner brought me into the first game," Wood said, "you figure it's only going to go one or two innings and it's going to end up one way or another. It just so happened that it went on and on."

By throwing 14 innings, Wood ended up with two wins in one day from two games that were spread over three days.

CAREER

Wilbur Wood spent parts of 17 seasons in the majors and won 164 games. He was on such a roll exhibiting what appeared to be a rubber arm in the early 1970s it seemed possible he could pitch practically forever with the knuckler putting no strain on his left arm.

But it was not his arm that did Wood in. In a May 1976 game, when he was again off to a good start to the new season, Wood was throwing against the Detroit Tigers. Outfielder Ron LeFlore got hold of a Wood pitch and slammed a line drive back to the mound. The ball struck Wood and broke his left kneecap.

Not only was Wood's season ended that year, when he came back from the injury he was not the same pitcher. Wood gave his comeback two seasons and retired at 36 in 1978.

Up until the fluke of a swing, there was every reason to believe Wood had a lot of pitching left in him. Instead, after leaving baseball, Wood went into the seafood business (he loves fishing) and then became a pharmaceutical representative. He continued to live in the Boston area near where he grew up.

Demonstrating his versatility, at different times during his career, Wood won The Sporting News Fireman of the Year Award for his relief pitching and The Sporting News Pitcher of the Year Award as a starter.

"I just couldn't do what I could do before I got hurt," Wood said of his physical situation after the damaging injury. "That took the fun out of it. When it was over, it was over. It was something you knew wasn't going to last forever anyway."

CARL YASTRZEMSKI

⟫⟫⟫⟫⟫⟫⟫⟫⟫⟫⟫ *THE SETTING*

The Boston Red Sox went from Ted Williams in left field for two decades to Carl Yastrzemski in left field for most of the next two decades, Williams retiring in 1960 and "Yaz," as he was called for short by almost everyone, taking over in 1961.

Yaz faced the enormous task of filling unfillable shoes, yet he did so admirably in his own way. He became one Hall of Famer following another. If Williams is on the short list of the most brilliant baseball hitters who ever lived, that was not something Yastrzemski could match. However, he was a superior fielder.

The new guy brought his own style and personality to the job and Yastrzemski patrolled left field at Fenway Park and developed the most intuitive understanding of the tricks and dents and angles of the Green Monster of anyone who ever camped with a glove beneath the tall wall.

As great as Williams was as a player starting in 1939 and departing after the 1960 season, his exit was not the tragedy in the lineup some felt would follow because the lucky Red Sox had a star-in-waiting.

It really was a remarkably fortunate situation for Boston to have someone of such great skill ready to step into the position and to also become a team leader. Yaz was only 21 when he joined the Red Sox and he stuck around Boston for 23 seasons, compiling a dazzling array of statistics and becoming a legendary figure in his own right. That was especially true during the "Impossible Dream" season of 1967 when he could do no wrong and won the American League triple crown.

As an impressionable youngster who had made Ted Williams his favorite player only to see him disappear into the ether when I was at such a young age, I was as happy as any Red Sox fan when Carl Yastrzemski proved to be the genuine article.

It was many years later, in my job as a sportswriter in Florida in 1977, however, when I finally got the chance to interview Yaz. It was a more tolerant time and the circumstances that gave me that opportunity would not arise today when the media and newspapers are more ubiquitous and reaching an individual player must be accomplished only through team channels. And then having the player be accommodating would be something that could only be hoped for, not guaranteed.

After some research, I figured out what hotel the Red Sox were staying at on a road trip to a specific city, picked up the telephone, called the hotel, and asked for Carl Yastrzemski's room. These days, it would be a sure-thing that a player would have a block on his hotel room phone preventing strangers from calling and would be relying on his personal cell phone for any communications. This was long before cell phone usage, however. There are numerous stories, as well, about professional athletes checking into hotels under fake names, or even silly names such as using the names of cartoon characters with only their loved ones knowing their temporary identities.

Carl Yastrzemski was registered at this hotel as Carl Yastrzemski and the front desk, no questions asked, put me right through. Of course, there was every chance he would not be in his room, even though it was the middle of the afternoon when the team was scheduled to play a night game.

What I did not count on, and surely neither did Yaz, who was not expecting to hear from me, was that my ring interrupted a nap. To his credit, after I introduced myself as a sportswriter who came from Boston, Yastrzemski did not hang up on me, was not curt, and cooperated in a chat before going back to sleep.

>>>>>>>>>>>>>>>>>>> **THE STORY**

It was 4:05 p.m. in the eastern time zone and the accommodations where the Red Sox were staying while they hung out preparing to play the Detroit Tigers was the Ponchartain Hotel. As it turned out, Yaz had not been accepting telephone calls through the front desk until 4 p.m., so my timing was pretty lucky.

Yastrzemski, of Polish heritage, grew up on Long Island, and a part of that region that seemed very distant and very different from nearby New York City. Yaz himself was a far different player in 1977, as 38 beckoned, than he had been at 21 when the Red Sox first beckoned.

He had earned himself a college degree from Merrimack College in North Andover, Massachusetts after beginning his studies at Notre Dame, from which he received a basketball scholarship, and then become a year-round resident of a small town in Florida. As his body aged, he developed off-season workouts that would keep it young, but he always took a vacation from serious baseball stuff after the end of the regular season for several weeks.

For an outfielder who packed some power, Yastrzemski was not an especially large athletic specimen. Baseball Reference describes him in his playing days as standing 5-foot-11 and 175 pounds. These days that's shortstop-sized.

"I start working out November 1," Yastrzemski said of his early preparations for the next season. "I do some hitting and running and keep it up right through spring training."

The Major League Baseball season starts around April 1 and the regular season ends around October 1. The schedule crams in 162 games with few days off. Since the games are so packed together and off-days often consumed by travel, Yastrzemski said he didn't do much of anything in the way of training when the team was in the heart of the season.

"I don't do anything special during the season, just play in the games," Yastrzemski said.

In the 45 years since this conversation took place, baseball has become more scientific, with analytics, revamping of the meaning of statistics, and the approaches taken by front offices and coaches shifting. Yet it still seems some of the same fundamental outlook applies to stepping into the batter's box as it always did.

"Concentration is the key to hitting," Yaz said. "It's all mental." He said he did not see any difference between the hard work of physical preparation and preparing the psyche.

At the start of that season, Yastrzemski had stroked 2,559 hits and had to be thinking ahead to reaching the goal of the elite company of those who topped 3,000. But he was hesitant to admit that outright.

"I would like to get them, but I won't really think about it until I get closer," he said. "If you think about that kind of stuff, it just slows you down. I just want to win games."

Winning games came at a premium for the Red Sox through the early stages of Yastrzemski's career. Boston was not a good team during the first half of the 1960s. The American League consisted of one, 10-team division and the Red Sox placed ninth in 1966. Then along came 1967, a wild pennant race, and the Sox emerging as AL winners to compete in the World Series.

That year is forever recalled as "The Impossible Dream" season in New England and Yaz was phenomenal. Not only did he lead the league in batting at .326, his 44 home runs and 121 runs batted in made him a rare triple crown hitting champion. But in this Most Valuable Player season those numbers did not even truly describe his success. Yaz also led the league with 112 runs scored, 189 hits, with a .418 on-base percentage and a .622 slugging percentage. Basically, he led the American League in everything.

It was no wonder that among his endorsements, Yastrzemski became a pitch man for something called "Yaz Bread," the staff of life. It was one of the greatest all-around seasons ever recorded by a player.

The Red Sox lost the World Series in seven games to the St. Louis Cardinals in 1967. They won another pennant in 1975 and lost in seven games to the Cincinnati Reds. It was July and Yaz was hoping his team could return to the Series in 1977.

"It's hard to think back," Yastrzemski said. "They did something we haven't done yet – win. When you start the season, everybody thinks they can win it. The Yankees? It takes more than talent."

Boston won a lot that year, finishing 97-64 for second place in the American League East, but did not reach the World Series. Yaz batted .296 with 28 homers and 102 RBIs.

》》》》》》》》》》》》》》 *CAREER*

Before Yastrzemski's career was over, he also played first base and took turns as a designated hitter for the Red Sox. His lifetime average was .285, he slugged 452 home runs and drove in 1,844 runs – five more than Ted Williams. Yaz's 3,308 games played are second all-time to Pete Rose's 3,562.

An 18-time All-Star, Yastrzemski did reach that milestone of 3,000 hits and kept right on counting until he stopped at 3,419. A three-time AL batting champion, Yastrzemski also impressed with his fielding, winning seven Gold Gloves.

Yaz retired at 44 in 1983 and was inducted into the Baseball Hall of Fame in 1989. Ted Williams had worn No. 9 with the Red Sox and that number was retired by the club. Yastrzemski wore No. 8 and that number was also retired.

When Yaz was in his seventies, the Red Sox unveiled a statue of him outside the right-field entrance to Fenway Park.

"This is as important to me as being elected to the Hall of Fame and having my number retired," Yastrzemski said at the ceremony in 2013. "It's a tremendous honor."

Many former teammates attended, including Jim Rice, who succeeded Yaz in left field and also was elected into the Hall of Fame, making for a spectacular trifecta at that position for the franchise over several decades.

Although in his 80s now, and rarely seen at baseball functions, Yaz does help the Red Sox as a roving instructor in the minor-league system. The Red Sox never won a World Series with Yastrzemski in uniform, but in the 2000s he was invited to throw out a first pitch at Series games hosted by the team in various years.

Yastrzemski's grandson, Mike, has been playing in the majors since 2019. That season, when the San Francisco Giants came to Boston for an interleague series, Carl Yastrzemski threw out a ceremonial first pitch – to Mike.

 Sources

Newspapers
Albany (New York) Times-Union
Anchorage Daily News
Baltimore Sun
Boston Globe
Casper (Wyoming) Star-Tribune
Chicago Sun-Times
Chicago Tribune
Cincinnati Enquirer
Columbus (Indiana) Republic
Cooperstown (New York) Crier
Dallas Morning News
Florida Times-Union
(Jacksonville)
Juneau (Alaska) Empire
Lawrence (Massachusetts) Eagle-
Tribune
Newark Star-Ledger
Newsday
New York Daily News
New York Times
Oneonta (New York) Daily Star
Pawtucket (Rhode Island) Times
Philadelphia Inquirer
St. Catherine's Standard
(Ontario,   Canada)
St. Louis Post-Dispatch
Seymour (Indiana) Tribune
Syracuse Herald-Journal
The Morning Journal (Lorain,
Ohio)
USA TODAY

Magazines
Boston Sports Record Weekly
Sports Collectors Digest
The Sporting News

Books
Diamonds In the Rough
Ernie Banks: The Life and Career
of "Mr. Cub"
Fergie: My Life from The Cubs
to Cooperstown.
Game of My Life: Chicago Cubs
Game of My Life: Chicago White
Sox
Game of My Life: Cincinnati Reds
George Altman: My Baseball
Journey from the Negro Leagues
to the Majors and Beyond
Juan Marichal: My Journey
from the Dominican Republic to
Cooperstown
White Sox Essential, Everything
You Need to Know to be a Real
Fan

Wire Services
Associated Press
United Press International

Websites
Call To The Pen
ESPN.com
Mlb.com
Sportsmemorabila.org

Film
Major League Baseball.com
stories from, when possible, I
tried to emphasize different
moments

About the Author

Lew Freedman is a prize-winning journalist who has written for the Philadelphia Inquirer, Chicago Tribune, Anchorage Daily News, and other newspapers. He has followed baseball his entire life and interviewed greats of the sport over the last 50 years.

Freedman is the author of more than 100 books. He, his wife Debra, and dog Boston — named after his hometown — live in Indiana.

>>>>>>>>>>>>>>>>>>>>>>>> **More to Explore**

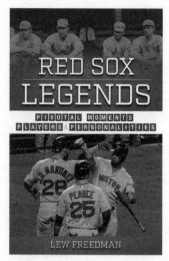

Red Sox Legends
$14.99 Paperback

Astro Legends, 2nd Ed.
$17.99 Paperback
Coming Spring 2024

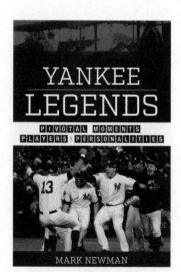

Yankee Legends
$14.99 Paperback

>>>>>>>>>>>>>>>> **More to Explore**

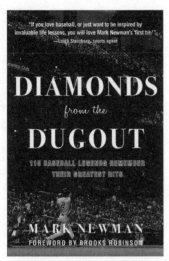

Diamonds from the Dugout
$24.99 Hardcover

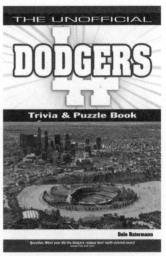

**The Unofficial Dodgers Trivia
and Puzzle Book**
$14.95 Paperback

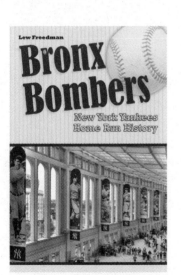

Bronx Bombers
$24.99 Paperback

Houston to Cooperstown
$27.95 Hardcover

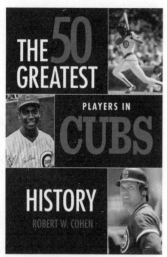
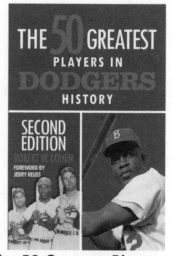
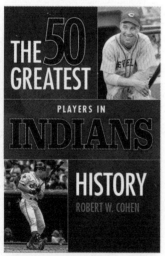

>>>>>>>>>>>>>>>> **More to Explore**

The 50 Greatest Tigers
$14.95 Paperback

The Little General: Gene Mauch
$22.95 Hardcover

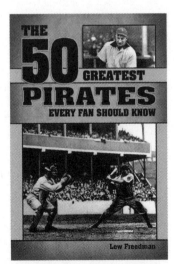

The 50 Greatest Pirates
$17.95 Paperback

**I Love the Work,
But I Hate the Business**
$16.95 Paperback

>>>>>>>>>>>>>>>>>>>> **More to Explore**

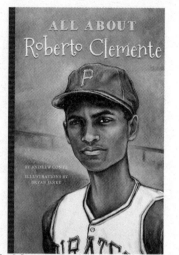

All About Roberto Clemente
$5.99 Paperback

All About Mariano Rivera
$5.99 Paperback